Decolonization(s) and Education

STUDIA EDUCATIONIS HISTORICA

Studies in the History of Education

Edited by

Marcelo Caruso / Eckhardt Fuchs / Gert Geißler / Sabine Reh / Eugenia Roldán Vera / Noah W. Sobe

VOL. 5

PETER LANG

Marcelo Caruso / Daniel Maul (eds.)

Decolonization(s) and Education

New Polities and New Men

PETER LANG

Bibliographic Information published by the Deutsche Nationalbibliothek
The Deutsche Nationalbibliothek lists this publication in the Deutsche Nationalbibliografie; detailed bibliographic data is available in theinternet at http://dnb.d-nb.de.

Library of Congress Cataloging-in-Publication Data
A CIP catalog record for this book has been applied for at the Library of Congress.

Printed by CPI books GmbH, Leck

ISSN 2195-5158
ISBN 978-3-631-67415-4 (Print)
E-ISBN 978-3-653-06771-2 (E-PDF)
E-ISBN 978-3-631-70848-4 (EPUB)
E-ISBN 978-3-631-70849-1 (MOBI)
DOI 10.3726/b17120

Peter Lang – Berlin · Bern · Bruxelles · New York · Oxford · Warszawa · Wien

This publication has been peer reviewed.

www.peterlang.com

Contents

Marcelo Caruso & Daniel Maul[1]

Decolonization(s) and Education
New Polities and New Men

In "Education for self-reliance" from 1967, the now famous policy paper about the educational challenges of the young state of Tanzania, President Julius Nyerere (1922–1999) pointed out the key importance he and many other independence leaders attributed to education in their project to radically break with the colonial past. There was "no use our educational system stressing values and knowledge appropriate to the past or to the citizens in other countries" Nyerere insisted. According to him it was "wrong if it even contributes to the continuation of those inequalities and privileges that still exist in our society because of our inheritance. Let our students be educated to be members and servants of the kind of just and egalitarian future to which this country aspires".[2]

When, some 150 years earlier, the Venezuelan educator Simón Rodríguez (1769–1854) published his considerations about the new "American societies" emerging from the fallen Spanish colonial order after 1808, he followed a similar rationale. Rodriguez, an early liberal and socialist thinker and one of Simón Bolivar's most influential teachers, expressed the same sense of newness in dramatic words in his discussion about the future of politics, culture, and education in Latin America: "Where should we search for models? Hispanic America is original; her institutions and governments have to be original; and the means for establishing both have to be original as well. Either we invent something new, or we will fail" (*inventamos o erramos*).[3]

To be sure, there were significant differences between the processes that led to the independence of the Latin American Republics in the early 19th century on the one hand and the liberation struggles surrounding the dissolution of the European colonial empires in Asia and Africa after World War II on the other.

---

1 We would like to thank the German Research Community (*Deutsche Forschungsgem einschaft*, DFG) for financially supporting both the conference held in Berlin in 2015 and the publication of this volume.

2 Julius K. Nyerere, *Education for Self-Reliance* (Dar es Salaam: Printed by the governement printer, 1967), 26.

3 Simón Rodríguez, *Sociedades americanas en 1828* (Caracas: Biblioteca Ayacucho, 1990), 88.

What Nyerere and Rodriguez shared however, was the project of creating new societies ridded of all remnants of the colonial past and in the key role they attributed to educational practices as a tool to reach this goal.[4] Nationalist leaders in both cases placed education at the heart of their quests to construct a new political order from scratch. In this sense, the following collection of essays tries to address this nexus by establishing a dialogue over time and across the space between these two historical experiences with a focus on its educational implications.

Locating educational discourses in decolonization – Building new polities and new men

Many nationalist leaders portrayed the necessity of a new political order as the culmination of the struggle for independence, and in doing so, they surpassed the mere political concept of decolonization and expanded the project of decolonization to the social and cultural realms. A quest for radical changes in politics and culture emerged after independence and fostered a sense of novelty and innovation with regard to education. The break with the colonial past was not only to be a political one. The break with the colonial political order would rather necessarily, as many independence leaders agreed, have to lead to new forms of education and schooling which, for their part, would have to be accompanied by and embedded in a profound revision of inherited institutions and practices. In many respects, new men had to build new polities and both, in turn, would be the result of educational practices. This sense of newness was by no means exclusive to utopian socialist thinking after World War II. Rather it was embedded in the particular dynamics that the quest for a post-colonial order unleashed, across geographical as well as ideological boundaries.

While conventional wisdom defines education as a field of action reproducing society in time, decolonization places broader and more radical demands on the field. New states perceived themselves as having a special need for education: given that independence and decolonization invariably implied to some degree a delegitimization of the existing social and political order, the reform of education was intrinsically connected to ideas of "revolution" and/or deep-running

4 Christopher J. Lee, "Anti-Colonialism: Origins, Practices, and Historical Legacies," in *The Oxford Handbook of the Ends of Empire*, ed. Martin Thomas and Andrew S. Thompson (London: Oxford University Press, 2018).

"modernization" projects.[5] When "new societies" had to be designed, established and consolidated, education acquired the role of a tool to both speed up and deepen these processes. Education had to do many things at the same time: it had to bridge the uncertainty associated with the new time, it had to strengthen the acceptance for new polities - often frail and contested - among its citizens. The need for such stabilizing practices was apparent. On yet a different level, education was also regarded as a major tool of emancipation in an international context. From the perspective of post-colonial elites, the building of new educational systems held a very practical meaning: the purposeful (re)integration of ex-colonies as independent states in the world market required at the very least well-trained citizens fit for competition.[6]

The outcome of these struggles that affected the educational sector – the primary institution of particular new polities – was neither evident nor necessary. On the contrary, it was to a high degree historically contingent. Even where nationalist movements had a clear ideologically founded concept of political independence, some of the basic features of the post-colonial societies remained highly controversial. Fainthearted attempts to build up a Spanish American confederation of republics well into the 1820s, later Pan-Africanism, Pan-Asianism and Pan-Arabism signaled that issues such as common identities and shared political projects, at least within some elites, were powerful forces in shaping decolonization(s).[7] This however did not necessarily unite those same elites in the nation-building process. In sum, during the process of decolonization, the very emergence of new polities had to be managed through measures of state building. Accordingly, education had not only a 'reproductive' function but also a 'productive' one: the invention of new polities. The urgent task of contouring

5 Corinna Unger, *International Development. A Post-War History* (London: Bloomsbury, 2018).

6 The high value attached to educational questions in the context of decolonization can be studied for instance with a view to the engagement of international organizations like UNESCO and ILO, UNIDO in the field. Unger, *International Development. A Post-War History*; Richard Jolly et al., *UN Contributions to Development Thinking and Practice* (Indiana 2004). Valeska Huber, "Planning Education and Manpower in the Middle East, 1950s and 1960s," *Journal of Contemporary History* 52, no. 1 (2017).; Martin Breuer, "Exploring the technical assistance activities of the International Labor Organization in the field of indigenous peoples: Development and Human Rights in the Andean Indian Program (1954–1968)," *Forum for Inter-American Research* (2018).

7 Vijay Prashad, *The Darker Nations: A People's History of the Third World, A New Press People's history* (New York: New Press: Distributed by W.W. Norton, 2007).

new political entities and giving them new forms of government invested education with an almost Messianic significance.

Focusing on the creation of new polities addresses an extremely important concern for actors at that time: It brings to light the hopes and anxieties by which people react to political and territorial rearrangements and the shifting societal patterns that accompany them. In a last grip on power, colonial powers often depicted autonomist and national liberation movements as a threat to security and prosperity and to associated independence with chaos and disorder. And indeed, in many cases, these dystopian views turned into threatening realities for the masses, when changing borders, loyalties and alliances marked the decolonization processes. We can see how the frequently traumatic experience of decolonization became in itself a powerful determinant in the elaboration of new educational policies. It was here, within the often-painful transition, that concepts of "liberation" and "self-determination" gained broader meaning, reaching far beyond mere political independence from the respective colonial powers. Whereas colonial education related to territory it had to stabilize, preserve and pacify, a new kind of social regime demanded cultural transformations of the utmost importance, such as general literacy, the creation of a modern citizenry, the imposition of new institutional rules, the contouring of a new kind of public sphere, etc. Education added substance and support to the lofty rhetoric that carried national liberation struggles of the 19th and 20th centuries. While phraseology of the most exalted liberalism accompanied the Latin American declarations of independence, socialist representations of society marked many of the liberation fights in the period after World War II. What both shared was the experience that proclamations were not enough: in order for the projects of liberation to succeed, the vocabulary had to take root in popular cultures. Educational efforts to make this language accessible and understandable affected both the education of the elites and common people.

Closely associated with polity building and societal change, the issue of the cultural and ethnic plurality of some of the new countries should also be taken into consideration. Many of the new polities faced the challenge of populations widely differentiated along ethnic, social or other lines. Post-colonial elites acted with a sense of urgency, launching ambitious programs of political and cultural homogenization in which education once again occupied a central role. While colonial rule had often privileged certain ethnic groups over others, the aspiration of the new political order was to re-shape collective identities under the new imperative of the "people". In the beginning an educational optimism dominated, and the redemption of certain groups within the new polities by means of the universal remedy of education was repeatedly propounded.

Although there is a consensus that post-colonial educational systems followed a path of institutionalization that in many ways resembled the Western and colonial approaches to schooling,[8] transformations in post-colonial education were by no means insignificant.

The noticeable focus on mass literacy was not the only aspect to constitute a qualitatively different approach from the more ambivalent strategies of colonial regimes.[9] Changes in curriculum content were considerable[10] as well as the re-arrangement of links between ethnic groups and schooling.[11] Moreover, the orientation of many post-colonial polities towards the socialist countries promoted changes in structure and prioritization that clearly marked breaks with colonial policies. The combination of new policies and new orientations also motivated a shift of perspectives on educational cooperation and aid on behalf of the former metropoles[12]. Most importantly, it attracted the attention of new actors such as the United States, which began to take a keen interest in gaining

8 See the arguments advanced in: Sarah Van Ruyskensvelde, Karen Hulstaert, and Marc Depaepe, "The cult of order: in search of underlying patterns of the colonial and neo-colonial 'grammar of educationalisation' in the Belgian Congo. Exported school rituals and routines?," *Paedagogica Historica* 53, no. 1–2 (2016).

9 Kate Skinner, "'It Brought Some Kind of Neatness to Mankind': Mass Literacy, Community Development and Democracy in 1950s Asante," *Africa: Journal of the International African Institute* 79, no. 4 (2009); Jeff Unsicker, "Tanzania's Literacy Campaign in Historical-Structural Perspective," in *National Literacy Campaigns. Historical and Comparative Perspectives*, ed. Robert F. Arnove and Harvey J. Graff (New York, London: Plenum Press, 1987); Dianne White Oyler, "A Cultural Revolution in Africa: Litaracy in the Republic of Guinea Since Independence," *The International Journal of African History* 34, no. 3 (2001). For a different approach, stressing continuities with late colonial times see Iris Seri-Hersch, "Towards social progress and post-imperial modernity? Colonial politics of literacy in the Anglo-Egyptian Sudan, 1946–1956," *History of Education* 40, no. 3 (2011).

10 Iris Seri-Hersch, "Did Friends and Enemies Change upon Decolonization? A Sudanese History Handbook for Elementary Schools, 1949–1958," in *Freund- und Feindbilder in Schulbüchern*, ed. Arsen Djurovic and Eva Matthes (Bad Heilbrunn/Obb.: Klinkhardt, 2010).

11 Tan Yao Sua, "Decolonization, educational language policy and nation building in plural societies: The development of Chinees education in Malaysia, 1950–1970," *International Journal of Educational Development* 33, (2013); Ting-Hong Wong, "Education and State Formation Reconsidered: Chinese School Identity in Postwar Singapore," *Journal of Historical Sociology* 16, no. 2 (2003).

12 Laurent Manière, "La politique française pour l'adaptation de l'enseignement en Afrique aprés les indépendances (1958–1964)," *Histoire de l'éducation*, no. 128 (2010).

influence in the education of the new post-colonial elites.[13] Their educational choices were invariably informed by an anti-colonial impetus and, at the same time, influenced – either by deliberate choice or necessity – by outside influences. After the Second World War, the Cold war served as a powerful force in this regard but international organizations like UNESCO equally provided an (in itself politically contested) international yardstick.[14]

Surely the timespan of decolonization is too long, the range of the problems too broad, and the geographical and political settings too different to capture all the richness of these different transformations in the present volume?[15] What the contributions collected in this book do instead, is to offer a novel and panoramic view on the multi-faceted role of education in decolonization processes over two centuries.

Filling a gap, advancing an agenda? The contributions

The contributions in this volume provide a diachronic perspective on decolonization and education spanning the 19th and 20th 18 centuries. They assemble local histories from places as varied as Argentina and India, Hong Kong and Mozambique and place them in their broader historical context. Connecting the local and the global, the contributions highlight the manifold transnational interactions that characterize educational discourses against the background of decolonization. Accordingly, decolonization in this volume features not as a concrete moment in time but rather as a process in which the quest to establish new cultural and political norms constitutes a common denominator in both time and space. The book addresses decolonizations, in a plural form, in order to grasp the diversity of historical situations in which the political and cultural dynamics of the nexus between education and the invention of new polities became apparent.[16] We argue that these processes were invariably complex and

---

13 Corinna R. Unger, "The United States, Decolonization, and the Education of Thirs World Elites," in *Elites and Decolonization in the Twentieth Century*, ed. Jost Dülffer and Marc Frey (New York: Palgrave macmillan, 2011).

14 Sunil Amrith and Glenda Sluga, "New Histories of the United Nations," *Journal of World History* 19, no. 3 (2008); Klaas Dykmann, "Only with the best intentions: International Organizations as Global Civilizers," *Comparativ* 23, no. 4/5 (2014).

15 David Strang, "Global Patterns of Decolonization, 1500–1987," *International Studies Quarterly* 335, no. 4 (1991).

16 From the wealth of literature on decolonization that shows the complexity of experiences under the heading of decolonization. Jan C. Jansen and Jürgen Osterhammel, *Dekolonisation. Das Ende der Imperien* (München: Beck, 2013); Nicola Miller, *Republics*

far-reaching – going beyond the mere delegitimization of foreign rule.[17] At the very least, by highlighting these attempts to create new men and new polities by means of educational reform, a process that reaches well into our own time, the articles in this volume open a window to the present.

All contributions point to the complexity of decolonization, exposing the tension between a fundamental break with the past and the continuities transcending the transfer of power. They emphasize various shades of transformation, adaptation and resilience enacted in these processes. They also capture both internal and external contexts when addressing education as a means of construction and renewal of polities and men. Beyond these common traits, some of the contributions look particularly at the entanglements between the colonial and the post-colonial, whereas a second group puts more attention on specific meanings and strategies used by particular actors. We briefly introduce the individual contributions following a chronological approach.

In his contribution about the discourse on 'colonial education' in 19th century Latin America, *Marcelo Caruso* shows the legitimizing role of the question of educational heritance in the decades after independence from Spanish colonial rule. In this earliest process of de-colonization, 'colonial education' became a common thread in public discourse in which at least two types of arguments were advanced. First, colonial education was added to the long list of colonial grievances that, in the view of the Latin Americans, made independence necessary and legitimate. Second, colonial education became a consistent argument when discussing why the new independent polities found such serious difficulties in consolidating a new political order. He concludes that this referencing to the educational past became a feature of scholarly and political discourses.

Certainly, the roots of decolonial projects reach far back to the colonial policies and experiences, as two contributions on India show. *Parimala Rao* analyses the strong links between the colonial and the post-colonial in her analysis of the history of nationalist educational proposals. In her account, the emergence of the first nationalist educational discourses – particularly from Bal Gangadhar Tilak – appear as a re-elaboration of an 'imperial idea' that critically continued

of Knowledge. Latin America in the 19th Century. (New York: Princeton University Press, Forthcoming 2019). After 1945: *Raymond F. Betts, Decolonization, 2nd ed., The making of the contemporary world* (New York: Routledge, 2004); Martin Shipway, *Decolonization and Its Impact: A Comparative Approach to the End of the Colonial Empires* (Massachusetts: Blackwell Pub., 2008).

17 We draw here from the distinction recently advanced by Jansen and Osterhammel, *Dekolonisation*, 7.

the practice of establishing modern education along the lines of class and gender hierarchization. The author shows that its underlying aim was the (re)construction of an imagined pre-colonial social order disrupted by British colonial rule. Moreover, Gandhi's famous educational proposals represented the spiritualization of this very imperial idea and did not pose an emancipatory alternative with regard to the questions of hierarchy and discrimination. Rao's contribution points to many key aspects of post-colonial education. It highlights its character as an elite project. Her argument about continuity directs our attention to the fact that anti-colonial movements as modern political forces partly resulted from the very educational schemes of colonial rule. Education constituted a primary tool in the fabric of independence and liberation. But this tool was still, following her reasoning, both imperial and socially conservative in outlook and purpose.

Catriona Ellis' contribution in turn addresses strategies and attached meanings in late colonial schooling through the lens of the autobiographical accounts of three different Southern Indian authors. Her analytical approach highlights the potential of autobiographical sources in recovering marginalized voices. Without ignoring the problematic side of this type of source, Ellis shows how self-testimonies, beyond simplistic concepts of authenticity, can help to open a 'ground-level' dimension of liberation struggles and decolonization. Within her sample of auto-biographies, Ellis' careful analysis brings to light common traits as well as differences: the experience of late colonial schooling, including questions of discrimination, as well as the dichotomization of time - between 'those days' and the present - all appear as resources used by the authors to strategically position their narratives in the post-colonial context. Ellis proposes a double approach to these critical sources: accordingly, one should consider not only their referential value with regard to late colonial education. Rather, she convincingly argues that it is their character as carriers of meaning that defines their high strategic value as an indicator for educational discourses in a post-colonial context.

Despite the diachronic view of decolonization taken in this volume, the end of World War II remains a unique turning point in many respects. This is certainly the case for countries like Korea, for which 1945 marked the end of a long period of Japanese colonial domination. *Michael J. Seth* presents the story of the run-up to the crucial Education Law in 1951, a landmark educational reference in the context of the emergence of a post-colonial South Korea. He depicts the key controversy between adherents of a single-track system and multi-track system as a reflection of a deeper-lying conflict. This conflict, Seth argues, pitched elitist/conservative ideas centered on basic education against progressive reformers inspired by American ideas of an educational system that promoted greater social mobility. As the author shows, decolonization featured prominently in these debates, in as much as the conflict played out in parts as a struggle for post-colonial legitimacy. One reason why the reformers eventually prevailed despite a parallel conservative and authoritarian turn in South Korean politics was that the elitist position was deeply tainted by many of its protagonists' collaborationist past under Japanese rule. The additional fact that their ideas were perceived by many as a mere reproduction of colonial educational realities under the Japanese significantly compromised their legitimacy.

In other parts of the world, World War II marked a watershed too. In Africa, for instance, it helped to foster a change in colonial policy that in the long run favored decolonization. *Hakeem Ibikunle Tijani*'s article on 'Nigerianization' of the educational system in the British West-African colony provides a rich and detailed account of this shift. Its focus is on the somewhat fluid period between late colonial rule and what historians Anthony Low and John Lonsdale have famously termed the "second colonial occupation" of Africa and the transitional phase leading eventually into independence of the British colony. The efforts for 'nigerianizing' technical and specialized staff within the state apparatus show a multi-layered conflict. Spanning the period between 1945 and the early years of independence in the beginning of the 1960s, Tijani reveals first and foremost the agency of local actors. Conflicts surrounding the build-up of new administrative capacities in the field of education needed for the consolidation and progress of the new polities played out on two different, but often intertwined levels: Between colonial and nationalist forces on the one hand and between different regions and ethnic groups within Nigeria on the other.

The rapid emergence of post-colonial polities after 1960 led to the swift dismantling of the major colonial empires. Yet individual, minor colonies continued to exist even under British and French authority. *Ting-Hong Wong*'s contribution shows how decolonization in multiple ways also provided a crucial background for the re-definition of colonial educational policies. The British Crown Colony of Hong Kong serves as an example. As a study in the micro-politics of educational institution building during decolonization, Wong's contribution also opens an otherwise often-ignored trans-colonial perspective. The author's object of study is the process preceding the founding of a Polytechnic Institution in Hong Kong during the early 1960s. Wong can show how the strategies implied by the main protagonists were informed by personal experiences with the reform of educational institutions gathered in different colonial and decolonizing contexts. In Wong's contribution, decolonization thus features as an incentive to create structures that would secure a degree of continuity after independence and stand the test of time even after the eventual dissolution of formal colonial rule.

The fall of the French and English colonial empires and their tremendous impact in world politics have also diverted attention from the latest processes of decolonization, particularly those of the Spanish and Portuguese last dominions. In her contribution, *Sónia Vaz Borges* addresses a model case of a liberation struggle accompanied by a whole set of educational strategies: Guinea-Bissau. In her analysis of the characteristics and impact of the Guinean liberation front's magazine *Blufo*, a novel militant and educational initiative aimed at 'youths', she calls our attention to the question of how the process of mobilization against colonial rule both used and transformed elements of traditional local cultures. Whereas the very name of the magazine referred to local notions of transitioning to adulthood, the idea of an age-related 'youth' as a clearly defined period was clearly a rupture in the local environment. By using and actualizing traditional notions about growing-up, independence fighters were transforming some aspects of this cultural resource. Moreover, the involvement of the Brazilian educator Paulo Freire as a reference in many initiatives in Guinea-Bissau opens a perspective in which South-South-cooperation and mutual observation are paramount.

Lastly, decolonization took place in the broader context of the Cold War and the existence of specific socialist entanglements throughout the world. The last two contributions address this theme from different perspectives. In their comparative analysis of educational transfers within the socialist world in the era of decolonization, *Tim Kaiser*, *Ingrid Miethe* and *Alexandra Piepiorka* present the establishment of a specific type of institution: the worker-peasant complementary education. Following their establishment and dissemination in postcolonial Vietnam and Mozambique, their discussion focuses on the crucial issue of the production of new forms of dependency, now within the socialist world-system, during decolonization. Their study offers surprising results: Applying a meticulously empirical approach, the authors can demonstrate that transfers were mostly locally activated and far from being imposed from the outside. The authors argue that local actors led the process all along, adapted the imported type of institutions to local needs and brought about genuine educational hybrids. By challenging the notion of new dependencies, the authors argue that these cases of educational transfers come close to an idea of 'true decolonization'.

Certainly, the socialist experience during decolonization was multi-layered and the colonial, understood as a set of representations constructing the other, also played a role during the process of socialist involvement in decolonization. Unequal relations between metropolitan and peripheral polities within the socialist cosmos resurfaces in *Jane Weiß*'s contribution on educational cooperation between the German Democratic Republic and Africa.

Weiß presents the perspectives of a different set of actors, among whom GDR officials feature most prominently. These actors were delegated to provide aid in building new educational systems in Africa under the banner of "socialist solidarity". Her analysis shows, that there is no easy answer to the question of the influence of these new "civilizers". The recipients' colonialist perceptions of educational aid and a genuine interest in the common goal of decolonization of education coexisted.

In conclusion, the contributions deal with some of the key dilemmas permeating the relationship between decolonization(s) and education. They analyze processes marked both by continuity and change, rupture and resilience. While they highlight decolonization as a project crucially driven by educational elites, they also show the end of empire as an open space and a springboard for the emergence of new voices and new ideas. The articles address discourses and representations as well as institutions and particular organizations. In all that, if there is another important result of the cases presented in this volume, it is that they often defy clear-cut dichotomies: the re-interpretation of roles leading to hybrid forms is the rule rather than the exception. Lastly, many of the analyses highlight transnational entanglements and the role of an 'outside' influence, be this the impact of US foreign policy, the institutionalization of socialist cooperation, or international organizations. As a collection of articles, they show how multi-faceted and fruitful the analysis of educational history in the transformative settings of decolonization can be.

Literature

Amrith, Sunil, and Glenda Sluga. "New Histories of the United Nations." *Journal of World History* 19, no. 3 (2008): 251–274.

Betts, Raymond F. *Decolonization. The Making of the Contemporary World*. 2nd ed. New York: Routledge, 2004.

Breuer, Martin. "Exploring the Technical Assistance Activities of the International Labor Organization in the Field of Indigenous Peoples: Development and Human Rights in the Andean Indian Program (1954–1968)." *Forum for Inter-American Research* 11, no. 3 (2018): 110–123.

Dykmann, Klaas. "Only with the Best Intentions: International Organizations as Global Civilizers." *Comparativ* 23, no. 4/5 (2014): 21–46.

Huber, Valeska. "Planning Education and Manpower in the Middle East, 1950s and 1960s," *Journal of Contemporary History* 52, no. 1 (2017): 95–117.

Jansen, Jan C., and Jürgen Osterhammel. *Dekolonisation. Das Ende der Imperien*. München: Beck, 2013.

Jolly, Richard, Louis Emmerij, Daram Ghai, and Frédéric Lapeyre. *UN Contributions to Development Thinking and Practice*. Indianapolis: Indiana University Press, 2004.

Manière, Laurent. "La politique française pour l'adaptation de l'enseignement en Afrique aprés les indépendances (1958–1964)." *Histoire de l'éducation* 128 (2010): 163–190.

Nyerere, Julius K. *Education for Self-Reliance*. Dar es Salaam: Printed by the government printer, 1967.

Prashad, Vijay. *The Darker Nations: A People's History of the Third World. A New Press People's History*. New York: New Press: Distributed by W.W. Norton, 2007.

Rodríguez, Simón. *Sociedades americanas en 1828*. Caracas: Biblioteca Ayacucho, 1990.

Seri-Hersch, Iris. "Did Friends and Enemies Change upon Decolonization? A Sudanese History Handbook for Elementary Schools, 1949–1958." In *Freund- und Feindbilder in Schulbüchern*, edited by Arsen Djurovic and Eva Matthes. 217–229. Bad Heilbrunn/Obb.: Klinkhardt, 2010.

Seri-Hersch, Iris. "Towards Social Progress and Post-Imperial Modernity? Colonial Politics of Literacy in the Anglo-Egyptian Sudan, 1946–1956." *History of Education* 40, no. 3 (2011): 333–356.

Shipway, Martin. *Decolonization and Its Impact: A Comparative Approach to the End of the Colonial Empires*. Massachusetts: Blackwell Publishing, 2008.

Skinner, Kate. "It Brought Some Kind of Neatness to Mankind: Mass Literacy, Community Development and Democracy in 1950s Asante." *Africa: Journal of the International African Institute* 79, no. 4 (2009): 479–499.

Strang, David. "Global Patterns of Decolonization, 1500–1987." *International Studies Quarterly* 335, no. 4 (1991): 429–454.

Sua, Tan Y. "Decolonization, Educational Language Policy and Nation Building in Plural Societies: The Development of Chinees Education in Malaysia, 1950–1970." *International Journal of Educational Development* 33 (2013): 25–36.

Unger, Corinna. "The United States, Decolonization, and the Education of Third World Elites." In *Elites and Decolonization in the Twentieth Century*, edited by Jost Dülffer and Marc Frey. 241–261. New York: Palgrave macmillan, 2011.

Unger, Corinna. *International Development. A Post-War History*. London: Bloomsbury, 2018.

Unsicker, Jeff. "Tanzania's Literacy Campaign in Historical-Structural Perspective." In *National Literacy Campaigns. Historical and Comparative*

Perspectives, edited by Robert F. Arnove and Harvey J. Graff. 219–244. New York, London: Plenum Press, 1987.

Van Ruyskensvelde, Sarah, Karen Hulstaert, and Marc Depaepe. "The Cult of Order: In Search of Underlying Patterns of the Colonial and Neo-Colonial, Grammar of Educationalisation' in the Belgian Congo. Exported School Rituals and Routines?" *Paedagogica Historica* 53, no. 1–2 (2016): 1–13.

White Oyler, Dianne. "A Cultural Revolution in Africa: Litaracy in the Republic of Guinea Since Independence." *The International Journal of African History* 34, no. 3 (2001): 585–600.

Wong, Ting-Hong. "Education and State Formation Reconsidered: Chinese School Identity in Postwar Singapore." *Journal of Historical Sociology* 16, no. 2 (2003): 238–263.

Marcelo Caruso

'To Forget Everything and to Learn Again.' Post-colonial Republican Order, 'Colonial Education' and Legitimacy in Nineteenth Century Latin America

Abstract The chapter analyses the discourse on 'colonial education' in nineteenth-century Latin America. It shows the legitimizing role of the question of educational heritance in the decades after independence from Spanish colonial rule. In this earliest process of de-colonization, 'colonial education' became a common thread in public discourse in which at least two types of arguments were advanced. First, colonial education was added to the long list of colonial grievances that, in the view of the Latin Americans, made independence necessary and legitimate. Second, colonial education became a consistent argument when discussing why the new independent polities found such serious difficulties in consolidating a new political order. The chapter concludes that this referencing to the educational past became a feature of scholarly and political discourses.

Keywords: Latin America, legitimacy, historiography, colonial schools

In 1918, in the city of Córdoba (Argentina), a broad student movement ignited against the inherited forms of governance and scholarship at Argentinean universities. This "university reform movement", in addition to having a major impact on educational and political circles in Latin America in the following decades, succeeded in imposing new forms of institutional governance and academic freedom.[1] With all the enthusiasm of a revolt, the young students published a manifesto addressed to all Latin Americans, which would turn into one of the best-known texts in the region during the twentieth century. Their passionate celebration of university reform began with a suggestive reference to Argentinean independence one century before: "Men of a free Republic, we have just finished breaking the last chain that, even in the twentieth century, tied us

1 Natalia Milanesio, "Gender and Generation: The University Reform Movement in Argentina," 1918, *Journal of Social History* 39, no. 2 (2005); Carlos Tünnermann Bernheim, *Noventa años de la Reforma Universitaria de Córdoba (1918–2008)* (Buenos Aires: CLACSO, 2008).

down to the old order of monarchic and monastic domination."[2] The students in Córdoba saw themselves as part of a broader liberating movement, the great movement for political independence that had begun a hundred years earlier to break the "first" chain of "monarchic and monastic domination".

It may be somewhat unexpected that revolting students after more than one hundred years of political independence still insisted in evoking colonial times for naming all things past, backward, or simply illegitimate. After all, Argentinians had governed the country since 1816 and they did it from the very beginning by favoring a break with colonial policies by founding republican institutions, through free commerce and a relatively ample, albeit only formal, enfranchisement of the male adult population. The meanings these students actualized in their manifest were both old and still effective: references to colonial times, including colonial education, persisted through the nineteenth century and became a political and scholarly pattern of argumentation with varied shapes and functions. The fascinating history of Latin American independence reverberated in these statements and expressed present hopes and past frustrations.

Initiated in 1808, Latin American independencies[3] led, in the long run, to the formation of 19 different polities out of four big colonial units called viceroyalties. Although shortly after independence preferences for a post-colonial political regime oscillated between monarchy and republic, all of these new polities eventually became republican regimes. Similarly, a strong tendency for leaving behind all traces of the old political regime prevailed on various societal levels from 1820 onwards. This process also entailed a good deal of utopian energy. The irruption of political modernity in the region reached a level and influence[4] that even progressive-minded European contemporaries considered too radical in many respects.[5] Aligning with a quite global

2 *Manifiesto Liminar de la Reforma Universitaria de 1918* (Buenos Aires: Ministerio de Educación de la Nación, 1985), 5.

3 I will focus on the former Spanish colonies, that is, I will set apart the particular process of independence in Brazil.

4 François-Xavier Guerra, *Modernidad e independencias. Ensayos sobre las revoluciones hispánicas*, 3 ed. (Mexico: Fondo de Cultura Económica, 2000); Jaime E. Rodríguez O., *La independencia de la América española* (Mexico: El Colegio de Mexico/FCE, 2005); Elías Palti, *El tiempo de la política. El siglo XIX reconsiderado* (Buenos Aires: Siglo XXI, 2007).

5 Jochen Gartz, *Liberale Illusionen. Unabhängigkeit und republikanischer Staatsbildungsprozeß im nördlichen Südamerika unter Simón Bolívar im Spiegel der deutschen Publizistik des Vormärz* (Frankfurt: Peter Lang, 1998).

pattern,[6] hopes and utopian ideas had given way to a more moderate and disillusioned approach by the middle of the century. The consolidation of the Latin American republics, mostly after 1850, became a rather patchy modern project, quite principled in its declarations but with increasingly conservative features.

In the following, I will explore the discourse on 'colonial education' in post-colonial times as a recurring motif in the construction of post-colonial legitimacy. The afterlife of 'colonial education' in post-colonial writings certainly played a role here, and came close to being a ghost haunting the new republics. I will treat the discourse surrounding colonial education as an ambiguous way of decolonializing educational practices and institutions. I do so by analyzing different works of Latin American intellectuals in the nineteenth century as the main leads into the discourse on colonial education in that time, using "discourse" in a loose Foucauldian way. Central elements of colonial education, the spread of universities, the lack of consistent elementary education and the dominance of the Jesuits until their expulsion from all Spanish American colonies in 1767, were amply referred to after independence as keys to understanding the ailments of the new republics.

I want to show that references to colonial education became an intellectual and political operation, in which statements were created for certain purposes and in specific situations through concrete actors (or groups of actors). The idea that the recurrent references to education in colonial times showed a supra-individual consistency and variation over a long time is part of my assumptions as well. Yet exploring colonial education as a discourse while constructing legitimacy in post-colonial times cannot include all types of discursive practices. Intellectual works – including early Latin American historiography – are therefore in focus. This implies that the impact this discourse had vis-à-vis wider audiences has to be treated separately. On the whole, this piece tells a story about the particular role of constructions of the past as one preferred source while constructing legitimacy in the post-colonial setting in Latin America.

Degraded, negative, purposeful: 'Colonial Education' in the early republican discussion

Critique against colonial education had already begun in the late colonial period as an element of wider criticism by supporters of the Spanish version of the

6 Christopher Alan Bayly, *The Birth of the Modern World, 1780–1914* (Massachusetts et al.: Blackwell, 2004).

Enlightenment against inherited educational structures. Education in the Jesuit colleges in particular was the subject of severe criticism.[7] Yet a more specific discourse on colonial education only ignited when the young republics, many of them still fighting against Spanish and loyalist troops, discussed their options for the future.

One major actor shaping this discourse was Simon Bolívar (1783–1830) himself, the military leader and politician from the Caracas upper class that would be decisive in the fight against the Spaniards in the Northern part of South America. Contrary to the rather simplistic image of the radical liberator that current political movements such as the Venezuelan *Chavismo* try to consolidate, Bolívar was – generally speaking – by no means a radical liberal. He was, for instance, more than a little cautious about the quick extension of political rights to the whole adult male population. Bolívar repeatedly evoked ancient republican orders and did not hide a racial bias against colored populations.[8] Yet, contrary to later racist discourses stressing differences between groups, Bolívar saw the main obstacle to the consolidation of the emerging republican order in the cultural environment. He strongly advocated for education according to the new principles of government. In the famous speech he rendered to the constitutional assembly of Gran Colombia at La Angostura in 1819, he described colonial rule as a combination of different "yokes": "The People of America, bound with the triple yoke of ignorance, tyranny, and vice, could not acquire either knowledge, power, or virtue."[9] Education, certainly, should become a key for the acceptance and stabilization of the new republican order. Yet education as he understood it was not only about learning new rules and principles. For Bolívar, to fight against "this abject state of depression" entailed a wider purpose: "Pupils of such

---

7 Enrique Villalba Pérez, *Consecuencias educativas de la expulsión de los jesuitas en América* (Getafe (Madrid): Dykinson, 2003); Martin Spiewak, *Das ferne Echo der Vernunft: das höhere Bildungswesen in Hispanoamerika im Zeitalter der Aufklärung* (Münster: Lit, 1993); Gregorio Weinberg, "The Enlightenment and some aspects of culture and higher education in Spanish America," in *Facets of Education in the Eighteenth Century*, ed. James A. Leith (Oxford: The Voltaire Foundation, 1977).

8 Aline Helg, *Liberty & Equality in Caribbean Colombia, 1770–1835* (Chapel Hill, London: The University of North Carolina Press, 2004); David Bushnell, *Simón Bolívar. Hombre de Caracas, proyecto de América. Una biografía*, Historias americanas (Buenos Aires: Biblos, 2002).

9 Simón Bolívar, *Speech of His Excellency General Bolivar at the Installation of the Congress of Venezuela in Angostura, on the 15th day of February 1819* (Angostura: Printed by Andrew Roderick, 1819), 4.

pernicious Masters – the lessons we received, and the examples we followed – were the most destructive. We were governed more by deceit and treachery than by force, and were degraded more by vice than by superstition. Slavery is the daughter of darkness, and an ignorant person is generally the blind instrument of his own ruin [...]."[10] In sum, colonial education was responsible for having formed "the habit of submission", as Bolívar called it.[11] And the task of the new republican education was first and foremost to erase this habit. Yet the second aspect of the new republican education was to inculcate the new political institutions vis-à-vis the new generations;[12] forgetting and restarting however was in the first decades after independence a leitmotiv in the cultural politics of the elites.

The second most important military leader during the independence wars, José de San Martín (1778–1850), was equally clear about the necessity of an extended and new education in order to consolidate the new order. He saw the legacy of the "fatal colonial education" in Peru as the main obstacle for a "moderate exercise

10 Ibid.

11 Ibid., 6.

12 Marcelo Caruso, "New Schooling and the Invention of a Political Culture: Community, Rituals and Meritocracy in Colombian Monitorial Schools, 1821–1842," in *Imported Modernity in Post-Colonial State Formation*, ed. Marcelo Caruso and Eugenia Roldán Vera (Frankfurt: Peter lang, 2007); Andrés Baeza Ruz, "Enlightenment, education, and the republican project: Chile's Instituto Nacional (1810–1830)," *Paedagogica Historica* 46, no. 4 (2010); Marcelo Caruso, "Independencias latinoamericanas y escuelas mutuas: Un análisis desde la perspectiva de la historia global (ca. 1815–1850)," in *História e Historiografia da Educação Ibero-Americana. Projetos, Sujeitos e Práticas*, ed. Claudia Alves and Ana Chrystina Mignot (Rio de Janeiro: Quartet, 2010); Marcelo Caruso, "Emotional Regimes and School Policy in Colombia, 1800–1835," in *Childhood, Youth and Emotions in Modern History*, ed. Stephanie Olsen (New York: Palgrave, 2015); Eugenia Roldán Vera, "Reading in Questions and Answers. The Catechism as an Educational Genre in Early Independent Spanish America," *Book History* 4 (2001); Eugenia Roldán Vera, "Order in the Classrom: The Spanish American Appropriation of the Monitorial System of Education," *Paedagogica Historica* 41, no. 6 (2005); Eugenia Roldán Vera, "Towards a logic of citizenship. Public examinatios in elementary schools in Mexico, 1788–1848: stateand education before and after independence," *Paedagogica Historica* 46, no. 4 (2010); Marcelo Caruso and Eugenia Roldán Vera, "El impacto de las nuevas sociabilidaes: Sociedad civil, recursividad comunicativa y cambio educativo en la Hispanoamérica postcolonial," *Revista Brasileira de história da educação* 11, no.2 (2011).

of the rights" achieved through independence and republican government.[13] His explicit support for new pedagogies like the Lancasterian model of schooling showed the association of political with pedagogical ruptures.[14] Bolívar's and San Martín's positions widely circulated in different South American countries – the speech at La Angostura for instance was published in the weekly press and in different pamphlets. The established argument of colonial education as a hindrance to sound republican development spread quickly. Echoes of this theme mushroomed among political elites. Manuel José Restrepo, who was in charge of the inner affairs of the Republic of Gran Colombia under the liberal-radical president Francisco de Paula Santander, voiced his conviction in his address to the Colombian congress in 1826 that colleges and universities had to undergo a deep transformation "like the one our political institutions have already suffered". To deliberately forget about the past was again at the center of the program: "it is certainly painful to have to forget most of the things that we have learnt under the Spaniard colonial education and to study again; but it is necessary in order to put ourselves on the path of the progress of our century and to obtain the place we aspire among the truly civilized nations."[15]

What kind of education was this colonial education and why did post-colonial elites take issue with it? First, colonial education was not simply "Spanish education", but rather a second hand, degraded form it. In an overview of the state of education during colonial times published in London in 1826, this degraded form of education was a main point: "It was not sufficient to deprive the Americans of the liberty of action, they were deprived of liberty of thinking as well."[16] Public establishments of education in the colonial time were "a monument of imbecility" full of bad books "full of errors and deceit; in all of them they presented

13 Decree from August 6, 1821. Printed in *Gazeta Ministerial Extraordinaria de Chile*, N°48 (August 29, 1821), 300–302, here 301.

14 Juan Fonseca, "'Sin educación no hay sociedad': las escuelas lancasterianas y la educación primaria en los inicios de la república (1822–1826)," in *La Independencia en el Perú. De los Borbones a Bolívar*, ed. Scarlett O'Phelan Godoy (Lima: Pontificia Universidad Católica del Perú, 2001). The association between Lancasterian schooling and overcoming colonial education was strong: See: Inacio Herrera, "Contestacion de la Camara de Representantes," in *Gaceta estraordinaria de Colombia*, April 27, 1824, 5.

15 *Esposicion que el Secretario de Estado del Depacho de Interior de la República de Colombia hace al congreso de 1826 sobre los negocios de su departamento* (Bogotá: Imp. de Manuel M. Viller-Calderon, 1826), 26.

16 Juan García del Río, "Revista del estado anterior y actual de la instruccion publica en la America antes española," *El Repertorio Americano* I(1826): 231.

words as knowledge and false doctrines as dogmas".[17] Degradation came from poor content that the new republics had to overcome: "An impenetrable veil hid from us the foreign languages, chemistry, natural history and the history of civil associations; a dark shadow separated us from the acquaintance of our own country, our planet and the general mechanics of the universe; we did not have the faintest idea about the relations that tie the Man to society and among societies."[18] This assessment from an exiled liberal leader did not stand alone. On the other side of the aisle, conservative authors equally condemned this education. In an early *Resúmen de la Historia de Venezuela* from 1841 the state of education in colonial times was presented as having been "in the most lamentable situation, being the education of the people completely useless and that of the higher classes incomplete in many respects."[19] Ecclesiastical centers of learning had emerged relatively late in Venezuela – contrary to the early establishment of universities in many colonial cities like Lima, Mexico, and Santo Domingo – and a printing press, subject to many regulations, opened only in the first years of the nineteenth century. In the view of early republicans, cultural achievements of that time were possible *in spite of* the restrictive colonial policies. The conservative author of this introduction into Venezuelan history regretted that the American colonies were cut off from all other scientific progress in fields like zoology, botany, chemistry, and physics as well as from the discussion of economic and political theories.[20] Adding insult to injury, the problem was not only the restricted range of knowledge circulating in the colonies, but also the way of its transmission: "To say the truth, colleges were only monastic enclosures where a lot of time got lost in religious practices […]. A severe regime or, better to say, harsh and tyrannical, early made the youth familiar with humiliating habits such as hypocrisy and lie; flogging punishments robbed them even of the idea of shame […]"[21] In sum, a wide consensus against this second-hand education united Hispanic Americans after independence.

Second, this consensus also included the effects of colonial education as having been invariably negative considering the task of building up new republics.

17 Ibid., 232.

18 Ibid., 235.

19 Rafael María Baralt, *Resúmen de la historia de Venezuela* (Paris: IMprenta de H. Fournier y Comp., 1841), 384.

20 Ibid., 388–91. Similar complaints in: Juan García del Río, "Revista del estado anterior y actual de la instruccion publica en la America antes española," *El repertorio americano* I(1826): 390–391.

21 Baralt, "*Historia de Venezuela*," 392–393.

Firstly, people outside of colonial schools were part of the overall gloomy picture. As the radical Central American philosopher, politician, and journalist José Cecilio del Valle (1780–1834) put it when he listed some "colonial crimes": "The condemnation of the natives to the most stupid ignorance, perpetuating their tutelage in consideration of the ignorance in which they were kept."[22] Secondly, even persons educated during the old colonial order were not suited to the new state of society: "Their instruction suffered from one thousand defects due to the systems of teaching; the small number of sciences cultivated at the University or the lack of books, the adherence to old methods, to formulations and so many other defects of colonial education [...]."[23] The consequences were obvious. An anonymous contemporary author that discussed "provincialism" as an urgent problem of his time in the context of Mexican politics, confirmed the negative image of the inherited educational practices and institutions. His adamant condemnation of the overly dominant religious element, the generally poor state in which schools found themselves in and the harming strategies of the Spanish colonists culminated in a characterization of the aims of colonial education as "getting accustomed to suffering, indolence, the almost sacred respect to the established authorities, ignorance, superstition, humiliation, obedience and distinction of classes". Moreover, "their habits [those of the Mexicans, MC] became fixed and have been passed over from generation to generation until the very present."[24] This was certainly not the only statement about "inexperience and colonial education" as the main causes of the "disgraces" affecting the new republics.[25] And this effect was deemed to run throughout as a structural one: in intellectual circles writers of different provenience lamented the long-term effects of colonial education as being felt "since centuries".[26]

Thirdly, this degraded and negative education was, as most writers agreed, not the work of a blind and simple stupidity; on the contrary it was seen as a

22 Exposition from 1829. Reproduced in: José Cecilio del Valle, *Obra escogida* (Caracas: Biblioteca Ayacucho, 1982), 103–104.

23 Manuel Tocornal, *Memoria sobre el primer gobierno nacional* (Santiago: Imprenta del Progreso, 1848), 17.

24 V. C., *Lijera reseña de los partidos, facciones y otros males que agobian a la República Mexicana, y particularmente al Distrito Federal* (Mexico: Imprenta de M. F. Redondas, 1851), 49.

25 José María Lafragua, *Memorandum de los negocios pendientes entre México y España* (Poissy: Tipografía de Arbieu, 1857), 54.

26 Agustín Rivera, *Pensamientos filosóficos sobre la educación de la mujer en México* (Mazatlan: Typ. y Casa Editorial de Valadés y Cia., 1908), 44.

purposeful effect of colonial rule: "All the efforts from Spain were directed towards brutalizing us. Spain put all kind of obstacles to our population, our education, our agriculture, our industry because they feared our progress and only desired our degradation."[27] Many decades later the feeling still prevailed that this education was a work of "high refinement in its malice".[28] Largely ignoring similar restrictive developments of education in Spain, critics of colonial rule saw in colonial education an intentional means of maintaining colonial hegemony: "It was convenient to them [the Spaniards, MC] to maintain the colonies in a state of ignorance and with the vices that loosen the Man from its native place, extinguish patriotic love, unnerve the spirits and debase persons."[29] Independence fighters constantly invoked episodes, in which colonial rule explicitly hindered educational progress. They listed numerous fruitless petitions from Buenos Aires, Yucatan, Guatemala and Quito asking for permission to establish new schools: "Thirty years ago, in the last century, cacique Juan Cirilo Castilla, wanted permission to establish a college for natives in his homeland Puebla de los Angeles. He died in Madrid without success."[30] Others continued to collect such grievances, such as the Venezuelan general José Antonio Páez (1790–1873), who had been a leader in the struggle for independence of his country from Gran Colombia in 1830. Decisions by the Spanish crown discouraging the establishment of schools for natives from 1785, the negative answer to the project of the city council of Buenos Aires for establishing a new School of nautical drawing (a project that the crown purportedly characterized as "presumptuous") and scattered evidence of Catholic officials defining the Christian doctrine as everything that the creole population of the Americas needed for her education were all constantly cited and kept inflaming the spirits.[31] Still, in the late nineteenth century authors described how some representatives of the colonial government had admitted with "insolent frankness", that it was the purpose of educational

27 "Ensayo histórico y politico sobre las Provincias del Rio de la Plata, desde el 25 de Mayo de 1810" *El Conciliador*, N°1, May 1827, 2.

28 "La felonía," *La América Ilustrada* (New York), II, N°25 (January 10, 1873), 10.

29 Juan Ignacio Gorriti, *Reflecciones sobre las causas morales de las convulsiones interiores en los nuevos estados americanos y examen de los medios eficaces para reprimirlas* (Valparaíso: Imprenta del Mercurio, 1836), 68.

30 García del Río, "Revista del estado anterior," 243.

31 José Antonio Páez, *Autobiografia*, vol. II (New York: Imprenta de Hallet y Breen, 1869), 184–85. Further cases of restrictive attitudes towards expanding education in the colonies in: García del Río, "Revista del estado anterior," 398–399.

politics to maintain the inferior status of the Hispanic Americans.[32] The case was clear: colonial rule implied a purposeful plan of keeping the Americans in a state of ignorance.

'Colonial Education' and the troubles of the new polities

One of the few virtues of colonial education in a retrospective view was its full compatibility with despotic rule. Particularly against the background of political instability after independence, this feature of colonial education became evident. In the words of the Argentinean writer and historian Andrés Lamas (1817–1891): "The elements of colonial life were connected – education and popular habits were in direct and immediate relationship to colonial policies."[33] This judgement echoed an older discourse coined by Montesquieu holding that education and political system had to be congruent. Others like the Mexican Simón Tadeo Ortiz de Ayala (1788–1833), advocated "a rational system of instruction (…) in harmony with the political regime adopted by the nation; without its development and operation, liberal institutions, in constant struggle against decadent habits, would only be beautiful theories […]".[34] He echoed a position already formulated in a project for elementary education addressed to the chambers of congress in Mexico in 1826: "A polity in which instruction is not in perfect harmony with the laws is untenable."[35] Now, under new republican circumstances, the probably unique positive effect of colonial education had lost its efficacy.

This retrospective view was quite understandable in view of the troublesome times the new republics had to face. Civil unrest, civil wars and confusion about the territorial distribution of some provinces overshadowed early hopes and favored a grim outlook on the future. 'Colonial education' continued to serve as a plausible explanation. For instance, the official gazette in Bolivia admitted

32 José Manuel Estrada, *Lecciones sobre la historia de la República Argentina dadas públicamente en 1868* (Buenos Aires: Librería del Colegio, 1898), 287.

33 Andrés Lamas, *Apuntes históricos sobre las agresiones del dictador argentino D. Juan Manuel Rosas contra la independencia de la República Oriental del Uruguay* (Montevideo: Imprenta Hispano-Americana, 1849), 18.

34 Tadeo Ortiz, *México considerado como nación independiente y libre, ó sean algunas indicaciones sobre los deberes mas esenciales de los mexicanos* (Burdeos: Imprenta de Carlos Lawalle Sobrino, 1832), 112.

35 Estevan Guenot, *Plan de educacion elemental y de varios establecimientos de utilidad y de beneficencia* (Mexico: Imprenta del ciudadano Alejandro Valdés, 1826), 5.

in 1829 that the negative opinion of some Europeans about the new polities in South America was grounded in troubling facts and in an exaltation of ideas "[...] we could never have acquired if we haven't had colonial education [...]".[36] Still in the Bolivian parliamentary assembly from 1846 the "defects of colonial education" helped to explain "the demoralization caused in the people through the untamed passions of the civil war".[37] From Costa Rica – "Liberty without reason" was the result of the "people that have no idea of true liberty because of colonial education [...]"[38] – to Mexico where colonial education equaled the "seeds of civil discord"[39] – this leitmotiv circulated. Progressive forces used this attribution of responsibility in the second half of the nineteenth century in order to discuss the further development of the young republics towards democracy. In the view of an early Chilean historian, "the prejudices of colonial education" promoted opposition to the "development of democratic ideas".[40]

Whereas the argument of colonial education affecting post-colonial political culture became a persistent pattern of discourse throughout the whole nineteenth century, a new kind of problem related to the question of economic progress and, particularly, free trade, came to be attributed to the effects of "colonial education" in the middle of the century: The Argentinean Juan Bautista Alberdi (1810–1884), a staunch liberal advocating free market policies, had no doubts that the gap between generous constitutional rights and the poor record of the new republics in matters of economic freedom was a "dangerous inconsequence" for the further development of the young republics. Following Rousseau's idea of "education through things" and not only through formal instruction, a notion Alberdi extended to all political and cultural conditions, he clearly blamed "colonial education" for being the main counterforce against economic progress.[41] The strong link between colonial rule and controlled and taxed commerce had educational effects that the modern republics now had to face. In a parliamentarian debate about the abolition of all customs in 1828, the project

36 "Esterior," *El Iris de La Paz*, N°6 (August 15, 1829): 2.

37 *Redactores de los Congresos Constitucionales de 1846 y Extraordinarios de 1847 y 1848* (La Paz: Litografías e Imprentas Unidas, 1924), 26.

38 "Pensamientos sueltos," *Mentor Costarricense* N°12 (March 25, 1843): 42.

39 Gustavo Baz and Eduardo L. Gallo, *Historia del ferrocarril mexicano* (Mexico: Gallo y Compañía, 1874), 157.

40 Daniel Barros Grez, *Pipiolos i Pelucones. Tradiciones de ahora cuarenta años* (Santiago: Imprenta Franklin, 1876), 262.

41 Juan Bautista Alberdi, *Elementos del derecho publico provincial, para la Republica Arjentina* (Valparaiso: Imprenta del Mercurio, 1853), 43–44.

had not only commercial purposes, but educational ones. It was an element of a wider policy of "encouraging and revitalizing" the population "taking them out from the nullity of commercial ideas in which they were immersed as a result of colonial education".[42] Interestingly enough, colonial education was even an argument for those few intellectuals advocating protectionist trade policies. One Chilean author characterized the old monopolistic trade system of the Spaniards as failing to elevate work to a social beneficial force: "they merely made a means of colonial education out of it".[43]

At least, three main economic aspects were linked to colonial education. First: "The bad colonial education has [...] deep roots", still causing a rejection of work and crafts among "decent people", who clearly prefer to be lawyers or medical doctors.[44] The argument was about the disdain for manual work and productive occupations in crafts and nascent industries, a pattern of meaning that continued well into the twentieth century.[45] Second, colonial education, as Alberdi had formulated, was a major obstacle for free trade. Next to factors like "passports, inner customs, the levy, sequestrations, kidnappers, police mistrust, local hatred", colonial education nourished "disastrous prejudices against change, among them against foreign trade" that stood in the way of the free flow of goods and capital.[46] Third, and as a consequence, re-education was needed in the view of these intellectuals of economic development. The sluggish pace of the progress of formal instruction demanded, in the view of some, a more resolute course of action. This was the case with the Mexican politician and writer José María Lafragua (1813–1875) when he addressed the constitutional assembly of 1846 in Mexico City in his capacity as minister of interior and foreign policies. He lamented that immigration, or "colonization", as many authors termed it at the time, had not been regulated in Mexico although liberal elites strongly supported it. Lafragua admitted that the causes of this failure were multiple. Yet "in my view, the most effective and powerful obstacle opposed to colonization has been the general upsetting reactions to the principle [of colonization, MC] and, then, in some regions, to the presence of foreigners; this is a precise effect

42 Valentín Latelier, *Sesiones de los cuerpos lejislativos de la República de Chile, 1811 a 1845* (Santiago: Imprenta Cervantes, 1893), 60.

43 Crisóval Valdez, "Estudios Histórico-Económicos," *Revista de Santiago* 3, no. 21(1849): 24.

44 Guillermo Prieto, *Lecciones elementales de economía política* (Mexico: Imprenta del Gobierno, 1871), 184.

45 Veronica Oelsner, *'Produzenten statt Parasiten': Entwürfe und Wirklichkeiten beruflicher Ausbildung im modernen Argentinien* (Frankfurt: Peter Lang, 2012).

46 Prieto, *Economía política*, 278.

of the prejudices coming from colonial education".[47] Again, during the polemic unleashed by the parliamentary treatment of the project of encouraging immigration into Mexico in the 1870s, a strong discussion about colonial inheritance ignited that explicitly included educational themes in the usual condemnatory formulations.[48] I will not elaborate on the ambivalent meanings that the notion of "colonization" for immigration may have actualized. Yet, one aspect is of utmost significance here, i.e. that the project of massive immigration was clearly seen as a large program for re-education of the population through a new "education through things" and costumes, those brought by purportedly industrious European immigrants.

Dissenting voices certainly existed, yet for a long time they were somewhat marginal. In one of the earliest research works on the field of history of education at the end of the nineteenth century, the discomfort of the author with the subject 'colonial education' was evident. "In our present view, the colonial period is a synonym of backwardness, obscurantism, barbarism, ignorance." The author, the historian José Manuel Frontaura Arana (1864–1904) lamented this situation and positioned his work vis-à-vis "the strong prejudice against everything that implied enlightenment and culture in Chile before independence." Among these prejudices, he quoted that general opinion sustained that during colonial times no elementary public-school system existed, which he strongly denied.[49] Yet this kind of consideration in a more 'Hispanistic' vein did not enter into the main corpus of scholarship, particularly in early historiography.

---

47 José María Lafragua, *Memoria de la Primera Secretaría de Estado y del Despacho de Relaciones Interiores y Exteriores de los Estados-Unidos Mexicanos* (Mexico: Imprenta de Vicente García Torres, 1847), 79–80. He clearly softened his stance a few years later, when he discussed the issue of religious tolerance in 1856. See José María Lafragua, "Discurso pronunciado por el Sr. Lic. Don José María Lafragua en contra de la Tolerancia de cultos, en la sesion celebrada en el Palacio Legislativo, el 1° de Agoto de 1856," in *Galería de oradores de México en el siglo XIX*, ed. Emilio del Castillo Negrete (Mexico: Tipografía de R. I. González e Hijos, 1878), 226.

48 Basilio Perez Gallardo, "La instruccion publica durante la dominacion española en México," in: *Polémica entre el Diario Oficial y la Colonia Española sobre la administración virreynal en Nueva-España y la colonización en México*, ed. Manuel López (Mexico: Imprenta Políglota, 1875).

49 José Manuel Frontaura Arana, *Noticias históricas sobre las escuelas públicas de Chile á fines de la era colonial* (Santiago de Chile: Imprenta Nacional, 1892), 5.

Historiography as a bridge for new generations

Whereas "colonial education" played a role in diagnosing disappointing developments in politics and economy, it also became a recurrent theme of early Latin American historiography. These works guaranteed that colonial education as an argument survived those who had experienced it. Resolutely negative descriptions of colonial education filled the pages of early liberal works of regional and national historiography, describing a rigid, restrictive and out-dated educational reality in colonial times as the quintessence of the hardships and injustices that the colonial regime had inflicted upon the Hispanic Americans. In addition, as already mentioned, the consistence of habits and education in this description was certainly both strong and condemnable.[50] Even when liberal elites were apparently more satisfied with the course of things, like in the case of Argentina in the second half of the nineteenth century, an attentive scrutiny of colonial education was still required. Although Argentinean authors saw their country complacently as being populated by very "generous, educated and intelligent" people "always more liberal and more progressive than their governments", they cautioned that the study of resistance to changes, a feature of colonial education, had to be consistently carried out.[51] Yet conservative historiography had developed a differentiated argument as well. Like in the voluminous *Historia eclesiástica y civil de Nueva Granada* (published 1869), conservatives clearly condemned both colonial education and the liberal attempts to overcome it. The ambitious educational plans followed by liberals and reformers, the argument went, were simply unrealistic and the "acclimatization among the people of Colombia to those doctrines advanced by Rousseau, Voltaire, Destutt de Tracy, Constant, Say, Bentham, Fritot…" was clearly doomed to fail.[52]

Clearly, the leitmotiv of colonial education persisted through different historiographical waves. A case in point is the characterization of José Gaspar Rodríguez de Francia (1766–1840), probably the impersonation of autocratic rule in post-colonial Latin America, who governed Paraguay with increasingly absolute powers between 1816 and 1840. The Chilean historian Manuel Bilbao

---

50 Eligio Ancona, *Historia de Yucatán desde la época más remota hasta nuestros días*, vol. II (Mérida: Imprenta de M. Heredia Argüelles, 1878), 531.

51 José Francisco López, *Estudio político de la República Argentina y un cuadro histórico del govierno municipal en los pueblos romanos y germánicos* (Buenos Aires: Imprenta, litografía y fundición de tipos de la Sociedad Anónima, 1875), 88.

52 José Manuel Groot, *Historia eclesiástica y civil de Nueva Granada*, vol. V (Bogotá: Casa Editorial de M. Rivas, 1893), 122.

(1827–1895), who wrote extensively about Francia and the Argentinean dictator Juan Manuel de Rosas, really focused on colonial education as a major factor in the making of these autocracies. With regard to Francia's dictatorship, causation was unambiguous: "Paraguay [...] was organized under the power of Dr. Francia, who, taking advantage of the colonial education, isolated himself from the revolution and from the contact with the world [...]".[53] The Argentinean psychiatrist and historian, José María Ramos Mejía (1849–1914), a staunch positivist who was about to become one of the major figures in Argentinean educational bureaucracy, later delivered a more detailed work of historical imagination on Francia. Fully imbued with positivistic views of history and reclaiming a truly scientific approach in his 'The neurosis of famous men in Argentine history' (1878), he linked Francia's colonial education with his posterior autocracy in pathological terms. Ramos Mejía claimed that Francia's pathological character had had deep roots in his complexion and early education, but the education he had received at the University of Cordoba in today's Argentina definitely reinforced his pathological tendencies. For Ramos Mejía, a "defective intellectual education" was an influence in producing "his extraordinary anomalies". For instance, he compared the experience of being exposed to four years of theological studies to that of a tumor spreading in a healthy body.[54] Lastly, the very content of that scholastic education was like "falling into troubled waters where the old Aristotelian ideas that circulated were confounded by the barbaric comments of the Arabs".[55] "This life of eternal intellectual masturbation had to be therefore necessarily harmful, that constant roaming of his mind oppressed by the shackles that tied him to the vague system of the Peripatetic school or to the old, moth eaten parchment venerated during the excessive ecstasies in which those colonial scholars failed."[56] Even if historiographical preferences changed from classic liberal to more positivistic and scientific views, colonial education proved a very productive theme for grappling with uncomfortable post-colonial realities.

Liberal historical accounts of colonial culture and education consistently devalued the main traits of colonial education.[57] Only very seldom were

53 Manuel Bilbao, *Historia de Rosas*, vol. I (Buenos Aires: Imprenta 'Buenos Aires', 1868), 69.

54 José María Ramos Mejía, *Las neurosis de los hombres célebres en la Historia Argentina* (Buenos Aires: Martin Biedma, editor, 1878), 14.

55 Ibid., 15.

56 Ibid., 17.

57 Felipe Barreda Laos, *Vida intelectual de la colonia (educación, filosofía y ciencias). Ensayo histórico crítico* (Lima: Impr. "La industria", 1909), 145.

references to "colonial education" not outright negative, for instance its characterization as "fraternal" in a History of Uruguay.[58] It was probably also the work of historians, now as authors of textbooks for schools, that propagated the popularity of colonial education as leitmotiv for explaining post-colonial developments and brought this argument to the revolting students quoted at the beginning of this text. With the expansion of primary and secondary education at the end of the nineteenth century some textbooks repeating the pattern of meaning conveyed the message to larger groups of the population. Introducing a textbook for primary and secondary schools in Guatemala, one anonymous author declared plainly: "I believe that the evils that affect Hispanic-American societies are the result of the poor colonial education whose atavism is still a heavy burden for us. To point out the defects of that education, to instill the youth with the conscious of them in the classrooms, to show them that intellectual laziness is overwhelming us and that the lack of ideals condemns us to be a people without energies is to advance the work of diffusion aimed at a better destiny."[59]

On the whole, "colonial education" became a quite effective means of legitimating one's position in the political arena in the post-colonial setting, and even was invoked to justify plans for "colonization" of the land in the work of some advocates of free market and "re-education" through transformation of the population by immigration. Lastly, it also acted as a historiographical recurrent motive in the major task of attaching meanings to the past, colonial and post-colonial.

Outlook: 'Colonial Education' and the construction of legitimacy in decolonization settings

A preliminary assessment of the discourse about 'colonial education' should take into account the widespread presence of this motive in political, scholarly and – probably – educational settings. There is no doubt that this reference suited the ideological needs of the elites of the fragile polities of early post-independence Latin America very well. They looked back to the colonial past and considered that the central problems of their polities were the outcome of deep, historical causation. They partly indulged in their political judgements by considering

58 Antonio Isidoro de Pascual, *Apuntes para la historia de la República Oriental ddel Uruguay desde el año 1810 hasta el de 1859*, vol. II (Paris: n.d., 1864), 474.

59 Prologue in: Rafael Aguirre Cinta, *Lecciones de Historia General de Guatemala* (Guatemala: Impreto en la tipografía nacional, 1899), XII.

the heavy inheritance of the habits produced by colonial education. Realities in Latin America, even in the early twentieth century, may not have been rosy and hopeful. The legitimacy of independence, republicanism and democracy was by no means affected by these disappointments. In this sense, colonial education as a discourse of seemingly consistent contours and functions, embraced equally by liberals, conservatives and later socialists, constituted a convenient resource for facing difficult realities.

In this sense, Latin American decolonization inaugurated a pattern of argument, in which the legitimacy of new political orders was strongly construed on the basis of historical insights. In cases, in which legitimacy is contested or fragile, actors may look for an 'outside' from which they borrow arguments that lend them additional meanings for constructing legitimacy. This operation, called externalization in the sociology of knowledge,[60] may refer to many sources. Actors may hint to experiences in other, more 'advanced' countries; they may refer to science or moral principles as well; or they may refer to history. Interestingly enough, decolonization processes favored a pattern of externalization in which references to the past, or to history gained a very significant place. Whether this constant referencing to the colonial past is a gain or a trap has worried several authors and intellectuals since independence. Yet the particular setting of decolonizing political and educational regimes in Latin America seems to have favored a strong historicizing gaze that eventually reached schools and became one of the elements in Latin American common sense discourses that definitely surfaced during the commemoration of the 500 years of the 'discovery' of the continent in 1992.

Literature

Aguirre Cinta, Rafael. *Lecciones de Historia General de Guatemala*. Guatemala: Impreto en la tipografía nacional, 1899.

Alberdi, Juan Bautista. *Elementos del derecho publico provincial, para la Republica Arjentina*. Valparaiso: Imprenta del Mercurio, 1853.

Ancona, Eligio. *Historia de Yucatán desde la época más remota hasta nuestros días*. Vol. II, Mérida: Imprenta de M. Heredia Argüelles, 1878.

60 Thomas Koinzer, "'Lehrfahrten für die Gesamtschule'. Educational Borrowing, Transfer und Externalisierung auf die amerikanische Comprehensive School," *Bildung und Erziehung* 62, no. 1 (2008); Jürgen Schriewer, "Vergleich als Methode und Externalisierung auf Welt: Vom Umgang mit Alterität in Reflexionsdisziplinen," in *Theorie als Passion*, ed. Dirk Baecker et al. (Frankfurt/M.: Suhrkamp, 1987).

Baeza Ruz, Andrés. "Enlightenment, Education, and the Republican Project: Chile's Instituto Nacional (1810–1830)." *Paedagogica Historica* 46, no. 4 (2010): 479–493.

Baralt, Rafael María. *Resúmen de la historia de Venezuela*. Paris: Imprenta de H. Fournier y Comp., 1841.

Barreda Laos, Felipe. *Vida intelectual de la colonia (educación, filosofía y ciencias). Ensayo histórico crítico*. Lima: Impr. "La industria", 1909.

Barros Grez, Daniel. *Pipiolos i Pelucones. Tradiciones de ahora cuarenta años*. Santiago: Imprenta Franklin, 1876.

Bayly, Christopher Alan. *The Birth of the Modern World, 1780–1914*. Malden/Mass.: Blackwell, 2004.

Baz, Gustavo, and Eduardo L. Gallo. *Historia del ferrocarril mexicano*. Mexico: Gallo y Compañía, 1874.

Bilbao, Manuel. *Historia de Rosas*. Vol. I, Buenos Aires: Imprenta 'Buenos Aires', 1868.

Bolívar, Simón. *Speech of his Excellency General Bolivar at the Installation of the Congress of Venezuela in Angostura, on the 15th day of February 1819*. Angostura: Printed by Andrew Roderick, 1819.

Bushnell, David. *Simón Bolívar. Hombre de Caracas, proyecto de América. Una biografía*. Historias americanas, edited by Carlos Mayo. Buenos Aires: Biblos, 2002.

Caruso, Marcelo. "New Schooling and the Invention of a Political Culture: Community, Rituals and Meritocracy in Colombian Monitorial Schools, 1821–1842." In *Imported Modernity in Post-Colonial State Formation*, edited by Marcelo Caruso and Eugenia Roldán Vera. 277–306. Frankfurt: Peter Lang, 2007.

Caruso, Marcelo. "Independencias latinoamericanas y escuelas mutuas: Un análisis desde la perspectiva de la historia global (ca. 1815–1850)." In *História e Historiografia da Educação Ibero-Americana. Projetos, Sujeitos e Práticas*, edited by Claudia Alves and Ana Chrystina Mignot. 19–42. Rio de Janeiro: Quartet, 2010.

Caruso, Marcelo. "Emotional Regimes and School Policy in Colombia, 1800–1835." In *Childhood, Youth and Emotions in Modern History*, edited by Stephanie Olsen. 73–94. New York: Palgrave, 2015.

Caruso, Marcelo, and Eugenia Roldán Vera. "El impacto de las nuevas sociabilidaes: Sociedad civil, recursividad comunicativa y cambio educativo en la Hispanoamérica postcolonial." *Revista Brasileira de história da educação* 11, no. 2 (2011): 15–52.

de Pascual, Antonio Isidoro. *Apuntes para la historia de la República Oriental del Uruguay desde el año 1810 hasta el de 1859*. Vol. II, Paris: T. Ducessois, 1864.

del Valle, José Cecilio. *Obra escogida*. Caracas: Biblioteca Ayacucho, 1982.

Esposicion que el Secretario de Estado del Depacho de Interior de la República de Colombia hace al congreso de 1826 sobre los negocios de su departamento. Bogotá: Imp. de Manuel M. Viller-Calderon, 1826.

Estrada, José Manuel. *Lecciones sobre la historia de la República Argentina dadas públicamente en 1868*. Buenos Aires: Librería del Colegio, 1898.

Fonseca, Juan. "'Sin educación no hay sociedad': las escuelas lancasterianas y la educación primaria en los inicios de la república (1822–1826)." In *La Independencia en el Perú. De los Borbones a Bolívar*, edited by Scarlett O'Phelan Godoy. 265–288. Lima: Pontificia Universidad Católica del Perú, 2001.

Frontaura Arana, José Manuel. *Noticias históricas sobre las escuelas públicas de Chile á fines de la era colonial*. Santiago de Chile: Imprenta Nacional, 1892.

García del Río, Juan. "Revista del estado anterior y actual de la instruccion publica en la America antes española." *El repertorio americano* I (1826): 231–253.

Gartz, Jochen. *Liberale Illusionen. Unabhängigkeit und republikanischer Staatsbildungsprozeß im nördlichen Südamerika unter Simón Bolívar im Spiegel der deutschen Publizistik des Vormärz*. Frankfurt: Peter Lang, 1998.

Gorriti, Juan Ignacio. *Reflecciones sobre las causas morales de las convulsiones interiores en los nuevos estados americanos y examen de los medios eficaces para reprimirlas*. Valparaíso: Imprenta del Mercurio, 1836.

Groot, José Manuel. *Historia eclesiástica y civil de Nueva Granada*. Vol. V, Bogotá: Casa Editorial de M. Rivas, 1893.

Guenot, Estevan. *Plan de educacion elemental y de varios establecimientos de utilidad y de beneficencia*. Mexico: Imprenta del ciudadano Alejandro Valdés, 1826.

Guerra, François-Xavier. *Modernidad e independencias. Ensayos sobre las revoluciones hispánicas*. 3 ed. Mexico: Fondo de Cultura Económica, 2000.

Helg, Aline. *Liberty & Equality in Caribbean Colombia, 1770–1835*. Chapel Hill, London: The University of North Carolina Press, 2004.

Herrera, Inacio. "Contestacion de la Camara de Representantes" In *Gaceta estraordinaria de Colombia*, April 27, 1824.

Koinzer, Thomas. "'Lehrfahrten für die Gesamtschule'. Educational Borrowing, Transfer und Externalisierung auf die amerikanische Comprehensive School." *Bildung und Erziehung* 62, no. 1 (2008): 11–29.

Lafragua, José María. "Discurso pronunciado por el Sr. Lic. Don José María Lafragua en contra de la Tolerancia de cultos, en la sesion celebrada en el Palacio Legislativo, el 1° de Agoto de 1856." In *Galería de oradores de México en el siglo XIX*, edited by Emilio del Castillo Negrete. 224–239. Mexico: Tipografía de R. I. González e Hijos, 1878.

Lafragua, José María. *Memorandum de los negocios pendientes entre México y España*. Poissy: Tipografía de Arbieu, 1857.

Lafragua, José María. *Memoria de la Primera Secretaría de Estado y del Despacho de Relaciones Interiores y Exteriores de los Estados-Unidos Mexicanos*. Mexico: Imprenta de Vicente García Torres, 1847.

Lamas, Andrés. *Apuntes históricos sobre las agresiones del dictador argentino D. Juan Manuel Rosas contra la independencia de la República Oriental del Uruguay*. Montevideo: Imprenta Hispano-Americana, 1849.

Latelier, Valentín. *Sesiones de los cuerpos lejislativos de la República de Chile, 1811 a 1845*. Santiago: Imprenta Cervantes, 1893.

López, José Francisco. *Estudio político de la República Argentina y un cuadro histórico del govierno municipal en los pueblos romanos y germánicos*. Buenos Aires: Imprenta, litografía y fundición de tipos de la Sociedad Anónima, 1875.

Manifiesto Liminar de la Reforma Universitaria de 1918. Buenos Aires: Ministerio de Educación de la Nación, 1985.

Michelena y Rojas, Francisco. *Exploracion oficial por la primera vez desde el norte de la América del Sur*. Brussels: Lacroix, Verboeckhoven y Cia., 1867.

Milanesio, Natalia. "Gender and Generation: The University Reform Movement in Argentina, 1918." *Journal of Social History* 39, no. 2 (2005): 505–529.

Oelsner, Veronica. *'Produzenten statt Parasiten': Entwürfe und Wirklichkeiten beruflicher Ausbildung im modernen Argentinien*. Frankfurt: Peter Lang, 2012.

Ortiz, Tadeo. *México considerado como nación independiente y libre, ó sean algunas indicaciones sobre los deberes mas esenciales de los mexicanos*. Burdeos: Imprenta de Carlos Lawalle Sobrino, 1832.

Páez, José Antonio. *Autobiografia*. Vol. II, New York: Imprenta de Hallet y Breen, 1869.

Palti, Elías. *El tiempo de la política. El siglo XIX reconsiderado*. Buenos Aires: Siglo XXI, 2007.

Perez Gallardo, Basilio. "La instruccion publica durante la dominacion española en México." In *Polémica entre el Diario Oficial y la Colonia Española sobre la administración virreynal en Nueva-España y la colonización en México*. 178–196. Mexico: Imprenta Políglota, 1875.

Prieto, Guillermo. *Lecciones elementales de economía política*. Mexico: Imprenta del Gobierno, 1871.

Ramos Mejía, José María. *Las neurosis de los hombres célebres en la Historia Argentina*. Buenos Aires: Martin Biedma, editor, 1878.

Redactores de los Congresos Constitucionales de 1846 y Extraordinarios de 1847 y 1848. La Paz: Litografías e Imprentas Unidas, 1924.

Rivera, Agustín. *Pensamientos filosóficos sobre la educación de la mujer en México*. Mazatlan: Typ. y Casa Editorial de Valadés y Cia., 1908.

Rodríguez O., Jaime E. *La independencia de la América española*. Mexico: El Colegio de Mexico/FCE, 2005.

Roldán Vera, Eugenia. "Order in the Classrom: The Spanish American Appropriation of the Monitorial System of Education." *Paedagogica Historica* 41, no. 6 (2005): 655–675.

Roldán Vera, Eugenia. "Reading in Questions and Answers. The Catechism as an Educational Genre in Early Independent Spanish America." *Book History* 4 (2001): 17–48.

Roldán Vera, Eugenia. "Towards a Logic of Citizenship. Public Examinatios in Elementary Schools in Mexico, 1788–1848: State and Education before and after Independence." *Paedagogica Historica* 46, no. 4 (2010): 511–524.

Schriewer, Jürgen. "Vergleich als Methode und Externalisierung auf Welt: Vom Umgang mit Alterität in Reflexionsdisziplinen." In *Theorie als Passion*, edited by Dirk Baecker, Jürgen Markowitz, Rudolf Stichweh, Hartmann Tyrell and Helmut Willke. 629–668. Frankfurt: Suhrkamp, 1987.

Spiewak, Martin. *Das ferne Echo der Vernunft: das höhere Bildungswesen in Hispanoamerika im Zeitalter der Aufklärung*. Münster: Lit, 1993.

Tocornal, Manuel. *Memoria sobre el primer gobierno nacional*. Santiago: Imprenta del Progreso, 1848.

Tünnermann Bernheim, Carlos. *Noventa años de la Reforma Universitaria de Córdoba (1918–2008)*. Buenos Aires: CLACSO, 2008.

V. C. *Lijera reseña de los partidos, facciones y otros males que agobian a la República Mexicana, y particularmente al Distrito Federal*. Mexico: Imprenta de M. F. Redondas, 1851.

Valdez, Crisóval. "Estudios Histórico-Económicos." *Revista de Santiago* 3, no. 21 (1849): 22–36.

Villalba Pérez, Enrique. *Consecuencias educativas de la expulsión de los jesuitas en América*. Madrid: Dykinson, 2003.

Weinberg, Gregorio. "The Enlightenment and Some Aspects of Culture and Higher Education in Spanish America." In *Facets of Education in the Eighteenth Century*, edited by James A. Leith. 491–522. Oxford: The Voltaire Foundation, 1977.

Parimala V. Rao

Imperial Roots of Nationalist Education Model in India 1880–1947

If you give education to the poor -
It "would teach them to despise their lot in life, instead of making them good servants in agriculture" (Tory MP Davies Giddy 1807)[1]
"The student may be unhappy and discontented in his peculiar position [...]" (Governor-General Auckland 1839)[2]
"teach him to be discontented with his lot." (Bal Gangadhar Tilak 1881)[3]
"do you wish to make a peasant discontented with his cottage or his lot?" (Mohandas Karamchand Gandhi 1909)[4]

Abstract The roots of decolonial projects reach far back to the colonial policies and experiences. The chapter analyses the strong links between the colonial and the post-colonial in the history of nationalist educational proposals. The emergence of the first nationalist educational discourses - particularly from Bal Gangadhar Tilak - appear as a re-elaboration of an 'imperial idea' that critically continued the practice of establishing modern education along the lines of class and gender hierarchisation. The author shows that its underlying aim was the (re)construction of an imagined pre-colonial social order disrupted by British colonial rule. Similarly, Gandhi's famous educational proposals represented the spiritualization of this very imperial idea and did not pose an emancipatory alternative with regard to the questions of hierarchy and discrimination. The chapter highlights the character of nationalist education as an elite project. Education constituted

1 Clyde Chitty, *Education Policy in Britain* (New York: Palgrave MacMillan, 2004), 5.
2 Minute by Auckland dated 24 November 1839, *Report of the General Committee of Public Instruction, 1840* (Calcutta, n.d., 1840), ix.
3 "Our System of Education: A Defect and a Cure," *The Mahratta* (May 15, 1881): 3–4.
4 Mohandas Karamchand Gandhi, *Indian Home Rule or Hind Swaraj* (Ahmedabad: Navjivan Press, 1938), 60.

a primary tool in the fabric of independence and liberation. But this tool was still both imperial and socially conservative in outlook and purpose.

Keywords: India, independence, nationalism, women, low castes

Introduction

The similarity in the ideas of a conservative member of the British parliament, the British governor-general of India who laid the foundation for its colonial education policy[5] and the most vocal anti-colonial leaders who have assumed an iconic status is quite extraordinary. Popular writings about the history of education in India assert that the British colonisers imposed English education while anti-colonial nationalism rejected it and that M. K. Gandhi produced the most original and revolutionary alternative.[6] The terms 'English' and 'English education', as used in the colonial records and the nationalist writings, denote modern education.

During the first ninety-three years (1757–1850) of its rule, the colonial state did not establish a single modern educational institution. It established Arabic and Sanskrit colleges and issued stipends and scholarships to study these languages. It incorporated nearly 70,000 indigenous vernacular schools by giving a small salary of five rupees to the teacher and established several schools where a "pre-colonial" vernacular curriculum was taught. Though the British liberals forced the colonial government to earmark 100,000 rupees a year for Indian education in 1813, the amount remained unutilised till 1823, and partially utilised till 1852–1853. During this period, few English schools were established by individual British officers, which were regularly closed down soon after the death or departure of their respective founders. Indians themselves established most of the modern educational institutions like the Hindu College at Calcutta, The Elphinstone College at Bombay, Pacheyappa College at Madras.

Two models of national education

The imperialist and nationalist historical narratives create binaries by side-lining the areas of convergence, co-operation and trans-national connections. In fact,

---

5 J. A. Richey, *Selections from Educational Records Part II* (Calcutta: Bureau of Education, 1922), 1.

6 See, Dharmapal, *The Beautiful Tree: The Indigenous Education in the Eighteenth Century* (New Delhi: Biblia Impex, 1983); Gauri Viswanathan, *Masks of Conquest: Literary Study and British Rule in India,* (London: Faber and Faber, 1990); Krishna Kumar, *Political Agenda of Education: A Study of Colonialist and Nationalist Ideas* (New Delhi: Sage, 1991).

the origin of the anti-colonial agitation itself was rooted in a transnational connection. Alan Octavian Hume (1829–1912), son of the radical Scottish member of British Parliament Joseph Hume, was the moving force behind the establishment of the Indian National Congress (INC) in 1885. The liberal Indian and British leaders who joined Hume opposed oppressive agrarian policies and campaigned for the introduction of compulsory and free education. They were idealists, rationalists, and humanists who refused to turn a blind eye on the traditional social disabilities suffered by women and lower castes and the abject rural poverty. They believed that economic and social transformation achieved through universalisation of education and political agitation for India's liberation from colonial rule should take place simultaneously.[7]

A group of leaders who called themselves as nationalists opposed this liberal agenda of the INC. The most prominent among them were Lajpat Rai (1865–1928), Aurobindo Ghosh (1872–1950), Bal Gangadhar Tilak (1856–1920) and Mohandas Karamchand Gandhi (1869–1948). These nationalist leaders could be divided into two categories: those who did embrace modern education and those who opposed it. Lajpat Rai and Aurobindo Ghosh supported modern education but insisted on teaching cultural, religious, and philosophical achievements in ancient India. Lajpat Rai was the first to raise the issue of "national education in 1883" two years before the establishment of the Indian National Congress. His primary concern was peculiar to his province of Punjab. When the British conquered Punjab in 1849, they rejected the Punjabi language which was spoken by the Hindus, Muslims and Sikhs as 'a dialect' and imposed Hindustani or what came to be later called Urdu in Persian script as the official language and the medium of instruction in schools.[8] This was resented by all the three communities. William Arnold, the first Director of Public Instruction, termed this opposition in a racist way by declaring that, "to an Asiatic, everything is distasteful, which is new."[9]

The resentment against the introduction of Hindustani was due to two reasons. Firstly, it was unfamiliar language and secondly, the British promoted Hindustani as the language of the Muslims other parts of India. This language

7 Parimala V. Rao, "Compulsory Education and Political Leadership in Colonial India," in *New Perspectives in the History of Indian Education*, ed. Parimala V. Rao (New Delhi: Orient BlackSwan, 2014), 151–159.

8 Parliamentary Branch, 1857–1858, vol. 42, Minute by Robert Montgomery, Judicial Commissioner minute dated 7 March 1853, 45–48, British Library, London.

9 Arnold's Second Report on Education in Punjab dated 25 June 1858; Richey, *Selections*, 300–303.

was spoken by people in and around Delhi, which was a seat of erstwhile Mughal Empire. This was a politically motivated stand to keep the two communities separate and prevent a possible threat of combined opposition to the colonial rule. Officials openly declared that "divide et imperia had always been our best policy and must continue to be so."[10] The Muslims in various parts of India spoke the language of their Hindu neighbours and used Arabic for religious purposes. They spoke Bengali in Bengal Presidency, Gujarati and Marathi in Bombay Presidency, Tamil and Malayalam in Madras Presidency. The colonial state argued that the Muslims had forgotten their culture and established separate schools for Muslims to teach Hindustani.[11] These schools were not successful; the Muslim boys studied in them could not get jobs as they had no command over the local language. But they were successful in promoting a distinct Muslim identity.

Lajpat Rai developed his ideal of national education as a reaction to this policy. He also held a very high status and position in the Arya Samaj, the revivalist organisation established by Dayananda Saraswati in 1875. He wanted "to instil pride in the Indian nation" by making Punjabi as the medium of instruction in the educational institutions and teach ancient India's cultural, and scientific achievements in addition to the modern curriculum.[12] His movement was region-specific.

Aurobindo Ghosh drew up a constructive plan for national education during the Swadeshi movement during 1905–1908. Aurobindo explained that the national education movement was an attempt "to rescue education from subversive to foreign and petty ends and to establish colleges and schools maintained and controlled by Indians which would give an education superior to the government-controlled education." Aurobindo insisted that "we must acquire for her the best knowledge that Europe can give her and assimilate it to her own peculiar type of national temperament. We must introduce the best methods of teaching humanity has developed, whether modern or ancient. All these we must harmonise into a system which will be impregnated with the spirit of self-reliance so on to build up men and not machines."[13] So the national education model promoted

10 General Department 23 of 1849, Establishment of schools. Maharashtra State Archives (MSA).

11 Ibid, General Department, 63 of 1824 (MSA).

12 Lajpat Rai, *Problems of National Education in India* (London: George Allen Unwin, 1920), 18–25.

13 Sabyasachi Bhattacharya, et al., *Educating the Nation* (New Delhi: Kanishka, 2003), 9–12, 33–38.

by Lajpat Rai and Aurobindo Ghosh proposed to teach patriotism along with the modern curriculum.

The second model was developed first by Bal Gangadhar Tilak and then by Mohandas Karamchand Gandhi. They rejected modern education as it supposedly destroyed the structures of hierarchy. This paper limits its analysis to the second group as its protagonists were the most vocal advocates of national education and exhibited vehement opposition to modern education.

The sources for national education

During the colonial period, two sources were available to build educational systems upon India's own pre-colonial system and the system as practised in England. Regarding the Indian system, the British officials and educators had conducted extensive village level enquiry and published reports for most parts of India. The Indian society was stratified in terms of caste, with Brahmins as priests and interpreters of sacred texts alone having access to the Sanskrit schools.

Vernacular schools, in contrast, were open to boys of all castes. Nearly two-thirds of students and a large portion of teachers in pre-colonial vernacular schools came from peasant and artisanal castes. In the Bombay Presidency, the village-wise data for Ratnagiri district is available. Here of the 1468 boys in schools 418 were non-Brahmin, and 393 belonged to artisanal castes, and the rest were Brahmins, Muslims and Jews.[14] In Ahmedabad district, of the 2,973 boys, 410 were Brahmins, 1,772 trading castes (Wani), 791 boys belonged to the peasant and artisanal castes.[15] In the Burdwan district, Bengal Presidency, out of 12,408 boys, 3,429 were Brahmins, and 4,361 were from artisanal castes, 750 boys came from untouchable castes. They studied with upper-caste boys in the same classroom.[16] Caste was largely disregarded in schools. High caste Brahmin and Muslim boys studied under non- Brahmin teachers.[17] Language and arithmetic formed the backbone of the curriculum in these schools. Vernacular translations of Sanskrit epics like *Ramayana* and *Mahabharata*, *Amara Kosha*, a treatise in

14 T. B. Jervis to the Secretary to the government dated 8 September 1824, General Department, 63 of 1824, (MSA).

15 Arthur Crawford to James Farish dated 20 September 1824, General Department, 92 of 1825, MSA.

16 Anathnath Basu, ed., William Adam, *Reports on the State of Education in Bengal 1835 and 1838* (Calcutta: University of Calcutta, 1941), 246–247.

17 Parimala V. Rao, "A Century of Consolidation and Resistance: Caste and Education in Maharashtra 1818–1918," *Occasional Paper NMML*, New Delhi, (2014): 5–6.

grammar were used to teach language and grammar. Arithmetic, including multiplication tables, was taught in all these schools. Some schools taught boys to "cast up accounts and to draw out a bill of exchange, book-keeping and calculate compound interest" in their curriculum.[18]

The majority of teachers and students were 'miserably poor,' and parents of the boys paid a monthly fee and occasional gifts to the teachers. The poor students received education gratis.[19] On average, the earnings of teachers were lower than that of agricultural labourers. In spite of the low economic status, poor teachers and students were well respected.[20] This was because of the underlying Indian belief that one could pursue knowledge only by giving up comforts and the Indian tradition had numerous examples, including that of Gautama the Buddha. So, the pre-colonial vernacular schools in India were open to boys from all castes, a very high standard of literacy and numeracy was taught, and the parents paid for such education. The chief drawback in terms of access was that girls were not allowed into these schools.

The education system in England

England too exhibited a similar trend in the pre-modern times. Richard Aldrich has quoted an instance of how "a beggar's brat could become a bishop, and sit among the peers of the realm and lord's sons and knights crouch to him." However, in the sixteenth century, the establishment of the Anglican Church legitimised social stratification.[21] The expansion of trade and Empire enabled the English elites to strengthen their position. The industrialisation further alienated the poor from education.[22] By the eighteenth century, two parallel systems of education emerged, wherein the elite children were prepared by either private tutors or expensive private 'preparatory schools' to enter exclusive secondary

---

18 Ramchandra V. Parulekar, *Survey of Indigenous Education in the province of Bombay 1820–1830* (Bombay: Asia Publishing House, 1951), xxxi–xxxv.

19 Rao, *New Perspectives*, 26.

20 Parimala V. Rao, "Promiscuous Crowd of English Smatterers': 'Poor' in the Colonial and Nationalist Discourse on Education in India 1835–1935," *Contemporary Education Dialogue* 10, no. 2 (2013): 223–225.

21 Richard Aldrich, *An Introduction to the History of Education* (London: Hodder and Stoughton, 1982), 13–14.

22 W. D. Halls, "Cultural ideals and elitist education in England," *Comparative Education Review, 15*(3) (1971): 317–329; Philip Gardner, "Literacy, learning and education," in *A Companion to Nineteenth-century Britain*, ed. Chris Williams (Massachusetts: Blackwell, 2004), 353–368.

schools called Grammar Schools. This type of institutions taught Greek, Latin, and mathematics, and served as a gateway to the universities.[23] The poor could send their children to Charity schools, Schools of Industry and Sunday schools which gave only rudimentary instruction in reading and reinforced the existing social stratification. Sunday schools were promoted by the social reformer Robert Raikes (1736–1811) who argued that for the children who worked the entire week, Sunday was a day of freedom, where "the misuse of Sunday appears by the declaration of every criminal to be their first step in the course of wickedness." The parents paid one dime per week. The Sunday schools thus aimed to keep the children occupied to prevent crime.[24]

The Schools of Industry were much more severe kind of system. As early as 1675 Thomas Firmian (1632–1697) had erected a spinning factory where children of four or five years of age were taught to read and spin. Towards the end of the seventeenth century, the English philosopher John Locke argued that "the children of labouring people are an ordinary burden to the parish, and are usually maintained in idleness so that their labour also is generally lost to the public till they are 12 or 14 years old." He, therefore, suggested that 'working schools' be set up in each parish in England for poor children so that they will be "from infancy [three years old] inured to work." He went on to outline the economics of these schools, arguing not only that they will be profitable for the parish, but also that they will instil a good work ethic in the children.[25] Several industrial schools set up in the early part of the eighteenth century taught gardening, carpentry, cobbling and printing to boys and spinning, knitting, sewing and straw-plaiting to girls. The work done by the children was sold, and proceeds went to their maintenance. If the child's earnings exceeded the cost of his keep, he was given a cash payment. The idea was to make schools self-supporting. In some schools of industry, children were taught reading and writing, but there was always the temptation to emphasise the occupational aspect to cover expenses. The boys' schools were largely a failure as their products did not command the market like

23 Stanley J. Curtis, *History of Education in Great Britain* (London: University Tutorial Press, 1965), 122; Richard S. Tompson, "The English Grammar School Curriculum in the 18th century: A Reappraisal," *British Journal of Educational Studies* 19, no. 1 (1971): 32–39; William A. L. Blyth, *English Primary Education: A Sociological Description* (London: Routledge and Kegan Paul, 1965), 30.

24 Curtis, *History of Education*, 193–199.

25 John Locke, "An Essay on the Poor Law," in *Political Essays*, ed. Mark Goldie (Cambridge: Cambridge University Press, 1997), 190–191.

those from girl's schools. These schools declined due to industrialisation as even very young children came to be employed in modern factories.

The underlying idea common to all three kinds of schools was that the poor ought to be trained to accept and internalize the existing social stratification. Even though the educational attainments of these children were in no way a threat to the elite monopoly of Grammar schools and the universities, it was still resented. It was argued that the education of the poor would result in discontent and rebellion. The poor occupied a position in society which had been assigned to them, and if they were to be labourers, they should be used to their position from the first.[26]

The *National Society for Promoting the Education of the Poor in the Principles of the Established Church* was established in 1811 in London. The society established a network of schools for the poor.[27] The purpose of the system was to "infuse [...] a cheerful and uniform subjection to all lawful authority," and to keep them away from "discontentment."[28] The Church wished that "the children to learn through their readers about the demarcation between rich and poor and the mutual dependence of each in a harmonious society. Contentment in the station of life to which God had assigned them was an important precept." A fable meant for children gave the example of what disaster would befall a person if the various parts of the human body went on strike in protest at the seeming greed and selfishness of the stomach. The fable explains that the stomach is to the body what the rich man is to the poor man in society, and concludes that "a rich man, even though he may care for no one but himself, can hardly avoid benefitting his neighbours."[29] Even this disciplining of children from the most impoverished section of the society was not free; the parents had to pay one shilling per quarter on first Monday in January, April, July, and October.[30] So the poor paid for being disciplined by the Church.

---

26 Curtis, *History of Education*, 195–199.

27 *First annual report of The National Society for Promoting the Education of the Poor in the Principles of the Established Church* (London, 1812), 5.

28 Phillip McCann, "Popular Education and Socialization and Social Control: Spitialfields 1812–1824," in *Popular Education and Socialization in the Nineteenth Century*, ed. Phillip McCann (London: Methuen, 1979), 1.

29 J. M. Goldstrom, "The Content of Education and Socialisation of the Working Class Child 1830–1860," in *Popular Education*, ed. Phillip McCann (London: Methuen, 1979), 98–103.

30 *First Annual Report of the National Society*, 36.

These measures were eventually opposed and countered by English liberals. They were successful in getting various education acts passed only after 1870 and compulsory and free education was successfully implemented throughout England.

The colonial state policy in India

The colonial state in India virtually followed the system that was practised in England. It closed down the schools established by the Scottish officers like Thomas Munro, T. B. Macaulay, Robert Shortread and others as they contained boys from "lower classes and miserable background".[31] It was while upturning Macaulay's Minute of 1835 by his own Minute of 1839 that governor-general Auckland argued that if modern education was given to the poor "the student may be unhappy and discontented in his peculiar position." It was not Macaulay's Minute but Auckland's Minute that laid the foundation for the educational policy of the colonial state. It encouraged the admission of the children of landlords and repeatedly told the headmasters to dismiss the boys from a poor background; it closed down over 100 schools as they had "no sons of the landed gentry." It carefully trained and appointed Brahmins as schoolmasters.[32] It openly opposed the admission of poor Brahmin as well as lower caste boys by stating that, "if the beggarly Brahmins are freely admitted into the government schools, what is there to prevent all the despised castes - the Dhers, Mahars from flocking in numbers [...] If education is open to men of superior intelligence from any community, and with such qualifications there would be nothing to prevent their aspiring to the highest offices open to native talent."[33]

In spite of these elitist measures, the poor students formed the majority of the school and college-going children during the colonial period. The British headmasters often ignored the government directives to remove poor students from schools.[34] Secondly, the missionaries extended free education to all. The leading members of the Indian National Congress like Dadabhai Naoroji and

31 Rao, "Promiscuous Crowd," 230–231.

32 Parimala V. Rao, "Modern Education and the Revolt of 1857 in India," *Paedagogica Historica*, no. 52, 1–2, (2016): 31.

33 The letter from the Governor of Bombay to the Board of Education of 24 April 1850, in: *Report of the Board of Education for the year 1849* (Bombay: Bombay Education Society's Press, 1851), 13.

34 W. Handford DPI Oudh to secretary to the Chief Commissioner of Oudh dated 24 November 1869, NAI, Home/Education, 3 August 1870 No. 8 A.

Gopal Krishna Gokhale who fought for radical social, economic and educational reforms had risen from poverty. So both the Indian tradition and the existing social reality pointed in the same direction; namely that, what India needed was equal educational access and good quality education for all.

Nationalising an imperial idea

The leading anti-colonial political leaders like Bal Gangadhar Tilak and Mohandas Karamchand Gandhi had, however, different ideas on what constituted an education for Indians. By rejecting the reformers as "anglicised, un-national leaders,"[35] Tilak and later Gandhi attempted to provide an alternative socio-educational philosophy that had a far-reaching impact on education.

Tilak came from a family of landlords, moneylenders and government officials. He entered the public arena in 1881, through his weekly publication *The Mahratta.* He used it effectively to oppose colonial policies and to attack the reformers. He defended the caste system in the name of "cleanliness," and declared that "the Hindu religion owed its existence to the caste system."[36] The term caste is a modern one, and the Hindu religious texts refer to this stratification as *chaturvarna* or four-fold division and the system which specifies how each caste should behave, follow certain occupations and punishment for those who transcend it is referred to as *varnashrama dharma.* Tilak used all three terms, sometimes in the same speech or editorial.

To begin with, Tilak was not against modern education. He actually declared that "we were an ignorant mass of people," before its "civilising influence."[37] However, he opposed the reformers' campaign for equal educational access for all sections of the society by arguing that, such a measure took the lower castes away from their traditional occupation and traditional existence:

> You take away a farmer's boy from the plough, the blacksmith's boy from the bellows and the cobbler's boy from his awl with the object of giving him liberal education, [...] you remove him from a sphere where he would have been contented happy and useful to those who depend upon him and teach him to be discontented with his lot and with the government.[38]

35 "How shall we do it? Editorial," *The Mahratta* (April 26, 1891): 2.
36 "The Prospects of Hindu Caste," *The Mahratta* (July 10, 1881): 1.
37 "The Functions of Our Universities," *The Mahratta* (Feb 15, 1885): 2.
38 "Our system of Education – A Defect and a Cure," *The Mahratta* (May 15, 1881): 3–4.

Tilak emphasised that teaching a modern curriculum for the lower castes had "no earthly use in practical life," and would actually "do more harm than good to them." He insisted that they should be taught "only those subjects which would be necessary for their living, [...] befitting their rank and station in life." They should be taught "most ordinary trades like those of a carpenter, blacksmith mason and tailor."[39] Later he urged the government to remodel the courses prescribed for rural schools and "introduce in them agricultural subjects such as preparing of soil, the tending of bullocks, the implements of husbandry etc."[40] He asked the colonial government to limit English education to affluent Brahmins and set up separate schools to meet the educational requirements of "variously civilized communities."[41] Against this background, it is hardly surprising that he openly opposed the admission of boys from untouchable castes into schools.[42]

What is interesting in these early discussions is that, Tilak although he called himself a nationalist, yet warned the colonial government "that the interests of the society and the government are similar [...] by placing the latest results arrived at by moral and political science in a young graduate's hand the government is encouraging the reformers to ask for extreme reforms in the society which would lead to reformers demanding similar extreme reform in the governance."[43]

By 1891, Tilak changed his stand. The British and Indian reformers were successful in getting the Age of Consent Bill passed. This Bill was introduced in the Imperial Legislature by Andrew Scoble and Dayaram Gidumal and was a limited measure, aiming at the abolishment of child marriage and meant to raise the marriageable age of girls to 12. During the debate, the reformers argued that the additional years secured in a girls' life could be used to educate them. Tilak vehemently opposed it by arguing that if girls were educated "India would lose its nationality its individuality as a separate nation".[44] By quoting the British newspapers, he argued that "the brain of a woman on an average weighed less by five ounces than that of a man."[45] He even stated that women reformers like Rakmabais, Pandita Ramabai "should be punished for the same reason as there

39 Ibid.

40 *The Mahratta* (Feb 21 1886): 5.

41 "The Educational Policy of the Government, Editorial," *The Mahratta* (March 3, 1889): 1.

42 "Admission of Mahar boys into government Schools," *The Mahratta* (March 26, 1882): 5–6.

43 "The Functions of our Universities I," *The Mahratta* (Feb 15, 1885): 2.

44 "Higher Female Education," *The Mahratta* (Aug 24, 1884): 2.

45 "Female Education," *The Mahratta* (Nov 13, 1887): 3.

is punishment for thieves, adulterers and murderers."[46] After the passing of the Age of Consent Act, Tilak became a vocal advocate of anti-colonial nationalism and national education. He placed the traditional caste hierarchy - *varnashrama dharma* at the heart of the Indian nationhood and argued that "had it not been for the influence of caste, the Hindu nation would have long ceased to exist." He asserted that activities of the reformers "would kill the caste and with it kill the vitality of the nation."[47] Since modern education undermined "respect for old institutions and beliefs" and led to "religious nihilism," it was a great impediment to Indian nationalism.[48] Tilak argued that religious and vocational education alone should form the basis of the curriculum to restore respect for "old institutions, old values and old idol". Tilak explained that with "old institution" he was referring to the caste stratification and by "old values" he hinted to the honour and respect paid by the lower castes to the "old idol", the Brahmins.[49] Since modern education had upturned all three, national education was vital to re-construct a strong Indian nation.[50] Tilak opposed the teaching of Sanskrit poetry or even Hindu philosophy. He explained that "much of the religious instruction should consist of dogma pure and simple. The schoolboys will have to be told dogmatically that there is God [...] of course; the schoolboy who wants an ocular proof of the existence of God will have to be caned into silence."[51]

Tilak and his supporters established national schools during the first phase of anti-colonial struggle (called the Swadeshi movement, 1905–1912). These schools were not popular with the people and soon disappeared. The quality of literacy that was advocated in the schools was very low. They opposed the efforts of Gopal Krishna Gokhale's Compulsory Education Bill 1912 and the efforts of the Maharaja of Baroda to implement compulsory education in his province.[52] During the public debates surrounding the passing of the Compulsory Education Bill, they argued that "the soul of education is really information; hence, it is sufficient to give information to boys." Since everybody loves to write his name,

46 "The Law for the Restitution of Conjugal Rights," *The Mahratta* (June 12, 1887): 2–3.

47 "The Caste and Caste alone has Power, Editorial," *The Mahratta* (May 10, 1891): 3.

48 "Mass Education Editorial," *The Mahratta* (Nov 30 1890): 2; "Moral and Religious Instructions in Schools," *The Mahratta* (March 17, 1901): 4–5.

49 "Caste Jealousies," *The Mahratta* (Feb. 26, 1888): 5.

50 "Religious Education in Schools and Colleges," *The Mahratta* (July 5, 1903): 318.

51 "Religion Education Suggestion Towards a Practical Scheme, Editorial," *The Mahratta* (July 3, 1904): 313.

52 "Moral and Religious Education," *Mahratta* (Apr. 10, 1910): 173; "Free Primary Education," *The Mahratta* (Apr. 24, 1910): 200.

he should be taught to do so. They also suggested "the appointment of a music master to play music in public and arrange slide shows of Hindu religious places to attract people."[53] Beyond this, the masses did not require education.

Tilak started the Indian Home Rule League, modelled after the Irish Home Rule League in 1916 to intensify his agitation against colonial rule. Home Rule aimed at the transfer of India's internal administration into Indian hands while India continued to be part of the British Empire. The justification he gave for Home Rule was that *chaturvarna* had declined under the influence of modern education and India needed Home Rule to protect *varnashrama dharma* – the caste system.[54] Tilak argued that "the colonial education discouraged students from learning anything from their elders about the actual surroundings [...] only in the national schools independent of government control, adequate education in making good citizen can be given."[55] In these schools the children should be taught "the theory of *karma* and the existence of god," and the pedagogy "is found in our *Puranas*" (Hindu Mythological stories).[56] The theory of *karma* in the Hindu religion provides justification for a person's low or high birth, and the *Puranas* upheld these justifications linking it up with the will of god. The instruction given to boys was mostly oral.[57] So, the aim of national education was to make children accept their caste and economic status in the society and not question them.

Two important issues can be deducted from these developments. Firstly, Tilak did not advocate the abolition of modern schools, colleges and universities. Secondly, the national education advocated by Tilak and comprised of religious and vocational education was essentially for the lower caste and lower class Indians. This meant that the affluent upper-caste Brahmins would have access to modern education and thereby control important positions of power, while the poor from the upper caste and the lower castes would be taught to accept the social and economic hierarchy. This was not based on the pre-colonial Indian education system but certainly derived from the class-based education system of the imperial rulers.

Tilak's national education could not be dismissed off as rhetoric produced during the time of anti-colonial struggle to cater to popular demand or to seek

53 "A Supplement to Primary Education," *The Mahratta* (May 14, 1911) 234–236.

54 "Brahmins not Brahmins," *The Mahratta* (Jan 7, 1917): 6; "The Tilak-Principle," *The Mahratta* (Jan 7, 1917): 6; "Varnashrama Dharma," *The Mahratta* (Jan 21, 1917): 34.

55 "Education for Citizenship," *The Mahratta* (Aug 26, 1917): 407.

56 *The Mahratta* (Apr 14, 1918): 178.

57 *The Mahratta* (Apr 14, 1918): 179.

the support of the more conservative sections of the society. His supporters controlled ten out of eleven municipalities in the Marathi speaking areas of the Bombay Presidency where they refused to expand educational infrastructure or support the admission of lower caste boys, let alone the education of girls.[58] They also refused to implement compulsory education even after the provincial Bill was passed in 1918.[59] Tilak, however, died on 1 August 1920, and the leadership passed on into the hands of Mohandas Karamchand Gandhi.

Spiritualising an imperial idea

If Tilak successfully nationalised the imperial idea of keeping the poor, girls and the lower castes from getting any meaningful education and emphasise religious instruction as real national education, Mohandas Karamchand Gandhi went a step ahead and spiritualised it. Gandhi was born into privilege; his father was a prime minister of the princely states of Porbandar and Rajkot. By his own admission, Gandhi was an average student and barely managed to pass the examinations,[60] yet he was sent to England for higher education. Later he went to South Africa in 1893 to represent a legal case of an Indian trader and spent the next 14 years there experimenting with and refining his social and political ideas. When the First World War broke out in 1914, he recruited volunteers for ambulance corps for the British. He returned to India in 1915. At that time the Indian National Congress was losing its liberal leaders one by one. The death of A. O. Hume (1912), Gokhale (1915), Dadabhai Naoroji (1917), William Wedderburn (1918) left the party virtually leaderless. Consequently, Tilak dominated the political arena. Gandhi supported the Home Rule agitation, but also engaged in the recruitment of young Indians as soldiers for the British army during the First World War, arguing that "we should become partners in the empire."[61] In 1919, the colonial government wanted to remove English as a medium of instruction in high schools, while retaining it in the universities. If implemented,

58 "Editorial," *The Mahratta* (Jan 25, 1890): 2; "The Poona Municipality. Editorial," *The Mahratta* (Jan 18, 1891) 3; "The Storm Against the Municipality Editorial," *The Mahratta* (Feb 8, 1891): 2.

59 "Free and Compulsory Education in Poona," *The Mahratta* (Aug 17, 1919): 394; "Nationalists and Compulsory Education," *The Mahratta* (Feb 29, 1920): 103.

60 Mohandas Karamchand Gandhi, *The Problem of Education* (Ahmedabad: Navajivan Publishing House, 1962), 54.

61 Appeal for Enlistment dated 22 June 1818, M. K. Gandhi, *Collected Works*, Vol.17 (New Delhi: Ministry of Information and Broadcasting, 1994), 83–85.

this measure virtually would have prevented thousands of high school students from entering the universities, and only Indian landed gentry who studied in exclusive schools alone would have been in a position to enter the universities. The landed gentry was known by various names like Talukdar, Inamdar, Jagirdar institutions, which denoted various demarcations within the landholders and Chiefs Colleges and Rajkumar Institutions where the sons of the Indian royal families studied. There was a widespread opposition, which was led by members of the Indian elite like Srinivasair, the advocate general of Madras, Krishna Nair, the Diwan (prime minister) of Travancore, or Sitanath Roy – one of the biggest landlords of Bengal. The colonial state could get support only from Gandhi, and the Lord Bishop of Madras, an Anglican Bishop, which is used to substantiate its final decision. The Bishop argued that "English is an intolerable burden on the students; foreign languages impose crushing weight upon the whole educational system of India. English has created cleavages between English educated and the mass of the population."[62] This was virtually a verbatim representation of ideas that Gandhi held regarding modern education. The British government, however, could not implement it immediately as the political agitation intensified.

Gandhi attacked modern education as early as 1908 in his book *Hind Swaraj* – Indian Home Rule. He denounced modern education as godless claiming that "India will never be godless, rank atheism cannot flourish in this land."[63] He attacked the modern curriculum by stating that:

> A study of geography, astronomy, algebra, geometry is false education and it is not for the millions. To give millions knowledge of English is to enslave them. Our ancient school system is enough. Character building has the first place in it, and that is primary education.[64]

Gandhi went on to argue as governor-general Auckland and Tilak had done before him, "do you wish to make a peasant discontented with his cottage or his lot?" He also declared that "our ancient school system is enough." Gandhi criticised the supporters of compulsory education as "those carried away by the flood of western thought."[65] Like Tilak, Gandhi too argued that modern education is "calculated to wean the masses from their traditional culture. They are never taught to have any pride in their surroundings, and the government

62 NAI, Education Proceedings, September 1919, A, No 1,

63 Mohandas Karamchand Gandhi, *Hind Swaraj or India's Home Rule,* 1908 (Ahmedabad: Navjivan Publishing House, 946 reprint), 67.

64 Ibid.

65 Ibid.

schools had entirely denationalized the masses."[66] During the compulsory education debate, Gopal Krishna Gokhale had suggested using eight annas (half a rupee) salt tax to fund compulsory education. Gandhi claimed that Gokhale was his political guru, but did not support Gokhale's Bill and later famously made his opposition to salt tax central to his anti-colonial struggle during 1930–1931.

Extraordinary political developments took place in India during 1919–1920. The post-war political reform earlier promised by the British did not lead to Home Rule. This frustrated the rank and file of the Indian National Congress. At the same time, the government passed the Rowlett Act under which anyone suspected of anti-British activities could be imprisoned for two years without trial. There was widespread protest against this law, and in one such peaceful meeting at Jallianwallah Bagh in Punjab, a British police officer opened fire, killing and injuring more than 1,000 unarmed persons. Around the same time, the Muslims in India began Khilafat – a pan-Islamic movement against the British, which added to widespread discontent among all sections of the society against the colonial rule.[67]

When Gandhi began his non-cooperation movement in 1919, as a part of the larger programme of boycotting the government offices and courts, he asked the students to boycott the schools and colleges. He and his supporters established national schools. These schools rejected the modern curriculum as well as the English language. Gandhi emphatically declared that:

> If I had the powers of a despot, I would today stop the tuition of our boys and girls through a foreign medium. If I had my way, I would certainly destroy the majority of the present text-books and cause to be written text-books which have a bearing on and correspondence with the home life, so that a boy as he learns may react upon his immediate surroundings.[68]

Gandhi argued that:

> The curriculum and pedagogic ideas which form the fabric of modern education are foreign, and till they are repudiated there never can be national education. The force that maintains society together is a series of high loyalties, loyalty to faith, calling, parents,

66 *Young India* (June 1, 1921).

67 Khilafat Movement (1919–1922) was a pan-Islamic movement launched by Abdul Hamid II the emperor of the Ottoman Empire which had lost its power after the First World War. He was also the Caliph (Khalif) the religious head of Muslims around the world. He whipped up religious frenzy as his regime was threatened by democratic and secular forces led by Mustafa Kemal Attaturk. Hamid appealed to Indian Muslims to over throw the British rule. The movement died out in 1922 when Attaturk over threw the emperor and established a secular government.

68 *Young India* (September 1, 1921).

> family, *dharma*. The ancient educational system in India certainly maintained a long tradition of pride and service.[69]

Elaborating on this, Gandhi explained that:

> When our children are admitted to schools, they do not need slate and pencil and books, but simple village tools which they can handle freely and remuneratively. This means a revolution in educational methods. Only, reading and writing would come during the last year when really the boy or girl is ready for learning the alphabet correctly. Text-books especially for children are for the most part useless when they are not harmful.[70]

These were exactly the issues that the nationalists and particularly Tilak had campaigned on for four decades. The only difference was that Tilak openly advocated it for the lower castes and classes, while defending the right of affluent Brahmins to modern education. Gandhi tactically avoided this mistake. He remained silent on higher education and did not ask for the abolition of English in higher education and the universities but directed his educational experiment to the masses.

The schools established by Gandhi and his supporters were called 'self-supporting' schools. The children as young as 6 years had to spin yarn which was sold and the money thus earned was used for giving salary to the teachers and upkeep of the schools. Gandhi declared that "if every school introduced spinning, it would revolutionise our ideas of financing education." He calculated that:

> The boy works at the wheel for four hours daily, he will produce every day ten *tolas* of yarn and thus earn for his school one *anna* per day. [...] A boy can earn 1-10-0 per month and a class of 30 boys would yield an income of 48-12-0 per month.[71]

Since the people who supported the non-cooperation movement did not show similar enthusiasm for his educational activity, Gandhi tried to convince them. He told the people that "of all the superstitions that affect India, none is so great as that a knowledge of the English language is necessary for imbibing ideals of liberty, and developing accuracy of thought."[72] He also asserted that "the government schools have unmanned us, rendered us helpless and godless."[73] In spite

69 *Young India* (March 20, 1924).

70 *Young India* (July 1, 1929); *Harijan* (December 1, 1933).

71 Bharatan Kumarappa, ed., Mohandas Karamchand Gandhi, *Towards New Education* (Ahmedabad: Navajivan Publishing House, 1953), 46; *Young India*, 2 February 1921.

72 Ibid, 11; *Young India* (April 27, 1921).

73 Ibid, 5; *Young India* (June 1, 1921).

of his persistent advocacy of the 'national education,' the schools were a failure. Gandhi himself admitted it when he said that "out of 30,000 boys and girls hardly one thousand are spinning on 100 charkhas at the rate of ½ hour per day. Hundreds of charkhas are lying idle and neglected." The attendance of untouchable and Muslim children was also poor.[74]

Gandhi insisted that his educational system was rooted in the Indian tradition by arguing that "the rishis taught without books. They only gave them a few mantras which the pupils treasured in their memories and translated in practical life."[75] He tried to convince the parents that the national schools would not become "spinning and weaving institutes."[76] But the children "would receive vocal instruction in elementary history, geography and arithmetic," and the children thus trained "would become silent revolutionaries."[77]

Though Gandhi labelled his self-supporting school system 'revolutionary', the colonial state had experimented it during the 1850s in his own state of Gujarat. At that time, the colonial state officials were horrified to find that most of the boys in government schools including the upper caste boys were from 'miserable background,' and even "a Cooli village had a school."[78] In 1850, the governor of Bombay ordered that there should be "strict limitation of superior education to the wealthy, who can afford to pay for it and to youths of unusual intelligence".[79] The officials in their reply admitted that their attempts "to bolster up a landed aristocracy have lamentably failed." Their efforts to maintain a school for the "wards of respectable natives" (aristocracy/landed gentry) in Belgaum was a complete failure.[80] The British thought that the failure of the school might have been due to the distance and also of its residential nature. So they decided to introduce a "self-supporting school system" through which the "respectable natives" would establish schools in their own locality for their children and prevent the admission of poor and lower caste children. They selected Uttarasanda, a rich village in Kheda district with a population of 3,477 and yielding revenue of 9,000 per annum for the experiment.[81] The education department set up a

74 Ibid, 25; *Young India* (August 7, 1924).
75 Ibid, 40; *Young India* (Jan 29, 1925).
76 Ibid, 28; *Young India* (March 12, 1925).
77 Ibid, 36; *Young India* (July 11, 1929).
78 NAI, Home/Education 1 July 1859, Nos. 6–7.
79 The letter from the Governor of Bombay to the Board of Education, dated 24 April 1850, *Report of the Board of Education* 1850, 13.
80 Ibid, 11.
81 W. Hart, Secretary to the Government of Bombay to the sec to the Government of India dated 5 November 1857. NAI, Home/Education, 2 July 1858, Nos. 1–3.

school for the rich landlords, traders and Brahmins. It asked them to contribute for its maintenance and gave them full powers to decide the admission of any child. The people of the village, including Brahmin priests, opposed it. The education department, after struggling to maintain the school for 18 months abandoned it.[82] The Director of Public Instruction declared that "it is framed to suit a state of society which does not exist."[83] Even in this elitist experiment, the colonial state put the burden on the affluent adults and not on the shoulders of the children. Gandhi, in turn, went even beyond the colonial state and did not see "anything wrong in the children as young as 7–12 paying for their education through work from the very threshold of their education."[84] Gandhi justified his educational ideas based on "securing to the students economic, social and spiritual freedom."[85]

The self-supporting schools were partially standing financially on their own feet, as the cost of constructing the school buildings, equipment as well as numerous recurring items of expenditure were covered for by the state. So Gandhi's Basic Education did not liberate education from the clutches of the state. What it actually did was to place the body and mind of a child under the control of the teacher. The schools worked for six hours a day out of which the child would work for four hours and the remaining two hours would be utilised for learning. Within these two hours, music, drawing and arithmetic were to be taught within a period of 40 minutes which allotted 13 minutes for each subject, while both social studies and general science were to be taught within a period of 30 minutes thereby devoting 15 minutes for each subject.[86] Since the salary of the teacher was derived from the labour of the child, there was a tendency to concentrate rather on labour than on the acquisition of knowledge. These schools worked for 288 days a year that is 24 days a month, without summer or winter break. So Gandhi's educational ideas like that of Tilak before him were not rooted in the Indian tradition or the pre-colonial school system. They were rooted in the oppressive school system designed for the British poor.

82 NAI, Home/Education 1 July 1859, Nos. 6–7.
83 *Report of the Director of Public Instruction, Bombay, 1857–1858* (Bombay: The Education Society Press, 1859), 56.
84 *Young India* (Feb 2, 1921); *Young India* (June 15, 1921).
85 Gandhi, *The Problem of Education*, 77.
86 Chunkat J. Varkey, *The Wardha Scheme of Education: An Exposition and Examination* (London: Oxford University Press, 1940), 75–85.

Concluding observations

Normally it is understood that in an anti-colonial struggle, the colonised either totally reject the colonial ideas and provide a viable alternative or incorporate certain positive ideas of the colonisers to strengthen the colonised to create strong resistance. However, in India, both Tilak and Gandhi took the most regressive ideas of the British rulers adopted them as their own. This happened because both Tilak and Gandhi defended the class of big landlords and held feudal interests. In 1879, after witnessing the untold misery suffered by the peasants due to famine Mahadev Govind Ranade and William Wedderburn drafted the Deccan Agriculturists Relief Act, and proposed to establish agricultural (Shetkari) banks. The Bombay government enacted both. According to the act, equipment and livestock of peasants were exempt from attachment by the landlords and moneylenders if the peasant failed to pay the loan. Tilak's entry into the political arena was by defending the right of the big landlords and money lenders (*inamdar, mamlatdar, khot, sowcars* etc) to send the peasant to jail for non-payment of debts. It is unparalleled in the history that an anti-colonial leader pleaded with the colonial state to arrest his poor compatriot peasants.[87] When Tilak was campaigning for the right of the landlords and moneylenders to send the peasants to jail, he maintained close contact with the Indian members of British communist party and published articles on Marxism in his own journals![88] How does one reconcile such a contradiction? Did the Indian born communist party members of the British parliament like Shapurji Saklatvala not read what Tilak wrote in his English journal? There are no definite answers to such fundamental questions since the entire gamut of research in independent India has been directed to the creation of hagiographies of anti-colonial leaders.

Tilak came from a family of big landlords and money lenders. He always argued that the colonial rule had "reversed the natural order of things," and it "liberated servants and women but enslaved the masters."[89] Tilak declared that "caste alone is the basis of Hindu nationality and to defend it, political freedom

87 Parimala. V. Rao, "New insights into the debates on rural indebtedness in the nineteenth century Deccan," *Economic and Political Weekly* 44, no. 04 (January 24 – January 30, 2009): 55–61.

88 J. V. Naik, "Lokmanya Tilak on Karl Marx and Class Conflict," *Economic and Political Weekly* 34, no. 18 (May 1–7, 1999): 1023–1025.

89 For full debates on caste and class interests of Tilak see, Parimala V. Rao, *Foundations of Tilak's Nationalism: Discrimination, Education, and Hindutva* (New Delhi: Orient BlackSwan), 2011.

and self-rule or *swarajya* was needed."[90]So the defence of feudal interests was fundamental to Tilak's anti-colonial struggle.

As a trained lawyer, Gandhi was much more sophisticated and nuanced in his arguments. As a politician who entered the political arena after the First World War, he had a peculiar advantage. In a world distressed by violence seen during the war and his appeal for non-violence made him an instant saint. Within four years of Gandhi's entry into politics, the westerners were comparing him to Christ and Buddha.[91] This too is an unparalleled situation. Though his style of non-violent agitation was drawn directly from various liberal political movements in Britain which he had witnessed during his stay in England, yet it was his projection of it in a spiritual language that caught the world imagination.

Gandhi did not come from a landowning family but was elite. His father was the prime minister of the Kathiawar kingdom (called princely state under colonial rule). In a feudal structure, defence of social and economic hierarchies are vital for maintaining the status quo. Gandhi regarded the rich, both the landed and business community, as the "trustees of the society." The British elites too thought that they were trustees of the society. There is a basic difference between the class system of Europe or elsewhere and the English class system. In the former system anyone by dint of merit and hard work could acquire wealth and enter into the elite class, while in the latter, the entry into the elite class is by birth alone. Brian Simon, the prominent British Marxist historian of education, has termed the peculiar English class system as 'the caste system'.[92] The 'English class system' is closer to the Indian caste system than the 'class system' of Europe. The defenders of the caste system in India and the defenders of class system shared the same values.

So when a member of the British parliament opposed the education of the poor because it would "result in discontentment and rebellion," or when a British governor-general did the same, it resonated with the thought of Indian political leaders who had similar interests to defend. Hence, there is an unbroken

90 "Editorial," *The Mahratta* (April 26, 1891): 2; "Editorial," *The Mahratta* (March 6, 1892): 3.

91 The poem 'Gandhi' by Mary Siegrist published in 1922 begins, "Who is it that walks the earth today? A Christ or Buddha on the common way", *Gandhi and the Non-Violent Resistance,* ed. Blanche Watson (Madras: Ganesh and Company, 1923), 1–3.

92 Brian Simon, *Education and the Labour Movement 1870–1920* (London: Lawrence and Wishart, 1974), 97. For the peculiar English class system and its control over education in England see Brian Simon, *The Two Nations and the Educational Structure 1780–1870* (London: Lawrence and Wishart, 1960).

link between the feudal thinking of the British and Indian elites. In 1909, when Gandhi stated that giving education to the poor would make them discontented with their cottage and their lot, the Auckland's Educational Minute of 1839 was not in the public domain. It was brought to the public domain only in 1919.[93] Still, Gandhi was able to reproduce it verbatim. This shows a close proximity of their thinking process. In the ultimate analysis, "nationalism is an ideology created by the elite to perpetuate surplus appropriation and class/caste interest."[94] Anti-colonial struggle in India produced new men who were wedded to old imperial educational ideas as it suited their agenda of upper caste/class control over the society.

Archives

British Library, London

National Archives, New Delhi

Maharashtra State Archives, Mumbai

Tamil Nadu State Archives, Chennai

West Bengal State Archives, Kolkata

Newspapers

The Mahratta, 1880–1920.

Young India, 1920–1932.

Literature

Aldrich, Richard. *An Introduction to the History of Education.* London: Hodder and Stoughton, 1982.

Basu, Anathnath, ed., and Adam William. *Reports on the State of Education in Bengal 1835 and 1838.* Calcutta: University of Calcutta, 1941.

Bhattacharya, Sabyasachi, Joseph Bara, and Chinna Rao Yagati (eds.), *Educating the Nation.* New Delhi: Kanishka, 2003.

Blyth, William A. L. *English Primary Education: A Sociological Description.* London: Routledge and Kegan Paul, 1965.

93 Henry Sharp, *Selections from Educational Records, 1781–1839* (Calcutta: Government Press, 1922).

94 Rao, *Foundations of Tilak's Nationalism,* 324.

Chitty, Clyde. *Education Policy in Britain.* New York: Palgrave MacMillan, 2004.

Curtis, Stanley J. *History of Education in Great Britain.* London: University Tutorial Press, 1965.

Dharmapal, *The Beautiful Tree: The Indigenous Education in the Eighteenth Century.* New Delhi: Biblia Impex, 1983.

First Annual Report of The National Society for Promoting the Education of the Poor in the Principles of the Established Church. London: n.d., 1812.

Gandhi, Mohandas K. *Indian Home Rule or Hind Swaraj.* Ahmedabad: Navjivan Press, 1938.

Gandhi, Mohandas K. *Hind Swaraj or India's Home Rule, 1908.* Ahmedabad: Navjivan Publishing House, 1946 reprint.

Gandhi, Mohandas K. *The Problem of Education.* Ahmedabad: Navjivan Publishing House, 1962.

Gandhi, Mohandas K. *Collected Works, Vol 17.* New Delhi: Ministry of Information and Broadcasting, 1994.

Gardner, Philip. "Literacy, Learning and Education," in *A Companion to Nineteenth-Century Britain,* ed. Chris Williams. Massachusetts: Blackwell, 2004, 353–368.

Goldstrom, J. M. "The Content of Education and Socialisation of the Working Class Child 1830–1860," in *Popular Education*, ed. Phillip McCann. London: Methuen, 1979, 98–103.

Halls, W. D. "Cultural Ideals and Elitist Education in England." *Comparative Education Review*, 15(3) (1971): 317–329.

Kumar, Krishna. *Political Agenda of Education: A Study of Colonialist and Nationalist Ideas.* New Delhi: Sage, 1991.

Kumarappa, Bharatan, ed., and Mohandas Karamchand Gandhi. *Towards New Education.* Ahmedabad: Navajivan Publishing House, 1953.

Locke, John. "An Essay on the Poor Law." In *Political Essays*, edited by Mark Goldie. Cambridge: Cambridge University Press, 1997.

McCann, Phillip, ed. *Popular Education and Socialization in the Nineteenth Century.* London: Methuen, 1979.

Naik, J. V. "Lokmanya Tilak on Karl Marx and Class Conflict." *Economic and Political Weekly*, 34(18) (May 1–7, 1999): 1023–1025.

Parulekar, Ramchandra V. *Survey of Indigenous Education in the Province of Bombay 1820–1830.* Bombay: Asia Publishing House, 1951.

Rai, Lajpat. *Problems of National Education in India.* London: George Allen Unwin, 1920.

Rao, Parimala V. “New Insights into the Debates on Rural Indebtedness in the Nineteenth Century Deccan.” *Economic and Political Weekly*, 44(04) (January 24 – January 30, 2009).

Rao, Parimala V. *Foundations of Tilak's Nationalism: Discrimination, Education, and Hindutva*. New Delhi: Orient BlackSwan, 2011.

Rao, Parimala V. “Promiscuous Crowd of English Smatterers’: ‘Poor’ in the Colonial and Nationalist Discourse on Education in India 1835–1935.” *Contemporary Education Dialogue*, 10 (2013): 223–225.

Rao, Parimala V. “A Century of Consolidation and Resistance: Caste and Education in Maharashtra 1818–1918.” *Occasional Paper NMML*, n° 54, New Delhi, 2014.

Rao, Parimala V. “Compulsory Education and Political Leadership in Colonial India.” In *New Perspectives in the History of Indian Education*, edited by Parimala V. Rao. New Delhi: Orient BlackSwan, 2014.

Rao, Parimala V. “Modern Education and the Revolt of 1857 in India.” *Paedagogica Historica*, 52, 1–2, 2016.

Report of the General Committee of Public Instruction, 1840. Calcutta, n.d., 1840.

Report of the Board of Education for the Year 1850. Bombay: Bombay Education Society's Press, 1851.

Report of the Director of Public Instruction, Bombay, 1857–58. Bombay: The Education Society Press, 1859.

Richey, J. A. *Selections from Educational Records Part II*. Calcutta: Bureau of Education, 1922.

Sharp, Henry. *Selections from Educational Records, 1781–1839*. Calcutta: Government Press, 1922.

Simon, Brian. *The Two Nations and the Educational Structure 1780–1870*. London: Lawrence and Wishart, 1960.

Simon, Brian. *Education and the Labour Movement 1870–1920*. London: Lawrence and Wishart, 1974.

Tompson, Richard S. “The English Grammar School Curriculum in the 18th Century: A Reappraisal.” *British Journal of Educational Studies*, 19(1) (1971), 32–39.

Varkey, Chunkat J. *The Wardha Scheme of Education: An Exposition and Examination*. London: Oxford University Press, 1940.

Viswanathan, Gauri. *Masks of Conquest: Literary Study and British Rule in India*. London: Faber and Faber, 1990.

Williams, Chris, ed. *A Companion to Nineteenth-Century Britain*. Massachusetts: Blackwell, 2004.

Catriona Ellis

Climbing the Coconut Tree: Three South Indians Use Their Personal Memories of Colonial Education to Influence the Decolonisation of Education after Independence

Abstract The chapter addresses strategies in late colonial schooling through the lens of the autobiographical accounts of three different Southern Indian authors. It highlights the potential of autobiographical sources in recovering marginalised voices. The author shows how self-testimonies, beyond simplistic concepts of authenticity, can help to open a 'ground-level' dimension of liberation struggles and decolonisation. The analysis brings to light common traits as well as differences: the experience of late colonial schooling, including questions of discrimination, as well as the dichotomisation of time – between 'those days' and the present – all appear as resources used by the authors to strategically position their narratives in the post-colonial context. This proposes a double approach to these critical sources: accordingly, one should consider not only their referential value with regard to late colonial education. Rather, she convincingly argues that it is their character as carriers of meaning that defines their high strategic value as an indicator for educational discourses in a post-colonial context.

Keywords: India, autobiographies, narrative, liberation struggle, late colonial schooling

K. Sreenivasan, a textile manufacturer who became Director of the South Indian Textile Research Association, wrote about his educational experiences in an autobiography entitled "Climbing the Coconut Tree" in 1980. Quoting both a favourite teacher and a local deity *Padmanabha*, Sreenivasan asked "how far can you support a man climbing a coconut tree?" to which the answer came "only as far as your hand can reach; after that he has to do the climbing himself".[1] This paper considers three South Indians who, in very different spheres, had reached the top of the coconut tree of life and wanted to assist others by documenting their own initial experiences of climbing and the hands which had

1 Kasthuri Sreenivasan, *Climbing the Coconut Tree: A Partial Autobiography* (Oxford: Oxford University Press, 1980).

helped them. The fragmentary memories contained within the autobiographies of Sreenivasan's contemporaries help us explore how elite adults remembered their childhood experiences of early education in the South of India between 1900 and 1947. All three were educated when the British were still the dominant political power, while the greater part of their careers and public life took place after decolonisation. I argue that a close look at the detail of their recollections of education, in particular the classroom as an educational space, the role of the teacher, the place of the curriculum and the experience of discrimination at school alongside the experience of more informal education at home, complicates our understanding of late colonial education. It also reveals the educational priorities of these individuals as adults and the close association between education, decolonisation and nation-building in the imagination and priorities of the post-independence educated middle classes.

The three individuals chosen for this study are A. P. J. Abdul Kalam (1931–2015), A. N. Sattanathan (1905–1991) and Malladi Subbamma (1924–2014). A. N. Sattanathan's autobiography *Plain Speaking: A Sudra's Story* was published in 2007, and was written as part of his work promoting the rights of the so-called Backward Classes.[2] The Backward Classes or *Sudras* in India are the lowest varna in the Hindu caste hierarchy and among the most socio-economically disadvantaged in society, but higher on the social scale than the Scheduled Castes or *Dalits*. Although elementary education for all castes had been promoted since the Commission on Indian Education in 1882, access to schooling remained limited for these lower caste groups. Born in 1905 in Sengottai, Tirunelveli District, Sattanathan became a lecturer in history in 1926, before joining the Superior Civil Service in 1929 and serving in the customs and excise department in the North East of India and at the United Nations until 1956. After retirement Sattanathan wrote his autobiography and published two books for children *The Jester, the Judge and the Minister,* and *Folk Tales from the South,* before becoming Chairman of the 1969 Tamil Nadu Backward Classes Commission.[3] The Commission supported the reservation of opportunities in education and the civil service for individuals from particular Backward Class groups, but also recognised the existence of a socio-economic group – which Sattanathan named an 'upper crust' or 'creamy layer' – within these classes which dominated the

2 A. N. Sattanathan, *Plain Speaking: A Sudra's Story* (Delhi: Permanent Black, 2007).

3 Tamil Nadu, "Government of 1971 Report of the Backward Classes Commission [A. N. Sattanathan, Chairman]. 3 Vols.," Madras: Director of Stationery and Printing.

benefits given by reservation.[4] Sattanathan continued as a public intellectual and commentator on Backward Castes issues until his death in 1990.[5] His autobiography was published seventeen years later by his granddaughter.

Avul Pakir Jainulabdeen Abdul Kalam climbed the coconut tree by a completely different route. He was born in 1931 into a large Muslim family in Rameswaram on Pamban Island, off the coast of Tamil Nadu. Kalam studied aeronautical engineering, receiving India's highest civilian honour, the Bharat Ratna, for his role in the development of India's ballistic missile program and nuclear missile tests in 1998. Between 2002 and 2007 Kalam became the consensus candidate for President of India, continuing afterwards as a public lecturer and writer with a particular focus on inspiring India's youth and on making India a developed nation by 2020.[6] After initially co-writing *Wings of Fire: An Autobiography* in 1999, Kalam went on to publish another 30 books outlining his philosophical and political ideas which centred round promoting religious (particularly Hindu-Muslim) toleration and encouraging youth participation in nation-building.[7] A further autobiography of his life as President was published in 2012, and another book of childhood memories in 2013 – *My Journey: transforming dreams into actions.*[8] In this, Kalam drew on his childhood – and particularly his family – as a key element to his public persona. Kalam passed away in 2015.

Malladi Subbamma initially struggled to climb the coconut tree, and attributed this to the lack of helping hands and often direct opposition by others. Her autobiography, *Fearless Feminist: an autobiography of a social revolutionary*, was published in 1994.[9] Subbamma was born in 1924 in Guntur district, and married when she was ten years old, although she remained at school until she was thirteen when her husband returned home having failed his college exams. After

---

4 A. N. Sattanathan, *The Dravidian Movement in Tamil Nadu and Its Legacy* (Madras: University of Madras, 1982), 38.

5 For example: Sattanathan, *The Dravidian Movement in Tamil Nadu.*

6 See A. P. J. Abdul Kalam and Yagnaswami Sundara Rajan, *India 2020: A vision for the new millennium* (New Delhi: Penguin Books India, 2002) or A. P. J. Abdul Kalam, *Indomitable spirit* (New Delhi: Rajpal and Sons, 2006).

7 A. P. J. Abdul Kalam and Arun Tiwari, *Wings of Fire: An Autobiography* (Hyderabad: Universities Press, 1999).

8 A. P. J. Abdul Kalam, *My Journey: transforming dreams into actions* (New Delhi: Rupa Publications India, 2013) and A. P. J. Abdul Kalam, *Turning Points: A Journey through Challenges* (New Delhi: HarperCollins Publishers India, 2012).

9 Malladi Subbamma, *Fearless Feminist: An Autobiography of a Social Revolutionary* (Hyderabad: Booklinks Corp, 1994).

looking after her five children Subbamma became a social worker campaigning on social reform issues such as literacy for women and the anti-liquor movement, becoming head of the Institute for the Advancement of Women in Hyderabad. A committed feminist and humanist, she authored a number of books on women's rights and edited the Telegu journal *Stree Swetcha or Freedom for Women*. Her autobiography was explicitly written to highlight her position as "a frog in the well due to the force of tradition" and the ways she overcame this.[10]

Despite disparate lives and career trajectories, the three autobiographies are tied by more than merely the geographical space of south India. All three became articulate 'new men' and 'new women' after independence, contributing to the formation of new ideas about the role and methods of education in ways which reflected their experience as children in the late colonial period. All three were educated in the local village school, and the transfer to secondary education represented a key moment of rupture in their lives which set them apart from their peers and ultimately confirmed their status as part of the elite. As adults, they were members of the educated middle classes and could trace their later success and change in socio-economic status directly to their educational opportunities. Central to my argument is that setting autobiographies alongside more recognised sources such as textbooks or official reports can add depth to our understanding of late colonial education. The idea that the transmission of knowledge through formal education was used to reinforce colonial power relationships, both by prioritising the knowledge and pedagogies of the coloniser and by using that knowledge to impose a system of moral and social control has been frequently and eloquently acknowledged.[11] That this control was contested by adults is evidenced in the extensive debates on policy, funding and curriculum between colonialists, missionaries, nationalists and social reformers.[12] However, there is a need for a more qualitative analysis of the pedagogical realities of the educational experience from the point of view of the child as the recipient. I view the child here as a competent social actor, who used their own agency to both accept and contest the control and knowledge transmitted in the

---

10 Subbamma, *Fearless Feminist*, 4.

11 Nigel Crook, ed., *The Transmission of Knowledge in South Asia: Essays on Education, Religion, History, and Politics* (Oxford: Oxford University Press, 1996); Bernard Cohn, *Colonialism and Its Forms of Knowledge: The British in India* (New Jersey: Princeton University Press, 1996).

12 Bhattacharya Sabyasachi, ed., *The Contested Terrain: Perspectives on Education in India* (Hyderabad: Sangam Books, 1998); Satadru Sen, *Colonial Childhoods: The Juvenile Periphery of India 1850*–1945 (London, New York, Delhi: Anthem Press, 2005).

classroom. These childhood experiences had a long term impact on the adult's later political outlook, views on pedagogy and ideas about the transformative impact of education.[13]

Contextualising autobiographies as a genre

Life histories, as "straddling the elusive divide between personal narrative and objective truth," allow some insight into the, albeit fragmentary, remembered experiences of children in education.[14] The autobiographies are used here as 'critical interventions', literary sources which fulfil a particular narrative function detailing social and cultural change.[15] Kalam's first autobiography *Wings of Fire* encompasses both "individual destiny and the social matrix in which it is embedded".[16] He writes to detail the "tribulations and triumphs of a small-town boy" linked to a history of the development of the missile programme: "it is a story of national aspiration and of co-operative endeavour".[17] His later account, written as part of his campaign to encourage youth participation in "nation-building", is a much more explicitly nostalgic description aimed at preserving the memory of his family.[18] Both books reflect the nature of Tamil autobiographies as a particular genre which A.R. Venkatachalapathy argues are much less about self-reflectivity or the public performativity of the self than autobiographies in Bengal or in the West.[19] More often, he suggests, Tamils discuss their autobiographies in terms of "excising the self", using their life stories as a 'public' source to detail social change.[20] Tamil autobiographies are usually structured around a binary of the difference between *antha kalam/intha kalam*, or "those days/these days" which

13 Chris Jenks, *Childhood* (London, New York: Routledge, 1996); Catriona Ellis, "Education for All: Reassessing the Historiography of Education in Colonial India," *History Compass* 7, no. 2 (2009): 363–375.

14 David Arnold and Stuart Blackburn, ed., *Telling Lives in India: Biography, Autobiography and Life History* (Delhi: Permanent Black, 2004), 4.

15 Kathryn Hansen, *Stages of Life: Indian Theatre Autobiographies* (London, New York, Delhi: Anthem Press, 2011).

16 Kalam, *Wings of Fire*, xiv.

17 Ibid., xiv–xv.

18 Kalam, *My Journey*.

19 Mines Mattison, *Public Faces, Private Voices: Community and Individuality in South India* (Berkeley, Los Angeles: University of California Press, 1994), 149.

20 A. R. Venkatachalapathy, *In Those Days There was No Coffee: Writings in Cultural History* (Delhi: Yoda Press, 2006), 175.

explicitly demonstrates change in wider society rather than the individual's life.[21] The decision to publish Sattanathan's most famous lectures alongside his personal story, is symptomatic of this.

Autobiographies have been increasingly used in the South Asian context as a significant expression of marginalised voices. Not merely marginalised on account of their age, all three autobiographers represent communities noted for their educational backwardness – Muslims (Kalam), Backward Castes (Sattanathan) and girls (Subbamma).[22] The autobiographies are used consciously as a site of resistance, and Sattanathan's editor highlights "his intimate knowledge and first-hand experience of social disadvantage and marginalisation" as well as laying claim to "his individuality, his agency in his own story".[23] Subbamma also uses her life story as a political tool to discuss gendered issues of education and child-marriage and as "a torch to show the way and provide the light in the darkness of ignorance, inequality and lack of education" in ways which would vindicate her own position as a social worker and give other women the 'courage' to write their own life stories.[24] Life stories are therefore politically significant because they provide an insight into the lives of children and of marginalised communities.[25] Both these groups are under-represented in traditional archival sources. They add a particular richness and humanity to the historical record of educational change. At the same time, as Bowen and Hinchy so eloquently argue, the context in which these autobiographies are produced often tells the historian more about the adult authors at the time of writing, than the historical experiences of children.[26]

Memories of formal education

All three of the autobiographers were educated in the late colonial period. Under the British, the avowed aim of elementary education after 1882 was "the

21 Venkatachalapathy, *In those Days,* 173.

22 For a wider discussion of educational backwardness see Parimala V. Rao, ed., *New Perspectives in the History of Indian Education* (Hyderabad: Orient Blackswan, 2014); Sanjay Seth, *Subject Lessons: The Western Education of Colonial India* (Durham: Duke University Press, 2007).

23 Editor Uttara Natarajan in Sattanathan, *Plain Speaking,* 3, 6.

24 Subbamma, *Fearless Feminist,* 4–5.

25 Antoinette Burton, *Dwelling in the Archive: Women Writing House, Home and History in late Colonial India* (Oxford: Oxford University Press, 2003), 26.

26 Zazie Bowen and Jessica Hinchy, ed. "Introduction: Children and Knowledge in India," *South Asian History and Culture* 6, no. 3 (2015): 319.

instruction of the masses, through the vernacular, in such subjects as will best stimulate their intelligence and fit them for their position in life".[27] Colonial education for the masses was designed to provide basic literacy and numeracy at village and city level. It was a form of social control, intended both to discipline the population into governable groups or 'educational communities' and to encourage loyalty to British institutions and ideals.[28] The structures were highly devolved, each Presidency being responsible for its own educational administration, particularly after the constitutional changes of 1919. Most schools – around 62% in the Madras Presidency – were run by local schoolteachers but received Grant-in-Aid funding from the government in exchange for using the specified curriculum and exams.[29] The 1920 Madras Elementary Education Act both reformed educational administration and allowed for the introduction of compulsory education at district level. It also contained a renewed commitment to education for all communities, not only the Brahmins or wealthy caste groups or even vocal minorities such as Muslims, but also to girls and to *dalits* or Untouchables who had been traditionally barred from formal schooling. In 1932 in the Madras Presidency 1.9 million boys were at school. This represented 33% of 5.8 million boys between the ages of five and fifteen years recorded in the 1931 census.[30] The figure for girls stood at 12.4 % significantly lower, which seems symptomatic for historical neglect on first sight, but could also be read as reflecting the growing recognition female education received by the 1920s.[31] With regard to Caste, by 1931 Scheduled Classes comprised 13.4 % of the school population, but only 26 % of Scheduled Caste boys went to school, while 57 % of Brahmins attended. All in all, the period from 1900 was characterised by gradual improvement in both the quantity and quality of elementary education, although the reports were more often a reflection of official aspirations and opinions than

27 National Library of Scotland. *Annual and Quinquennial Reports of Director of Public Instruction (Madras Presidency) (1906–1907)*, 27.

28 Seth, *Subject Lessons*; Gauri Viswanathan, *Masks of conquest: Literary Study and British Rule in India* (New York: Columbia University Press, 2014); Crook, *The Transmission of Knowledge.*

29 NLS: *Annual and Quinquennial Report of Director of Public Instruction (Madras Presidency) 1921–1922 to 1926–1927*, 7.

30 NLS: *Annual and Quinquennial Report of Director of Public Instruction (Madras Presidency) 1927–1928 to 1931–1932*, 83.

31 Sita Anantha Raman, *Getting Girls to School. Social Reform in the Tamil Districts 1870–1930* (Calcutta: Stree, 1996).

the reality.[32] All this took place in a changing context in which the mass nationalist movement gained momentum politically, and also invested more emphasis and resources in its educational ideals. There was also a rise in popular support for other movements for social and political reform, often based around marginalised communities such as Muslims or women. These movements manifested themselves differently in South India and reflected the distinctive historical, social, economic, and linguistic context of the Madras Presidency. This included unique patterns of landholding and taxation, of religious observance and a less hierarchical caste structure than the North, with Brahmins comprising only 3 % of the population.[33] Politics were dominated by the anti-Brahmin Justice Party, rather than the Indian National Congress, and by the late 1930s there was a flourishing Dravidian nationalist movement, largely based around the Tamil language. This too was closely linked to education and was galvanised by opposition to the imposition of Hindi within secondary schools.

A detailed focus on the memories of elementary schooling reveals the disjunction between the official narrative and the actual experience. The official reports from the 1890s onwards recognised the physical symbolism of the modern school building, and the pedagogical impact the physical space of the classroom had in changing everyday behaviour.[34] It normalised particular practices such as sitting on benches or using black boards, and helped students to internalise colonial values of self-discipline, cleanliness and modernity. By contrast, Kalam remembered his first school Rameswaram Panchayat Primary school as a building by the sea with a thatched roof and 400 pupils, divided into classes of around 55 children.[35] Sattanathan's first school, which he joined at the age of 5 was an "old-fashioned primitive single teacher school" which functioned in a "shed at the end of our street".[36] It comprised 30 pupils and was recognisably "an institution bound to the old village economy, which believed in co-operative

---

32 Latika Chaudhary, "Determinants of Primary Schooling in British India," *The Journal of Economic History* 69, no. 1 (Mar 2009): 269–302.

33 David Washbrook, *The Emergence of Provincial Politics* (Cambridge [u.a.]: Cambrige University Press, 1976); Christopher Baker and S. A. Washbrook, *South India: Political Institutions and Political Change 1880–1940* (Delhi: Macmillan, 1975); Eugene Irschick, *Dialogue and History: Constructing South India, 1795–1895* (Berkley, Los Angeles: University of California Press, 1994).

34 Nita Kumar, *Lessons from Schools: The History of Education in Banaras* (Delhi, London: Sage, 2000).

35 Kalam, *My Journey*, 36.

36 Sattanathan, *Plain Speaking*, 29.

self-sufficiency" so that children could be educated in their own village. He moved on to a larger Malayalam medium school about half a mile away, and then relocated at the age of seven or eight to live with his sister about twelve miles away so that he could attend the local Christian Mission School and learn English. He described this latter school as having "extensive playgrounds and shady avenues of trees and an atmosphere conducive to" providing an education which led to a profession.[37] Kalam too included a photograph of a white building with the plaque "Let not thy winged days be spend in vain. When once gone, no gold can buy them back again."[38] There is a clear association in the minds of both writers between the regularity and order of the secondary school building and the structured and modern educational experience they enjoyed. This reflected a view of education in the literary binaries of these days/those days which suggested a transition from tradition to modernity. It clearly positioned both men as eager to promote modern education a means of encouraging social mobility. The experiences of both men were atypical, however, and the impact of the school as a physical symbol of colonial modernity in the village community should not be overplayed in the lives of the vast majority of school-attending children.

Central to the school experience was the modern teacher who (according to official reports) inherited the role of the traditional guru as the *only* conveyor of legitimate knowledge in the classroom. His authority was to be enhanced by his own morally sound character and his association with the colonial state. In practice, the curriculum was carefully prescribed by the Education Department giving the teacher little autonomy and the calibre of recruits was generally poor because of poor professional and monetary incentives.[39] This is seen most clearly in Sattanathan's memories of schooling. His first teacher was a "kindly old man", personally caring but antagonistic to modern pedagogical methods and a frequent practitioner of the monitorial system, leaving his nephew in charge if required elsewhere.[40] In his second school, the teacher was condescending but kind, aware of both his own superior caste background as a Brahmin but also his low socio-economic status.[41] By contrast, the majority of his lower secondary teachers were "mediocre, colourless". The exception was the headmaster, a "good disciplinarian

37 Ibid., 34–36.

38 Kalam, *Wings of Fire.*

39 Krishna Kumar, *Political Agenda of Education: A Study of Colonialist and Nationalist Ideas* (Delhi, London: Sage Publications, 1991).

40 Sattanathan, *Plain Speaking*, 30.

41 Ibid., 32.

and administrator", and a "man of culture and wide intellectual tastes", both temperamentally and intellectually capable to be a teacher, who contributed to educational policy as a member of the Travancore Education Department.[42] This reflects the limitations of the source material, which evidences Sattanathan's own educational success and later approach to pedagogy and school discipline, and surely must be read as a very adult evaluation of the teacher's charisma. Kalam similarly describes teachers who were a "lasting influence" and who "instilled in all the children a sense of their own worth".[43] Situating progress in the person of the modern schoolteacher, Kalam emphasised the teacher's ability to develop the pupil's character, again reflecting the author's adult beliefs which highlighted the role of the teacher as an agent of change in society.

Krishna Kumar argues that colonial teachers were effectively dictators, exercising power within the classroom based on both a claim to superior knowledge and a position in society.[44] Often this was reflected in discipline. Subbamma's experience was of a teacher who "was disposed to become angry often" and who disciplined children by making them stand in a bending position.[45] She remembered "the chastisement of being hit with a cane twig. It was no exaggeration to state that no pupil escaped punishment at his hands," although the adults in her family thoroughly approved his methods. Sattanathan also recalled his Brahmin teacher who seemed to draw satisfaction from bullying low caste pupils.[46] Again these examples were associated with traditional teaching methods in contrast to the more modern techniques advocated by the Education Department and were presented to convey the image of a system in decline. Sattanathan details one of the most vivid experiences of unfair discipline recalled in any south Indian autobiography and devotes a whole chapter to the incident. At the age of eight he missed a day of school and caught up by copying everything from the notebook of a classmate, including the teacher's corrections. The young Sattanathan was accused of the "terrible crime" of forging signatures, recalling that he could not understand what he had done wrong.[47] Beaten and humiliated, "the severe manhandling I got unnerved me and I made up my mind that I would have nothing more to do with that school or the teacher".[48] In response he ran away by

42 Ibid., 49.
43 Kalam, *Wings of Fire*, 9, 13. Also Kalam, *Indomitable Spirit.*
44 Kumar, *Political Agenda.*
45 Subbamma, *Fearless Feminist*, 20.
46 Sattanathan, *Plain Speaking*, 51.
47 Ibid., 40.
48 Ibid., 41.

train but was found and returned to his family. He recalls that when the teacher was confronted by his father, he "seemed to have realised the unfairness of the punishment and was convinced of my sincerity and earnestness", and he was sheepishly accepted back to school.[49] The commentary by Sattanathan reveals his analysis as an adult, which credited the teacher with the ability to change, highlighted his own spirit of forgiveness and emphasised both the short-term pain and longer term psychological impact of the beatings. However, this incident also reveals the common disciplinary strategies of the colonial school and the reluctance of adults in authority to listen to children in ways which appear to be typical. While running away cannot form part of a grand narrative of resistance to adult authority, as a "weapon of the weak" it reveals a degree of agency for children that is not often found in the traditional narrative of colonial education.[50] This discussion both reveals the limitations of any education system, and provides a clear connection between the structures of colonial education and violence against children which the authors are eager to leave in the past as they themselves contribute to new reformulations of the education system after decolonisation.

While textbooks are frequently used to provide an insight into curriculum changes and the subject matter of education, autobiographies provide some indication of the pedagogical strategies used to communicate this knowledge to children. Others, such as Nita Kumar, have demonstrated that the very ways in which knowledge was conveyed within the classroom brought home to the pupils values of imperial citizenship and the rule of law.[51] However, while they were intended to justify the colonial state they ultimately contributed to undermine it.[52] Probably because these values were internalised they were hardly discussed within the autobiographies, perhaps also because adults find it more interesting to record exceptional teaching. Subbamma recalls rote learning and writing on palmyra leaves, which serves to highlight the difference between these days of present and those days of her childhood. Her clearest memories were of positive reinforcement through competition in class, either about grades,

49 Ibid.

50 James C. Scott, *Weapons of the Weak: Everyday Forms of Peasant Resistance* (New Haven: Yale University Press, 2008).

51 Kumar, *Lessons from Schools.*

52 Seth, *Subject Lessons*; Topdar, Sudipa, "'Duties of a 'good citizen': colonial secondary school textbook policies in late nineteenth-century India," *South Asian History and Culture* 6, no.3 (2015): 417–439; Viswanathan, *Masks of Conquest*; Bellenoit Hayden, *Missionary Education and Empire in Late Colonial India* (London: Routledge, 2015).

about language learning or in the activities organised by the local women's Stree Hitaishini Mandali such as races, debates, essays and music competitions, as well as material objects - the pencils and other small prizes - they received.[53] Sattanathan recalled a particularly inspiring history teacher who had a "flair" for military history.[54] He also remembered frequent games and sports, a personal memory of what Sen and Mills argue was crucial to the colonial and nationalist projects in the formation of athletic masculinities.[55] Later, at the local secondary school he remembered an exceptional art teacher who taught through visual representations of nature and geography meaning "his contribution to the study of geography and history was greater than that of the teachers of those subjects".[56] It appears that the lessons which were actively remembered into old age – and thought worth recording – were those which engaged the child's imagination. Similarly in his book *Indomitable Spirit* Kalam claims he received his "vision for life" at the age of ten when the teacher took his class to the coast to teach anatomy and flight through watching the seabirds, having failed to successfully explain the principles of flight in the classroom.[57] Pedagogically the use of 'practical examples' was effective, but the impact on Kalam's young life was immense providing him not just with "a special feeling" but with "a goal and a mission for my life."[58] The extent to which the memory became self-fulfilling in the light of his later career path in space and aviation is very difficult to judge. While the exceptional or the inspiring is recounted, this should be balanced by the uninspiring boredom of schooling and difficulty in rote-learning the scripts, arithmetic and spelling which was the most abiding memory for many. At the same time, all three give an insight into learning in ways not found in any other source material.

Identity and the experience of discrimination

For many children the enduring memory of school was discrimination based on their identity. All three autobiographers use detailed memories of past discrimination as a voice of resistance at the time of writing, claiming authority for

53 Subbamma, *Fearless Feminist*, 34.
54 Sattanathan, *Plain Speaking*, 39.
55 James H. Mills and Sen Satadru, *Confronting the body: The Politics of Physicality in Colonial and Post-Colonial India* (London, New York, Delhi: Anthem, 2004).
56 Sattanathan, *Plain Speaking*, 50.
57 Kalam, *Indomitable Spirit*, 25–27.
58 Ibid.

their current campaigns for inclusion using the innocence and authenticity of the child's voice.[59] These campaigns included Subbamma's activism for gender equality, Sattanathan's critique of caste discrimination and Kalam's emphasis on religious tolerance. From the reforms in 1884, the colonial bureaucracy was concerned with categorising the population into "educational communities" as a means of measuring educational backwardness and providing strategies to improve opportunities for the disadvantaged.[60] Since only roughly 10 % of girls attended school in 1931, Subbamma notes her privileged status being allowed to study in a small village school up to the age of eight years (4th grade), the minimum prescribed for basic literacy.[61] After her wedding, she continued her education until the marriage was consummated when she was thirteen, despite the opposition of her orthodox Hindu grandmother. This privileged access had a profound effect on her later life and her campaign for what she perceived to be the intertwined causes of humanism and literacy for women, blaming the poor socio-economic condition of women on conservative Hindu gender ideologies. On the other hand, while Sattanathan's elder sister was married at the age of eleven, she had never been to school and had worked in paid employed from the age of five.[62] This was not a particular source of concern to Sattanathan, although he detailed his discomfort at the domestic abuse she suffered.[63]

Caste discrimination was also significant. Equal access to education was established in principle by the 1930s, and was encouraged by the Madras Education Department, which also threatened to withdraw government funding from all schools which refused admission to Scheduled Caste pupils.[64] However, even when access was granted, the experience of caste discrimination *within* the classroom remains a recurring theme in the autobiographies.[65] The access of children from low caste and Dalit backgrounds remains an explosive site of political contestation in post-colonial South India, despite equal access to education being

59 Morrison, Heidi *Childhood and Colonial Modernity* (London: Palgrave Macmillan, 2015).

60 Seth, *Subject Lessons*.

61 Subbamma, *Fearless Feminist*, 30.

62 Sattanathan, *Plain Speaking*, 34.

63 Ibid., 34–39.

64 Quinquennial Report of Director of Public Instruction (Madras Presidency) 1916–1917 to 1921–1922, 66.

65 Deepa Sreenivas, "Telling Different Tales: Possible Childhoods in Children's Literature," *Childhood* 18, no. 3 (2011): 316–332.

established in the constitution in 1950.[66] Subbamma acknowledged her privileged position as a member of a high caste, but also recognised the physical manifestations of status within the schoolroom: "As I was the grand-daughter of a property-owning woman and the daughter of a pleader I was permitted to sit on a mat of palmrya leaves."[67] Sattanathan's perspective is particularly interesting, though closely associated with his role as the Scheduled Caste chair of the 1969 Tamil Nadu Backward Classes Commission. He described his first Tamil Brahmin teacher as an "obscene petty tyrant" and records that:

> "the man had no hesitation about displaying his contempt for pupils who were not of his caste. He had the intellectual arrogance of his caste, though he himself had no intellectual attainments. If a cultivator's son did not recite the Tamil verse properly, he would taunt him saying, 'why don't you stick to your plough?' His general abuse was, why should not the erring pupil take to the barber's razor instead of wasting time in a school not meant for him […]"[68]

The result was that "this teacher produced in me almost a revulsion towards learning Tamil." Sattanathan was keen to portray this experience as representative rather than exceptional, and as symptomatic of a wider societal problem. He later evaluated the ways in which Brahmins benefited from British education and argued "they had not culture enough to appreciate that the gift of education which they had in their hands should be given impartially to all their students, and not humanity enough to have sympathy with the underdog."[69] He criticised the long-term impact of "hatred of the Brahman" as a result of their "lack of humanity, and traditional arrogance" not just as recognised fact, but again as authenticated by personal experience – "if there was a pupil from a very low caste, his life was made unbearable by petty acts of discrimination and ostracism". He attributed this to the fact that "in rural areas the respect for the Brahmin and tolerance of his arrogance was so deeply engrained in popular tradition, that the non-Brahmin students seldom noticed, much less protest against, the display of arrogance and superiority". By contrast, Sattanathan describes a Christian catechist, whose son became his good friend, whom he describes as 'kindly', as zealous and whose "grievance against Hinduism was in respects of its social order – the caste system. In that we were in agreement".[70] Sattanathan used his autobiography to

66 See Eleanor Zelliot, "Dalit Initiatives in Education, 1880–1992," in *New Perspectives in the History of Indian Education*, ed. Parimala V. Rao (Hyderabad: Orient Blackswan, 2014).

67 Subbamma, *Fearless Feminist*, 20.

68 Sattanathan, *Plain Speaking*, 51.

69 Ibid., 52.

70 Ibid., 84.

highlight past discrimination, mostly in order to demonstrate how society had changed and progressed between those days and these days, but also to emphasise his political campaign of opposition to Brahmanical dominance. His three lectures in 1982 at the University of Madras, for example, are simply a different genre – social history rather than autobiography – to convey that same message. In these lectures he traced the social and political history of the Dravidian Movement as an anti-caste movement based on the idea that "the idea of superiority and inferiority by birth or calling is no longer tenable", and evaluating the different strategies employed by different caste groups to combat this.[71] The autobiography thus needs to be read as both a memory of childhood hardship and as a contemporary political statement in a less overtly campaigning genre.

Kalam's experience of identity was diametrically opposite to this, again reflecting his political perspective and campaign for the peaceful co-existence of religions.[72] Ultimately, he was chosen by the major political parties as President in 2002 because of his professional status as a scientist but also because as a Muslim he was seen as a unifying force, or a reassurance to the Muslim minority community despite the political dominance of the Hindu nationalist Bharatiya Janata Party.[73] Kalam described his personal experience of religious discrimination in a number of his autobiographies. Although his father was Imam of the local mosque, Kalam's three best friends were from orthodox Hindu Brahmin families, an extension of his father's close friendship and regular contact with the local Hindu and Catholic priests.[74] Kalam recounted that in 5th Standard a new teacher separated him from his friend after noticing the material symbols of their religion – the Muslim cap and the Hindu sacred thread. In the first account the father of his friend, the Imam, rebuked the teacher "that he should not spread the poison of social inequality and communal intolerance in the minds of innocent children."[75] In the second account, all three religious leaders confronted the teacher about intolerance being allowed to "infect the minds of the youngest members of society," causing the teacher to apologise.[76] While the two versions demonstrate subtle differences not unlike the retelling of oral history, they also re-emphasised Kalam's personal belief that children accept difference and

71 Sattanathan, *The Dravidian Movement in Tamil Nadu*, 4, 21.

72 See for example his website: http://www.abdulkalam.com/kalam/theme/jsp/guest/myprofile.jsp, Accessed November 6, 2015.

73 Kalam, *Turning Points*.

74 Kalam, *My Journey*, 33; Kalam, *Wings of Fire*, 8–9.

75 Kalam, *Wings of Fire*, 8–9.

76 Kalam, *My Journey*, 39.

prejudice is a learned behaviour and intolerance should be dealt with "firmly and openly".[77] This was a "strategic use" of childhood to make a political claim that the shared experience of childhood was sufficient to overcome adult violence, whether physical or intellectual, and the adult structures of caste and religious identity, both inside and outside school.[78] It is also an attempt by all three writers to envisage a new set of school contexts and values which are fundamentally reformed by political independence and are as central to decolonising the classroom as the overt attempts to reform the curriculum.

Learning outside the classroom

It is also important to consider education received outside the classroom, and how this contributed to the three individuals' experiences of education, and their later views on how to reform the education system. These forms of learning were barely recognised by the Education Department, but are crucial to our understanding of how children learnt; it helps us to better contextualise their moral and cultural values, and how they negotiated the various knowledge hierarchies of colonial India.[79] Considering education only through institutions is both gendered and hierarchical, for even by the 1930s the majority of children still received no formal school education and the very limited numbers of those who did rarely progressed beyond the elementary level. The formal-informal binary reflected one of the most rigid ideological boundaries of colonial modernity. It was perpetuated in the new patriarchies of the independence movement and reflected a symbolic division between home and the world, the private and the public. In this binary the middle class home was imagined as a site of pure Indian values and culture, existing outside the gaze of the colonial state.[80] At the same time, the homes of the lower classes were sites of backwardness and a threat to the modernising project and were to be regulated and reformed.[81]

---

77 Ibid., 36.

78 Malavika Karlekar and Rudrangshu Mukherjee, ed., *Remembered Childhood: Essays in Honour of Andre Beteille* (Oxford: Oxford University Press, 2010); Morrison, *Childhood and colonial modernity*, 102; Sen Satadru, *Traces of Empire: India, America and Post Colonial Cultures* (Delhi: Primus Books, 2014).

79 Kumar, *Lessons from Schools*; Nita Kumar, *The Politics of Gender, Community and Modernity: Essays on Education in India* (Oxford: Oxford University Press, 2007).

80 Partha Chatterjee, *Nation and Its Fragments* (New Jersey: Princeton University Press, 1993).

81 Sen, Colonial Childhoods.

Educators both strove to protect traditional values and shared anxieties over the way knowledge was preserved, changed and transmitted to younger, vulnerable generations by "untrustworthy people" – the poor, the illiterate, the female, the old, all those who had not themselves received a modern education.

The way this debate played out in the lives of children is demonstrated in the life histories. In addition to her schoolwork, Subbamma was taught skills relevant to a high caste Brahmin girl, such as learning to play the harmonium as well as household management, skills which reflected her social positioning in the gender and caste hierarchies of south India and her adult prospects as wife and mother.[82] As responsible for her instruction at home, her grandmother used oral traditions and "stories of chaste housewives, duties of women prescribed by Manu and other moral anecdotes" which had been passed down the generations and which initiated her into the "duties to be performed by different castes at different stages of life."[83] Her unquestioning acceptance of this as a child was challenged in later life, but she argued that "to get rid of those ideas it took me thirty years of my early life". This process proved to be central to her character formation and not least to her later career as a feminist which stood in direct opposition to Hindu orthodoxy, which she saw as justifying the oppression of women.[84] It is important to recognise the contribution of informal education, but also not to romanticise it. Education in the home also involved socialisation into the norms of the community which was often "a violent and painful process" in which children were "constrained" into pre-determined social categories and hierarchies, not dissimilar to the impact of formal education.[85]

Subbamma's experience contrasts with the two male autobiographers, who have a much more nostalgic memory of informal education. Both Kalam and Sattanathan directly compare the knowledge systems of school and home, and their relative impact on both childhood and later life. Kalam attended Qur'an school as part of his initiation into the Muslim community but attributes his emotional stability rather to his parents and friends.[86] As a child he spent considerable time with Samsuddin, the local newspaper vendor, and his sister's husband Jallaluddin, both of whom provided a loving and supportive atmosphere, gave

82 Subbamma, *Fearless Feminist*, 23.

83 For a wider discussion see Gloria Goodwin Raheja and Ann Grodzins Gold, *Listen to the Heron's Words: Reimagining Gender and Kinship in North India* (Berkeley, Los Angeles: University of California Press, 1994).

84 Subbamma, *Fearless Feminist*, 22.

85 Jenks, *Childhood*, 22.

86 Kalam, *My Journey*, 7–8, 25.

spiritual and moral input and encouraged his formal studies.[87] Despite gaining technical competence in modern education, Kalam argued that he can "unhesitatingly attribute my subsequently manifested creativity to their company in my childhood".[88] Sattanathan recalled his illiterate father's 'astounding' knowledge of the epics, and his place at the centre of the family recounting them. However, when Sattanathan himself could read, "Father then suggested that I should read a chapter or a few pages of these epics every day in the evening so that all the family could listen."[89] This was reflected in his father's insistence that his son should focus on formal education with the objective of securing a bureaucratic posting, despite being a skilled musician himself. His father continued to emphasis the role of cultural and religious knowledge within in the family, thereby reinforcing his position as the authority figure in the home who could decide which knowledge was to be transmitted. At the same time, the performance of this knowledge was undertaken by his son, who was qualified because of his modern education at school. Sattanathan's life thus exemplified the difficulties in negotiating between different knowledge systems; the introduction of alternative forms of authority within the family through literacy, and the generational impact of modern education in situating legitimate knowledge and skills in youth. At the same time, Sattanathan acknowledged the long-term impact of reading the epics both as sources of "emotional and intellectual satisfaction" and as a source of moral guidance, in contrast to many of his compatriots.[90] This points again to the complexity of decolonising education, given the variety of knowledge systems at play in children's lives.

New men and women of post-independence India

It is important to situate these memories in the ongoing education debates of post-independence India. The constitution in 1950 guaranteed the right to education for all and attempts were made to decolonise both curriculum and pedagogy. In practice, this has taken much longer to achieve, and there remain concerns about the number of children from marginalised communities who continue to remain outside the school system and for whom it has little practical

87 Ibid., 66.
88 Kalam, *Wings of Fire*, 8.
89 Sattanathan, *Plain Speaking*, 79.
90 Ibid., 80.

benefit.[91] This was, for example, recognised in the Right of Children to Free and Compulsory Education Act 2009 which again reaffirmed the obligation of the government and local authorities to provide and enforce free and compulsory education for all children between the ages of 6 and 14 years, regardless of sex, religion or caste. All three autobiographers were highly committed to the project of modern education. All three regarded the expansion and decolonisation of education essential for building the new Indian nation and continuing its success as a leading global economic power at a time when modern, secular education is perceived to be under threat and to have even caused the gap between the elite and the rest of the population to widen.[92] They all use their own lives as proof of the success of modern education in escaping poverty, ignorance and backwardness and as evidence of progress and social change, and while their childhood memories induce nostalgia, they are firmly situated in 'those days' of the past.

In her book on childhood and colonial modernity in Egypt Heidi Morrison reflects on the extent to which the autobiographies she studied mirror the current social, political, economic and cultural priorities of the era in which they were written. She argues that rather than revealing the experience of children themselves, they tell us more about the anxieties about class, identity and gender norms and the new state apparatus in the post-colonial era.[93] By using autobiographies as a genre, Morrison argues that the authors make "strategic use of childhood", because childhood memories are a way of claiming authenticity, innocence and non-bias but are at the same time actually a way of controlling a representation of the child in the past for current purposes and to demonstrate support for modern education.[94] While still useful as source material, this appears true in the case of South India too. Subbamma's life work was explicitly intended to help free women from patriarchal structures and combat both overt and unconscious misogyny. Her intention was to "express unambiguously while felling the trees of poisonous ideas" which continues to limit the life choices of women.[95] This is seen too in her childhood memories and the events and relationships she chose to record, particularly her relationship with orthodox females. Similarly, all of Sattanathan's work was infused with his opposition to Brahmin domination with its favoured

91 Sarada Balagopalan, *Inhabiting Childhood: Children, Labour and Schooling in Postcolonial India* (London: Palgrave Macmillan, 2014).

92 Balagopalan, *Inhabiting Childhoods*; Sanjay Srivastava, *Constructing Post-Colonial India: National Character and the Doon School* (London: Routledge, 1998).

93 Morrison, *Childhood and Colonial Modernity*, 6.

94 Ibid., 102, 121.

95 Subbamma, *Fearless Feminist*, 3–4.

access to educational and economic resources. His goal was to change mind-sets so that these injustices are no longer considered acceptable or inevitable by those who are oppressed. He did this by recounting his very personal experiences of domination and his own feelings of despair and injustice. Kalam too dedicated his life to the technological development of India and to education and toleration between the Hindu and Muslim communities, and employs his prior experiences as a child to gain authority to further these goals. Even the narrative structure of the autobiographies is used to highlight social change, the difference between tradition and modernity, the colonial and the post-colonial, 'those days' and 'these days'. The experience of education influenced all of these writers and their views of what post-colonial education should be and what it could achieve. At the same time, all three autobiographers make strategic use of memoirs to push an educational agenda, which gains authority based on the 'truth' found in their own experiences as children. The choice of what to record and how to record it is perhaps more reflective of the authors' views of how to decolonise education and their agendas for social and educational reform in the last decades of the twentieth century than an accurate portrayal of their lives as children.

Reading along as well as against the grain also highlights the role of the child as the recipient of education. This helps us to take seriously the agency and subjectivity of the individual child as a historical actor. A qualitative study of autobiographies reveals nuances within the classroom that are not discussed in the historical literature regarding the experience of buildings and the key memories of teachers and curriculum, as well as intense and exceptional events such as corporal punishment. Listening to children's mediated voices gives a deeper understanding of both the short and long-term personal impact of discriminatory education practices. These add richness to our understanding of the power and limitations of colonial education policy, and give agency to the children who peopled the classrooms. They also challenge us to see the limitations of formal schooling, and the variety of ways in which children learn. The memories of the lived experience of the recipients of education, however fragmentary, help us to understand the multiplicity of hands which helped the child to climb the coconut tree.

Literature

Annual and Quinquennial Reports of Director of Public Instruction (Madras Presidency), 1900–1940. National Library of Scotland.

Arnold, David, and Stuart Blackburn, ed. *Telling Lives in India: Biography, Autobiography and Life History*. Delhi: Permanent Black, 2004.

Baker, Christopher, and S. A. Washbrook. *South India: Political Institutions and Political Change 1880–1940*. Delhi: Macmillan, 1975.

Balagopalan, Sarada. *Inhabiting Childhood: Children, Labour and Schooling in postcolonial India*. London: Palgrave Macmillan, 2014.

Bellenoit, Hayden J. A. *Missionary Education and Empire in Late Colonial India, 1860–1920*. London, New York: Routledge, 2015.

Bhattacharya, Sabyasachi, ed. *The Contested Terrain: Perspectives on Education in India*. Hyderabad: Sangam Books, 1998.

Bowen, Zazi, and Jessica Hinchy, ed. "Introduction: Children and Knowledge in India." *South Asian History and Culture* 6, no. 3 (2015): 317–329.

Burton, Antoinette. *Dwelling in the Archive: Women Writing House, Home and History in late Colonial India*. Oxford: Oxford University Press, 2003.

Chatterjee, Partha. *Nation and Its Fragments: Colonial and Postcolonial Histories*. New Jersey: Princeton University Press, 1993.

Chaudhary, Latika. "Determinants of Primary Schooling in British India." *The Journal of Economic* History 69, no. 1 (Mar 2009): 269–302.

Cohn, Bernard. *Colonialism and Its Forms of Knowledge: The British in India*. New Jersey: Princeton University Press, 1996.

Crook, Nigel, ed. *The Transmission of Knowledge in South Asia: Essays on Education, Religion, History, and Politics*. Oxford: Oxford University Press, 1996.

Ellis, Catriona. "Education for All: Reassessing the Historiography of Education in Colonial India." *History Compass* 7, no. 2 (2009): 363–375.

Hansen, Kathryn. *Stages of Life: Indian Theatre Autobiographies*. London, New York, Delhi: Anthem Press, 2011.

Irschick, Eugene. *Dialogue and History: Constructing South India, 1795–1895*. Berkeley, Los Angeles: University of California Press, 1994.

Jenks, Chris. *Childhood*. London, New York: Routledge, 1996.

Kalam, A. P. J. Abdul. *Indomitable Spirit*. New Delhi: Rajpal & Sons, 2006.

Kalam, A. P. J. Abdul. *Turning Points: A Journey through Challenges*. New Delhi: HarperCollins Publishers India, 2012.

Kalam, A. P. J. Abdul. *My Journey: Transforming Dreams into Actions*. New Delhi: Rupa Publications India, 2013.

Kalam, A. P. J. Abdul. http://www.abdulkalam.com/kalam/theme/jsp/guest/myprofile.jsp. Accessed November 6, 2015.

Kalam, A.P.J. Abdul, and Arun Tiwari. *Wings of Fire: An Autobiography*. Hyderabad: Universities Press, 1999.

Kalam, A. P. J. Abdul, and Yagnaswami Sundara Rajan. *India 2020: A Vision for the New Millennium*. New Delhi: Penguin Books India, 2002.

Karlekar, Malavika, and Rudrangshu Mukherjee, ed. *Remembered Childhood: Essays in Honour of Andre Beteille*. Oxford: Oxford University Press, 2010.

Kumar, Krishna. *Political Agenda of Education: A Study of Colonialist and Nationalist ideas*. Delhi, London: Sage Publications, 1991.

Kumar, Nita. *Lessons from Schools: The History of Education in Banaras*. Delhi, London: Sage, 2000.

Mattison, Mines. *Public Faces, Private Voices: Community and Individuality in South India*. Berkeley, Los Angeles: University of California Press, 1994.

Mills, James H., and Satadru Sen. *Confronting the Body: The Politics of Physicality in Colonial and Post-Colonial India*. London, New York, Delhi: Anthem, 2004.

Morrison, Heidi. *Childhood and Colonial Modernity*. London: Palgrave Macmillan, 2015.

Raheja, Gloria G., and Ann Grodzins Gold. *Listen to the Heron's Words: Reimagining Gender and Kinship in North India*. Berkeley, Los Angeles: University of California Press, 1994.

Raman, Sita A. *Getting Girls to School. Social Reform in the Tamil Districts 1870–1930*. Calcutta: Stree, 1996.

Rao, Parimala V., ed. *New Perspectives in the History of Indian Education*. Hyderabad: Orient Blackswan, 2014.

Sattanathan, A. N. *The Dravidian Movement in Tamil Nadu and Its Legacy*. Madras: University of Madras, 1982.

Sattanathan, A. N. *Plain Speaking: A Sudra's Story*. Delhi: Permanent Black, 2007.

Scott, James C. *Weapons of the Weak: Everyday Forms of Peasant Resistance*. New Haven: Yale University Press, 2008.

Sen, Satadru. *Colonial Childhoods: The Juvenile Periphery of India 1850–1945*. London, New York, Delhi: Anthem Press, 2005.

Sen, Satadru. *Traces of Empire: India, America and Post Colonial Cultures*. Delhi: Primus Books, 2014.

Seth, Sanjay. *Subject Lessons: The Western Education of Colonial India*. Durham: Duke University Press, 2007.

Sreenivas, Deepa. "Telling Different Tales: Possible Childhoods in Children's Literature." *Childhood* 18, no. 3 (2011): 316–332.

Sreenivasan, Kasthuri. *Climbing the Coconut Tree: A Partial Autobiography.* Oxford: Oxford University Press, 1980.

Srivastava, Sanjay. *Constructing Post-Colonial India: National Character and the Doon School.* London: Routledge, 1998.

Subbamma, Malladi. *Fearless Feminist: An Autobiography of a Social Revolutionary*. Hyderabad: Booklinks Corp, 1994.

Tamil Nadu, "Government of 1971 Report of the Backward Classes Commission [A.N. Sattanathan, Chairman]. 3 Vols." Madras: Director of Stationery and Printing.

Topdar, Sudipa. "'Duties of a 'Good Citizen': Colonial Secondary School Textbook Policies in Late Nineteenth-Century India." *South Asian History and Culture* 6, no. 3 (2015): 417–439.

Venkatachalapathy, A. R. *In Those Days There was No Coffee: Writings in Cultural History.* Delhi: Yoda Press, 2006.

Viswanathan, Gauri. *Masks of Conquest: Literary Study and British Rule in India.* New York: Columbia University Press, 2014.

Washbrook, David. *The Emergence of Provincial Politics.* Cambridge: Cambridge University Press, 1976.

Zelliot, Eleanor. "Dalit Initiatives in Education, 1880–1992." In *New Perspectives in the History of Indian Education.* Edited by Parimala V. Rao. Hyderabad: Orient Blackswan, 2014.

Michael J. Seth

Education, Nation-Building and the Quest for Legitimacy in South Korea

Abstract The chapter presents the story of the run-up to the crucial Education Law in 1951, a landmark educational reference in the context of the emergence of a post-colonial South Korea. He depicts the key controversy between adherents of a single-track system and multi-track system as a reflection of a deeper-lying conflict. This conflict pitched elitist/ conservative ideas centered on basic education against progressive reformers inspired by American ideas of an educational system that promoted greater social mobility. As the author shows, decolonization featured prominently in these debates, in as much as the conflict played out in parts as a struggle for post-colonial legitimacy. One reason why the reformers eventually prevailed despite a parallel conservative and authoritarian turn in South Korean politics was that the elitist position was deeply tainted by many of its protagonists' collaborationist past under Japanese rule. The additional fact that their ideas were perceived by many as a mere reproduction of colonial educational realities under the Japanese significantly compromised their legitimacy.

Keywords: South Korea, Education Law, school system tracking, legitimacy, collaboration

South Korea was one of the few post-colonial states that emerged after World War II to reject the education system created by its former imperial rulers. An entirely new educational system was established in the years after liberation from Japan, beginning with the U.S. military occupation, 1945–1948 and continuing during the early years of the Republic of Korea, 1948 to 1952. Partly, this speed by which education was decolonized was due the unusual nature of the country. Decolonization was part of the process of nation-building. This was difficult in most former colonies since few possessed culturally or ethnically homogenous populations.[1] South Korea, on the other hand, was one the most ethnically homogeneous societies in the world, inheritor of a thirteen century-old unitary state, possessing a strong sense of its cultural uniqueness.

Yet in many ways South Korea's post-colonial situation resembled other newly independent states after 1945. The nation had largely inherited its school system

1 Dane Kennedy, *Decolonization: A Very Short Introduction* (Oxford: Oxford University Press, 2016), 70.

built by a former colonial state for its own purposes. Less than half the adult population had any formal schooling, only 5 percent had a secondary education, and its only university existed primarily for Japanese residents – only a third of its students were Korean. From liberation in 1945, there was a general consensus that the country needed a system that reflected Korean needs. The only debate was what kind would be most appropriate. After considerable internal debates the Republic of Korea between 1949 and 1955 created an educational system that was a radical departure from the system imposed on the country by its former colonial masters.

The effort to decolonize education was not easy since all textbooks were in Japanese and half the nation's teachers had been Japanese nationals who were repatriated at the end of the war. There was a severe lack of trained personnel at all levels. Furthermore, the country was desperately poor. Even as late as 1960, South Korea's per capital income was below that of Ghana or Haiti.[2] Yet, despite these problems this early period also witnessed a remarkable expansion of schooling at all levels, an expansion that went on despite the political turmoil, the severe economic problems and the horrendous death and destruction brought about by the Korean War.

The Kingdom of Korea had a state-funded educational system dating to the tenth century. At the time of its "opening" by Japan in 1876 the educational system consisted of thousands of village schools that were funded by parents and roughly 200 county schools funded by the royal government. The county schools were designed to prepare young men for entry into state service through the civil and military entrance examination and entry into them was limited to the aristocratic *yangban* elite. Literacy rates among males was fairly high by premodern standards with about half the male population possessing a basic reading knowledge. At the same time less than one in twenty females were literate.[3]

This premodern system disintegrated after 1876 to be replaced by a haphazard system of mainly American-run Protestant mission schools, a numbers of state institutions and various private schools. The first comprehensive modern educational system was established by the Japanese during the colonial occupation of Korea, 1910–1945. It was based on the educational system of the

2 Michael J. Seth, "South Korean Education: A National Obsession," in *The World Leaders in Education: Lessons from the Successes and the Drawbacks of their Methods*, ed. Hani Morgan and Christopher Berry (New York: Peter Lang, 2015).

3 See Michael J. Seth, *Education Fever: Society, Politics and the Pursuit of Schooling in South Korea* (Honolulu: University of Hawaii, 2002).

home country which in turn took its main inspiration from imperial Germany. Students attended six years of elementary school. These were followed by either a five-year academic preparatory or five years of vocational school. The latter was terminal while academic secondary school students could go on to a college preparatory and a three years university program. Originally there was a dual education system in Korea, one for Koreans and one for Japanese residents who made up about four percent of the population. Education was compulsory for Japanese but not for Koreans. The operating system was thus separate but equal. Throughout the thirty-five years colonial occupation the expansion of the school system proceeded slowly at all levels. Partly this was because Japanese authorities felt that Koreans did not need higher levels of schooling since more of the professional, managerial and administrative positions in the colony were held by the resident Japanese. Even the sole university was established primarily to serve the local Japanese community. Colonial education proceeded so slowly that it led to a pent-up demand for schooling. Some of this was met unlicensed private schools operated by Koreans of various backgrounds but their degrees were not recognized by the colonial government. Those who could afford it went to Japan for secondary and tertiary education. When Japan invaded China in 1937 it placed the entire empire on a wartime footing. At this time the Japanese began a policy of forced assimilation of Koreans requiring to adopt Korean names and register at Shinto shrines. Education was used as a means of carrying out this policy of erasing a separate sense of Korean identity. Korean content was reduced and then disappeared from the curricula and in 1940 all instruction was in Japanese only. The use of education to erase a sense of Korean identity became a source of deep resentment.

Decolonization of education under the U.S. Military Government, 1945–1948

The decolonization of South Korean education began under the United States Military Government in Korea (USAMGIK) which carried out educational policies based on those that the U.S had formulated for the occupation of Germany and Japan. The underlying principle was that the creation of a democratic education would be fundamental to the larger project of creating a democratic society. This could we be interpreted as a sort of new colonial education, this time American rather than Japanese. At the same time it was actively embraced by a number of reformers in South Korea and called "New Education Movement" (*sae kyoyuk undong*). The "New Education Movement" was rooted in the American progressive educational philosophy that emphasized equal opportunity for all and the development of self-reliance and individual responsibility. It encouraged student participation in the classroom in order to stimulate an active discovery method of learning in which the student would learn that there was no absolute right or wrong answer to most questions and to pursue a pragmatic approach to problem solving. It was an educational philosophy that stressed the acceptance and encouragement of individual difference and the belief that students should be taught to think for themselves, and the idea that change was desirable. The American concept of progressive education envisioned an education in which parents, community leaders, and teachers would decide what to teach and how to teach it. This meant that educational administration needed to be decentralized and teachers and schools had to be given considerable autonomy.

American progressive education was not new to Koreans. A small number of the Korean educations had studied in at Teachers College, Columbia University, a center of Deweyism. Many other Koreans had been exposed to American pedagogy at Presbyterian and Methodist schools in Korea. But the ultra-nationalist turn in the Japan after 1930 limited intellectual inquiry and made it hard to openly question the school system imposed by the colonial administration. Many Korean educators, writers, journalists and intellectuals saw American progressive education as "providing a foundation for the reconstruction of the social order into a progressive cultural identity."[4] Its appeal was partly that it was diametrically opposed to Japanese colonial pedagogical concepts that stressed authority rather than questioning, conformity rather than individual. Colonial education was elitist rather than democratic, and centralized rather than allowing for local participation and local needs. This idea of elitist education was associated with the early tracking of students into vocational and academic tracks. The ideal was a general secondary schooling that was not terminal but open to the possibility advance to higher education.

In fact, the first initiative toward educational reform came not from the ill-prepared and initially poorly organized American military government but from a small number of prominent U.S.-trained Korean educators Yu Ŏk-kyôm, O Ch'ŏn-sŏk, Paek Nak-chun (George Paik), and Kim Hwal-lan (Helen Kim), who formed the Korean Committee on Education in September 1945. All of whom were respected educators. All had at some point in their schooling had studied at American institutions. O Ch'ŏn-sŏk, for example, attended Teachers College at Columbia University, belonged to an American affiliated Christian

4 Noel F. McGinn, *Education and Development in Korea* (Cambridge: Harvard University Press, 1980), 36.

church and was an enthusiastic believer that the United States offered a model of democracy, prosperity and progress for Korea to follow.[5] Kim Sŏng-su, one of the country's wealthiest citizens and an educational philanthropist, served as the chairman. They discussed plans for sweeping educational reform including the implementation of a system of education patterned after that of the United States.[6] Kim Sŏng-su left the committee and Yu Ŏk-kyŏm succeeded him as chairman. Subsequently, the committee continued to meet until May 1946, serving as an advisory body to the Americans in the Bureau of Education, as the former Ministry of Education had been remained, recommending its reorganization and advising on the reopening of schools, the dismissal of Japanese personnel, and the appointment of educational officers. At the recommendation of the committee, USAMGIK established the National Committee on Educational Planning which met from November 1945 until the spring of 1946.[7] The purpose of the committee was to develop the "fundamental philosophy of Korean education based on democratic principles and practices" and to reorganize "Korean education in accordance with that philosophy." In order to carry this out, the work of the committee was to be "predicated upon a balance between native cultural aims and modern American educational influences."[8] Thus, the educational reform efforts under the U.S. occupation of South Korea were as much the product of a small enthusiastic group of Korean educators as it was of the Americans.[9]

The committee reports recommended changes that brought South Korean education closer to the American example. Most prominent was the proposed adoption of the 6-3-3-4 year educational system. Six years of primary education would be universal, followed by three years of middle school and three years of high school, leading to a four-year college education. The committee recommended that the two-track system of vocational and academic (university-bound secondary schooling) be abolished for a single track. This move was

5 Son In-su, *Han'guk kyoyuksa [History of Korean Education]* (Seoul: Munŭmsa, 1987), 1, 805–806.

6 O, Ch'ŏn-sôk, *Han'guk sin kyoyuk-sa [History of the New Education in Korea]* (Seoul: Hyôndae Kyoyuk Chisa Ch'ulp'an-sa, 1964), 104, 108–109.

7 Ibid., 108–109.

8 United States Army Military Government in Korea, *Summation of the United States Military Government Activities in Korea* (Seoul: USAMGIK, March, 1946), 19.

9 Han Suk Hoo, "Influence of Foreign Ideas in the Making of National Education System: The Case of Japan's Education Planning for Colonized Korea," *KEDI Journal of Educational Policy* 7, no. 1 (2010): 91–114.

intended to bring the country's schooling in line with the principle of equal opportunity, a principle regarded by advocates of progressive education as an essential feature of a democratic society. The Americans, upon endorsing these proposals, added their own recommendations for a unitary educational structure and a separate middle and high school, eliminating the old system whereby children decided their life's vocation when they finished elementary school. The Americans also proposed that no type of middle or high school, nor any type of course, was to be terminal so that a student in a technical program could switch to a college-bound one. This flexibility was in accordance with prevailing American educational theory which stressed the need to give the individual child more personal freedom and responsibility, thus promoting individualism, the foundation of a democratic society. In addition, American advisors supported equal opportunity for girls at all levels and argued for the need of coeducation at the secondary school level.[10]

Perhaps the most important leader of the movement for *sae kyoyuk* was O Ch'ŏn-sŏk. With the sponsorship of the Department of Education, O Ch'ŏn-sŏk ran a summer workshop at Seoul National University in 1946.[11] The first of a series of similar programs, it introduced the concepts of progressive education to hundreds of Korean teachers. Another series of workshops conducted by Hyojae Primary School principal, Yun Chae-ch'ŏn, was designed to introduce these new education concepts to elementary school teachers.[12] Since there was a widespread fascination with the new educational theory among Korean educators, workshops, seminars, and education manuals were distributed by U.S. educational officials were eagerly received. However, the Americans did not carry out any major structural reforms. Their occupation was too brief and they were most concerned with establishing political stability and prevent communist subversion. They also faced the militant opposition of many leftist students and teachers who sought to create a socialist society. Leftist teachers formed the *Chosŏn Kyoyukcha Hyŏphoe* (Korean Teachers Federation) in February 1946, the

---

10 Donald K. Adams, "Education in Korea 1945–1955," (Ph.D. diss., University of Connecticut, 1956), 65–78; Nam Byung Hun, "Educational Reorganization in South Korea Under the United States Army Military Government 1945–1948," (Ph.D. diss., University of Pittsburgh, 1962), 3–97.

11 Eiko Seki, "An Endeavor by Koreans toward the Reestablishment of an Educational System under the U.S. Military government," *East-West Education* 5(1) (Spring 1986): 44–66.

12 Hyojae Kungmin Hakkyo, *Hyojae kusibinyôn-sa [Ninety-Two Year History of Hyojae Elementary School]* (Seoul: Hyojae Kumgnin Hakkyo, 1987), 78.

first grass-roots teachers organization in Korean history.[13] It became affiliated with the pro-Communist labor organization, the *Chŏnp'yŏng*.[14] Opposition to the U.S. occupation and to conservative Koreans it was promoting resulted in frequent shutdowns of schools. By early 1947, fifty-seven of the nation's high schools and colleges were closed due to campus unrest.[15] The result was that the American occupation made full use of the Japanese trained police force to arrest hundreds of teachers and ultimately maintained the highly centralized educational system of the colonial period. The U.S. endeavor to "democratize" schooling thus ran into conflict with the efforts to create an anti-Communist political order in South Korea.

Establishing a new educational system, 1948–1951

As a result of the brief nature of the U.S. occupation and its preoccupation with anti-Communism and security issues South Korea began its existence as an independent entity in the summer of 1948, without having determined the nature of its educational system. The new nation inherited the old Japanese educational structure slightly modified by the U.S. Military Government. It also inherited the plans, which had been drawn up prior to independence by Koreans and Americans for reforming schooling along the lines of the U.S. education system. With these two models before it, the South Korean government had, as one of its first tasks, to decide on the type of educational system that was to serve the nation for the next decades. Educational debates were influenced by awareness of developments outside of Korea, references suggest that some educators followed education reforms in American occupied Germany and especially in Japan that continued after the Americans left South Korea in 1948. Debates on educational developed sometimes echoed the arguments made by reformers and conservatives in Japan.[16]

---

13 Han'guk Kyoyuk Yôn'guso, *Han'guksa ken-Hyôn taep'yôn [Essays on Modern and Recent Korean History]* (Seoul: Han'guk Kyoyuk Yôn'guso, 1994), 450–451.

14 Taehan Kyoyuk Yônhaphoe, *Taehan kyoryôn sasipnyônsa [Forty-Year History of the Korean Federation of Educators' Associations]* (Seoul: Taehan Kyoryôn Yônhaphoe, 1987), 4.

15 Yi Chae-o, *Haebang hu Han'guk haksaeng undongsa [History of the Student Movement After Liberation]* (Seoul: Hyông-sa, 1984), 74, 88–92. For an example of U.S. official fears of campus unrest see *Summation* (April 1946), 191.

16 See Masako Shibata, *Japan and Germany under the U.S. Occupation: A Comparative Analysis of Post-War Education Reform* (Maryland: Lexington Books, 2008).

While officials, educators and journalists discussed just how to structure the new educational system, a pent-up demand for schooling animated the public. Meeting this demand was a high priority for the Republic of Korea (South Korea) under the regime of Syngman Rhee (1948–1960). While South Korea was ethnically homogeneous and did not face the sectarian divisions than many former colonies were enmeshed in, it was riven by ideological conflicts between leftists and rightists reflecting a split in the nationalist movement that had dated from the colonial period. Furthermore, the South Korean state was the product of a divided nation. From the onset, the division of the nation into two rival regimes was almost universally regarded as tragic and unacceptable. Its new division was based on an arbitrary boundary with no geographical or cultural logic to it. Families found themselves divided, and the hundreds of thousands of refugees from the north living in the south created a powerful lobby for reunification. Koreans generally conceived of the South Korean state as a temporary unit to function only as long as it took to reconstitute a united Korea. Meanwhile, the South Korean state found itself in competition with a North Korean political entity which offered an alternative version of national development. A serious problem of the South Korean state as it competed for legitimacy with a rival claimant to the mantle of nationalism, was the weak nationalist credentials of its leadership. The majority of the officials serving the new state were tainted with collaboration. Although the bureaucrats and politicians were little different from the vast majority of Koreans who had simply compromised with the Japanese authorities as they tried to maintain their daily lives, the political and moral authority claimed by the state was undermined by the fact that it was commanded and served mainly by those who had not only cooperated, but often prospered under colonial rule. To gain legitimacy the new/old elite sought to respond to the public desire to school their children. It sought to build a school system that could accommodate children of all school ages, while opening up the possibility of social mobility through education to all families. It also needed to demonstrate that it was rejecting the Japanese colonial administration with its elitist concept of schooling.

As officials, members of the National Assembly, educators and journalists discussed the type of educational system to be established they focused on two main issues: whether to maintain the separate academic and vocational tracks, and whether or not to decentralize the school system. The Rhee administration proposed to eliminate the narrow aperture to an elite academic university-oriented path inherited from the colonial period to adopt the more open American system that avoided early tracking and in which no type of primary or secondary schooling was terminal. Proponents of the open, flexible, American system held that is was based on the principle of egalitarianism and would serve to produce a society that was democratic, open at all levels, with equal opportunity the central operating principle. But for some Koreans, the American-inspired schooling system was a dangerous innovation that would erode standards and hinder the development of an education structure suitable for Korean needs, that for large numbers of vocationally trained workers and literate farmers, and a small number of higher trained professionals and managers. Adherents of this view called for a system that would provide a specialized, multi-tracked schooling that would maintain the best of pre-liberation education.

While everyone denounced the authoritarian style of the colonial system, and the need to some greater input by teachers and the public, many advocates of the American-style school system also aimed at instituting a system of local school boards. Opponents of decentralized education sought to either limit the role of the education boards as much as possible, or to not carry out the experiment at all. They argued that the need for a strong, centralized, coherent administration outweighed the need for local authority and they were unwilling to risk the disorder and incompetency of autonomous, local educational administrative bodies. Another related issue concerned the belief in uniform education. How could uniformity of content and standard be guaranteed without central control and supervision? Accompanying this issue was the question of educational autonomy. This meant freeing the MOE and the proposed school boards from the general administrative and coercive organs of the state, in particular from the Ministry of the Interior (*Naemubu*), which controlled both the administration of local government and the police. It also meant creating an education system operated by teachers and professional educators who would enjoy autonomy of decision making and security of position free of arbitrary intervention from the non-educational organs of government.

Educators were also concerned about whether and how to adopt American instructional methodology. Would it be suitable for Korea? Would it promote a democratic and prosperous society and moral citizens? And what type of curriculum would be best suited to serve this purpose? In the public debate over the establishment of a new educational system, however, attention was mainly focused on how open the system should be to access to higher levels of education and how centralized and uniform it should be. U.S. educational reformers helped spark a lively debate among Korean educators on the type of education they wanted for their nation. Much of this debate occurred in the framework of educational organizations. In 1948, there were three main organizations for the promotion of educational ideas in South Korea: the *Sae Kyoyuk Yŏn'guhoe* (New Education Research Society), the *Munhwa Kyoyuk Hyŏphoe* (Culture and

Education Association), and the *Chosŏn Kyoyuk Yŏn'guhoe* (Korean Education Research Society). The largest of these the *Sae Kyoyuk Yŏn'guhoe* was organized by advocates of the so-called new education, as American Deweyism was called. Among its leaders were O Ch'ŏn-sŏk and Yun Chae-ch'ŏl. Most of its members had been exposed to American education either by attending school in the United States, attending an American missionary school or being a student of an American-trained educator.

While leftist opposition to education reforms was effectively repressed in the way of anti-communism that characterized both the U.S. occupation and the Rhee regime, a more nationalist tone was characteristic of another educational organization the *Chosŏn Kyoyuk Yŏn'guhoe.*[17] Its founder An Ho-sang, who became South Korea's first minister of education, had been educated in Germany, where he studied philosophy. He adopted a blood and soil ultra-nationalism, the extolled the racial purity of the Korean people and disparage the U.S. as "a carnival of peoples."[18] They tend to be critical of both the American and Japanese education systems insisting that Korea must develop its own system, not blindly imitate others. Although they were not always clear or consistent just what this "Korean system" would look like they tended to have a more vocational education for the masses and a smaller elite track for the professional and managerial class. It would also be centralized to insure uniform and high standards. In other words, a system not very different from the colonial one.

South Korean educators had much in common. Part of this was due to the suppression of leftist opposition which placed limits on the range of views that could be expressed. But more important, almost all Korean educators shared the view that education could produce a prosperous and strong nation. This tremendous faith in education was heavily influenced by the traditional Confucian belief in the role of education in transforming the individual and society, a belief that was amplified by the Japanese idea of using education to create a rich and powerful state and American ideals of education for all. Additionally, all South

---

17 The *Chosôn Kyoyuk Yôn'guhoe* was founded in August, 1946 under the title *Minju Kyoyuk Yôn'guhoe* (Democratic Education Research Society) and changed its name in December, 1946. See Hong Ung-sôn, *Kwangbok hu e sin kyoyuk undong 1946–1949, Chosôn kyoyuk yôn'guhoe rûl chungsim ûro [The New Education Movement after Liberation, 1946–1949, Centered on the Chosôn Educational Research Society]* (Seoul: Taehan Kyogwasô, 1991), 45–63.

18 An Ho-sang, *Minjujuûi ûi yôksa was chôngnyu [History and Varieties of Democracy]* (Seoul: Ilmin Ch'ulp'an-sa, 1953), 239.

Korean writers on education appear to have shared the traditional view of the intellectual and educator as the conscience of the nation, and saw education as the legitimate means of selecting the leadership of society. At the same time, they sought to achieve uniformity in education content. Nor, as subsequent events demonstrated were these beliefs confined to the elite. At all levels of Korean society there was a faith in education as the basis for creating a new nation and for conferring moral, political, and social leadership among those who had studied hardest. This placed the issue of education not on the periphery but at the center of public discourse in the new South Korean state. All believed in thoroughly Koreanizing the curriculum (Koreans were still using some translated Japanese texts in 1948).

All these issues played out in the National Assembly which devoted five weeks to debate over the education law in the fall of 1949. Conferences were held every morning, starting in early November to work out an acceptable bill, but by mid-November the Education Law had become the main issue in the Assembly, delaying other bills.[19] No other single issue occupied so much time in debate during that year. The debate centered on fundamental differences in educational policies. The National Assembly presented a draft for an education system that essentially resembled the prewar Japanese system with its early sorting of students into specialized tracks. The Ministry of Education with its many American trained members presented a proposal that that followed the 6-3-3-4 system with a unitary single track. There was general agreement on a universal, compulsory six-year elementary schooling, but little agreement on any other specifics. Nationalist feeling ran strong and proponents of both models were careful in arguing that they were creating a Korean educational system and not implementing a purely borrowed one. Supporters of both versions attacked the other for uncritical foreign borrowing. Ironically the stigma of being "Japanese" was attached to both versions. The MOE version was defended by its supporters as "proper for Korea and because every other country has adopted this system."[20] At the same time supporters of the National Committee version attacked the current system as too American and unsuitable for Korea's needs. Framers of the MOE version were also accused of merely translating the American inspired 1947 Fundamental Education Law of Japan. What was needed, critics charged, was a truly Korean educational law, not a copy from another country. Responding to these charges, the Minister of Education, An Ho-sang, in a newspaper interview, replied that

19 *Tonga ilbo*, (Nov 24, 1949).

20 *Kukhoe sokkirok* [Minutes of the National Assembly], (October 31, 1949): 553.

"whether it is American or Japanese, we will adopt whatever is best." The MOE proposal, however, he added, was "far from being Japanese."[21] In turn opponents lambasted the National Assembly draft as adhering to the prewar imperial Japanese system.

Debate over a single or multi-tracked system

The most important issue in the formulation of the education law proved to be over how open the educational system should be at the higher levels. Politicians, officials, and educators who argued for separate vocational and academic middle schools asserted that a common, general three-year middle school was a luxury that Korea could not afford. And they further maintained that greater emphasis should be placed on career training. These arguments carried considerable weight in the National Assembly, and by November, there was a strong push for a four-year academic or vocational middle school, followed by a two-year college preparatory school for university-bound students, and higher technical schools for vocational middle school graduates.[22] Practical as these arguments may have been, they ran counter to a broad-based push for access to education occurring throughout Korea, which was in part a result of the pent-up aspiration for education brought about by the restrictive policies of the Japanese colonial government. Everywhere, private secondary schools and colleges were springing up to meet this demand. Thus, there were two related reasons for supporting single-track education: to create a democratic and truly egalitarian society rather than a more rigidly structured, elitist society; and to keep the gate of opportunity from narrowing to an academic track available only to a university-bound few.

Related to this issue was the problem of separated middle and high schools. In the MOE version, secondary education was divided, American style, into a three-year middle school and a three high school, and any separate channel of education would come only at the three year high school level. This, however, posed a problem since it would mean that existing secondary schools would have to be separated leading to a multiplicity of administration. Furthermore, opposition to the creation of separate middle and high schools came from parents in major cities such as Seoul who, having succeeded in gaining entry into one of the prestigious middle schools, viewed with dismay the prospects of competing again for entry into an academic high school.

21 *Chosôn ilbo*, (Sep 21, 1949).

22 *Kukhoe sokkirok*, (Nov 3, 1949): 631–648; *Chosôn ilbo*, (Nov 17, 1949).

During the subsequent debate no clear agreement could be reached, and a bewildering variety of modifications were proposed. Some suggested maintaining a single track system but reducing secondary school to four years.[23] Most Assemblymen wanted a single institution of secondary education that would be of two types: academic or vocational, others argued that this would force students to decide upon a career while they were still in elementary school.[24] But supporters of vocational secondary education maintained that there was a need to begin vocational education early and that academic students needed a long rigorous preparation for college.[25] Many also strongly opposed efforts to eliminate separate middle and high schools. According to American educational theory, the middle school gave children a longer time to develop their abilities and determine where their aptitude and interests were, while the high school was the point in adolescents' education when they began to select courses suitable for the preparation for their life's work. Eliminating the separate stages of middle and higher secondary school for a more career-oriented single middle school seemed to some a regressive step, especially, at a time when Japan was adopting the American system and rejecting the very system that many Assemblymen sought to re-impose in a modified form.

The debates revealed a divide between professional educators in and out of the Ministry of Education who supported the 6-3-3-4 system and the majority of other Assemblymen who supported a system closer to the one in which they had been educated, or had served through the bureaucracy that administered it. South Korea's educators sought a more radical break with colonial education, not just greater nationalist credentials, but because they sought to create a more vibrant democratic society based on equal opportunity; and they saw the United States and its education system as a progressive, successful society that could serve as a model for Korea. The National Assembly prevailed and on 26 November 1949, this National Assembly by a comfortable margin voted for the 6-4-2(4)-4 system: six-year elementary school, followed by either a four-year academic middle school, or a four-year vocational middle school.[26] Those attending the four-year academic middle schools could attend a two-year college preparatory school and continue on to four years of university. Vocational middle school students could continue on to a two or four-year technical school,

23 *Kukhoe sokkirok*, (October 31, 1949): 559.

24 *Kukhoe sokkirok*, (Nov 25, 1949): 1181.

25 *Kukhoe sokkirok*, (Nov 5, 1949): 794; *Kukhoe sokkirok*, (Nov 25, 1949): 1181.

26 *Kukhoe sokkirok*, (Nov 26, 1949): 1186.

which would be the terminus of their educational advancement. Specialized normal secondary schools, under strict national supervision, would serve as still another specialized track for teachers. This system was almost identical with the Japanese colonial system. One difference though was that middle school had been shortened from five to four years.

Supporters of multi-track secondary school were careful to avoid references to the colonial system but instead cited the example of Germany with its bifurcation of secondary education into *realschule* and *gymnasium* as an example of professional excellence and a realistic approach to schooling. They also spoke of the need to limit university enrollment to the numbers of intellectually trained people the economy could absorb. These supporters feared that there was already a surplus of college graduates. This was seen by its supporters as a sound practical decision. As one of the authors of this change, Assemblyman Yi Chae-ik, explained "for a poor country like Korea...trained persons are needed who can finish education in a very short time."[27] The same group also rejected the idea of local school boards.

The Japanese colonial system had been characterized by separate teacher training in secondary schools and colleges. It also maintained rigorous standards of teacher training. Many wanted to retain both features which were considered inseparable but others wanted to integrate the higher normal schools with the universities to create a more liberal atmosphere for teacher training and lower the standards for teacher training in order to cope with teacher shortages. On this issue, the Fundamental Education Law of 1949 ended with a compromise which created two-year teacher training schools (*sabŏm hakkyo*) for middle school graduates, and college level schools that would be open to all secondary school graduates. Instead of highly professional training that would have required six years of post-middle school training, which would have restricted the number of teachers available, teachers at the primary school level needed only two years of specialized training. But a more professional college level educational training was available for secondary school teachers.

As part of the effort to create mass literacy many educators and politicians called for the exclusive use of the Korean alphabet (*han'gŭl),* but conservative Koreans insisted that the prestigious *hanmun* (Chinese characters) be included as well. Proponents of the indigenous Korean alphabet appealed to nationalist sentiments since the Korean script had become a symbol of Korean uniqueness

27 *Kukhoe sokkirok*, (Nov 26, 1949): 1185; Gilsang Lee et al., *The History of Education in Korea: A Sourcebook* (Bundang, Korea: Academy of Korean Studies, 2015), 30–34.

and ingenuity. Moreover, by avoiding the extremely arduous task of learning Chinese characters, Korean would be much easier and literacy could spread more quickly. But mastery of *hanmun* had long been a mark of the educated man and a source of pride for the *yangban* elite, and many educated Koreans were reluctant to abandon a difficult system of writing that they had spent years mastering. Conservatives feared it would also make the country's traditional culture less accessible to a newer generation. The issue was never resolved. Initially Chinese characters were taught along with the Korean alphabet, then in the 1960s and 1970s the state moved toward exclusive use and instruction in *han'gŭl*, but the Ministry of Education reversed itself in the 1980s and 1990s when Chinese characters were again taught along with the Korean alphabet.

As enacted by the National Assembly in 1949, the educational system maintained far more of the features of the Japanese colonial education than the reformers in the Ministry of Education found acceptable. Almost immediately initiatives to revise the Education Law were put forward. With the support of the state-sponsored Korean Federation of Educators Associations (KFEA), held a series of meetings in each province. These meetings organized special committees to lobby for the revision of the law (*hakche sujŭng simŭi-hoe*) urging the restoration of the 6-3-3-4 system.[28] As a result two revisions of the Education Law in 1950 and in 1951 restored almost all the original, American-based elements. In the end, attacked as elitist and unprogressive, and as harking back to the discredited system that Japan itself in defeat had repudiated, the multi-track system was rejected, and the upper level secondary school system was revised. In place of the two-year college preparatory school and the two to four-year higher technical school, the MOE proposal for a uniform three-year high school (*kodŭng hakkyo*) was approved on 9 February 1950. The new system was 6-4-3-4: six years of primary school, four years of middle school, three years of vocational or academic high school, and four years of college or university. Also consistent with the emphasis on equal opportunity, legislators dismissed a suggestion by one Assemblyman that the high school entrance exam be limited to middle school students.[29]

28 *Kukhoe sokkirok*, (Feb 9, 1950): 554–555; *Chosôn ilbo*, (Feb 12, 1950).
29 *Chosôn ilbo*, (Feb 10, 1950).

Conclusion

South Korea's process of decolonization of education was concluded when the Education Law was finalized in 1951. The multi-track and highly centralized education system was replaced by a more uniform system that made no tier of education terminal. It was to be universal and broadly accessible at all levels. Central control was balanced with elected local school boards that would insure teacher and community input. There are a number of reasons why South Korea discarded much of its inherited colonial education. The Japanese policy of treating Koreans as second class citizens in their own country, and their policy of coercive assimilation led to stigmatize all institutions associated with them. Moreover, the defeat of the Japanese Empire in 1945 undermined its claims to represent a successful form of modernity. Koreans looked to the victors and liberators-the Soviet Union and the United States as models of progressive societies. However, with the creation of two rival Koreas, the United States became the only acceptable model for educators, officials and reformers in the South. Not all South Koreans were comfortable with adopting the American model, but many were and those that opposed them found it difficult to defend educational ideas that adhered too closely to the colonial system.

The discourse over educational reform indicated that the main issue at stake was not just to rid the school system of its colonial past but more positively to create a new kind of society different from both its colonial and pre-colonial heritage. This was to be a society that was democratic, that allowed for a high degree of social mobility and that was based on the principle of equality of opportunity. To accomplish these goals, education had to be not only Korean in content but broadly accessible, and non-elitist. Educational issues were important, since Koreans inherited a belief in the transformational value of education that was reinforced by the Japanese and American examples. Intellectuals and politicians of all stripes saw education as the means for creating the basis for a modern, progressive Korean nation. Education was universal and compulsory at the primary level and open at the higher levels. The new school system was based on the belief that the opportunity for promotion to higher levels of schooling should remain open to all, and that children should not be assigned a low level terminal tracked early in life. Although the system underwent a number of minor revisions, these fundamental features have remained a permanent part of the South Korean structure of formal learning.

Few newly independent nations after 1945 rejected their colonial educational structures. South Korea's change was made easier by Japan's own educational reforms, but was also an indication of the strong desire of South Koreans to seek to improve the life chances of their younger family members through educational advancement and to avoid placing them into fixed terminal tracks. The new system had an enormous impact on South Korea's subsequent development, helping to shape the nation's "education fever." By allowing the possibility for advancement at every level of schooling, the way was open for unrelenting competition at every rung of the educational ladder. Many Koreans saw no point of schooling as terminal, but each step as only a preparation for the next. This attitude created an enormous desire for higher levels of schooling. It would also inadvertently undermine vocational education since vocational education came to be seen as an unfortunate way station on the path to a more desirable non-vocational university education.[30]

The new educational system indeed Korean. Few schools even taught the Japanese language; and all words of Japanese origins were purged from textbooks, dictionaries and publications. Yet it was not a total break with the colonial education system. The local school boards that were established in 1952 to decentralize the system were not effective in establishing community control over the schools, and were abolished in 1961. The colonial practice of centralized direction of schooling continued. The Ministry of Education maintained complete control over all curricula and established detailed regulations for all private schools. Even the school uniforms worn by secondary students were virtually the same black military styles of the colonial period until this vestige of the past was abolished in the early 1980s. Teachers training programs, pedagogical methods and even the physical layouts of the schools resembled those of the colonial period. But the ending of tracking, the commitment to equal access, the egalitarian ideology promoted in the schools, the disdain for vocational schooling, and, of course the Korean content of the curriculum all were breaks with the colonial past.

Literature

Adams, Donald K. "Education in Korea 1945–1955." Ph.D. diss., University of Connecticut, 1956.

Chae, Jae-Eun, and Hee Kyoong Hong. "The Expansion of Higher Education Led by Private Universities in Korea." *Asia Pacific Journal of Education* 29(3) (2009): 341–355.

30 Jae-Eun Chae and Hee Kyoong Hong, "The Expansion of Higher Education Led by Private Universities in Korea" *Asia Pacific Journal of Education* 29, no. 3 (2009): 341–355.

Chosŏn ilbo [Chosun Daily Newspaper].

Han, Suk Hoo. "Influence of Foreign Ideas in the Making of National Education System: The Case of Japan's Education Planning for Colonized Korea." *KEDI Journal of Educational Policy* 7(1) (2010): 91–114.

Han'guk Kyoyuk Yôn'guso. *Han'guksa ken-Hyôn taep'yôn [Essays on Modern and Recent Korean History]*. Seoul: Han'guk Kyoyuk Yôn'guso, 1994.

Hong, Ung-sôn. *Kwangbok hu e sin kyoyuk undong 1946–1949, Chosôn kyoyuk yôn'guhoe rûl chungsim ûro [The New Education Movement after Liberation, 1946–1949, Centered on the Chosôn Educational Research Society]*. Seoul: Taehan Kyogwasô, 1991.

Ho-sang, An. *Minjujuûi ûi yôksa was chôngnyu [History and Varieties of Democracy]*. Seoul: Ilmin Ch'ulp'an-sa, 1953.

Hyojae Kungmin Hakkyo. *Hyojae kusibinyôn-sa [Ninety-Two Year History of Hyojae Elementary School]*. Seoul: Hyojae Kumgnin Hakkyo, 1987.

Kennedy, Dane. *Decolonization: A Very Short Introduction*. Oxford: Oxford University Press, 2016.

Kukhoe sokkirok [Minutes of the National Assembly of the Republic of Korea].

Lee, Gilsang and Michael J. Seth (eds.). *The History of Education in Korea: A Sourcebook*. Bundang: Academy of Korean Studies, 2015.

McGinn, Noel F. *Education and Development in Korea*. Cambridge/Mass.: Harvard University Press, 1980.

Nam, Byung Hun. "Educational Reorganization in South Korea Under the United States Army Military Government 1945–1948." Ph.D. diss., University of Pittsburgh, 1962.

O, Ch'ôn-sôk. *Han'guk sin kyoyuk-sa [History of the New Education in Korea]*. Seoul: Hyôndae Kyoyuk Chisa Ch'ulp'an-sa, 1964.

Seki, Eiko. "An Endeavor by Koreans toward the Reestablishment of an Educational System under the U.S. Military government." *East-West Education* 5(1) (Spring 1986): 44–66.

Seth, Michael J. *Education Fever: Society, Politics and the Pursuit of Schooling in South Korea*. Honolulu: University of Hawaii, 2002.

Seth, Michael J. "South Korean Education: A National Obsession." In *The World Leaders in Education: Lessons from the Successes and the Drawbacks of their Methods*, edited by Hani Morgan and Christopher Berry. New York: Peter Lang, 2015.

Shibata, Masako. *Japan and Germany under the U.S. Occupation: A Comparative Analysis of Post-War Education Reform*. Maryland: Lexington Books, 2008.

Son, In-su. *Han'guk kyoyuksa [History of Korean Education]. 2 vols.* Seoul: Munŭmsa, 1987.

Son Sik. "Yahak Movement in South Korea." *Convergence* 37(1) (2009): 51–57.

Taehan Kyoyuk Yônhaphoe. *Taehan kyoryôn sasipnyônsa [Forty-Year History of the Korean Federation of Educators' Associations]*. Seoul: Taehan Kyoryôn Yônhaphoe, 1987.

Tonga ilbo [Tonga Daily Newspaper] (1949).

United States Army Military Government in Korea. *Summation of the United States Military Government Activities in Korea.* Seoul: USAMGIK, March, 1946.

Yi, Chae-o. *Haebang hu Han'guk haksaeng undongsa [History of the Student Movement After Liberation]*. Seoul: Hyông-sa, 1984.

Hakeem Ibikunle Tijani

Nigerianization as Decolonization. Human Capacity Development in Nigeria 1945–1960

Abstract The chapter deals with the 'Nigerianization' of the educational system in the British West-African colony. Its focus is on the somewhat fluid period between late colonial rule and what historians have termed the "second colonial occupation" of Africa and the transitional phase leading eventually into independence of the British colony. The efforts for 'nigerianizing' technical and specialized staff within the state apparatus show a multi-layered conflict. Spanning the period between 1945 and the early years of independence in the beginning of the 1960s, the author reveals the agency of local actors. Conflicts surrounding the build-up of new administrative capacities in the field of education needed for the consolidation and progress of the new polities played out on two different, but often intertwined levels: between colonial and nationalist forces on the one hand and between different regions and ethnic groups within Nigeria on the other.

Keywords: Human Capacity Development, Nigeria, Nigerianization, experts

Introduction

The year 1904 marked the beginning of British hegemony in Nigeria, with effective pacification of the people in the area north and south of the Benue and Niger Rivers. Throughout the pre-World War II era, efforts were made to establish structures that would ensure effective implementation of the British "civilizing" mission in Nigeria. One of the major structures was the establishment of the Secretariat in Lagos, and administrative offices in the provinces and districts throughout the country. The post-World War II period remained one of the defining moments in modern African history, marking the end of European rule in many colonies. Between 1945 and 1960, Nigeria was transformed from a colony to a self-governing country where Nigerians assumed administrative positions as part of the transfer of power. The discourse about European transfer of power after World War II is that transition in a given colony typically depended on two factors: the level of pressure for change in the colony and the response to the inevitable by the corresponding colonizing power. Roger Fieldhouse has identified the forces that shattered the "complacent air of dignified peaceful and paternalistic progression towards eventual independence in British Africa."[1]

1 Roger Fieldhouse, "Cold War and Colonial Conflicts in British West African Adult Education, 1947–1953," *History of Education Quarterly* 24, no. 3 (1984): 359–371.

What has not been emphasized is that, in many cases, the colonial powers themselves began to initiate policies and methods aimed at ensuring a smooth transition from European colonial civil servants to African civil servants wittingly and unwittingly. In addition, persuasion rather than force was also an instrument of attaining most policies aimed at decolonization of the civil service. In Nigeria, conservative and liberal nationalists were involved in a peaceful devolution of power leading to independence on October 1, 1960.[2] No doubt, the part and process of "inventing new nations and nationalisms" and mentoring "New Men and New Polities" became irreversible after World War II.

Contextualizing Nigerianization

Nigerianization, therefore, was [and still is] about ensuring that Nigerians are trained to staff various sections of the civil service as part of British style "modernization." Nigerianization is thus, defined as British efforts to develop the human capacity in colonial Nigeria, reform of the civil service, and the general transformation of Departments to Ministries with budgetary power. In this essay, I posit that Nigerianization was the most important element within the wider process of pacification, "modernization", and the development of human resource capacity in the most populous colony in the British Empire. The year 1948[3]

2 Africanists such as Ade-Ajayi, Adu-Boahen, Aluko, Robert Tignor, Samir Amin, Segun Osoba, and others have since challenged the imperial school led by Robinson and Gallagher. The imperial school, in the words of Tignor, is defined as "robustly Anglophobic; it is entirely rooted in the imperial archive; it conflates the official mind with the real world of [West] African economics and politics; and it employs the views of elite groups when dealing with subalterns." See Robert Tignor's review of David K. Fieldhouse, *Merchant Capital and Economic Decolonization: The United Africa Company, 1929–1987* (Oxford: Clarendon Press, 1994) *The Journal of African History* 38, no. 3 (1997): 514–515; Olajide Aluko, "Politics of decolonization in British West Africa 1945–1960," *History of West Africa* 2, eds. J. F. Ade Ajayi and Michael Crowder (London, 1974); C. Young, "Decolonization in Africa," in *Colonialism in Africa 1870–1960*, eds. L. H. Gann and P. Duignan (Cambridge: Cambridge University Press, 1970).

3 Examples are: Gabriel O. Olusanya, *The Evolution of the Nigerian Civil Service, 1861–1960* (Lagos: University of Lagos, 1975); Henry N. Nwosu, *Political Authority and the Nigerian Civil Service* (Enugu: Fourth Dimension Pub., 1985); Dayo Olopade, "The Nigerian civil service and change," *ASCON: Journal of Management* 8, no. 1, 2 (1989); Adele J. Bamgbose, "The Nigerian Civil Service: Past and Present," *ASCON – Journal of Management* 12, no. 1, 2 (1993): 31.

remained a pivotal moment in the process that began with British declaration of her Majesty's government over Lagos in 1861.[4] It was pivotal because it jolted the men on the spot and the Colonial Office into the reality of need to engage the nationalists through reforms and devolution of duties and functions either as Ministers or heads of government parastatals. It also marked the beginning of many nationalists demands and constitutional changes. Riots in Accra in 1948, and the irredentist Zikists call for revolution in Nigeria, are examples of events unfolding and the need for training of skilled and degree holders to assume leadership roles across the regions in Nigeria. The contents for skill training, and the location of degree training opportunities were monitored with a still anti-communist measures by the colonial and nationalists governments as it was in the Gold Coast, Burma or the British Caribbean.

Similarly, the process of Nigerianization was not without its politics that began at the Ibadan Conference in 1950, and again during the 1953 Lagos Conference where the nationalists began to see the process differently, and even threatened to secede if their terms were not met. Sir Arthur Richard's effort, directed at regional governments, was perceived as a threat to skilled and qualified N. that would man various middle cadre positions. Even the attempt to address this alongside other constitutional matters led to the 1950 Ibadan Conference where the gory side of ethnicity and the reality of dearth of manpower throughout the colony was emphasized. In fact, the disparity between the North and the rest of the regions was key to the establishment of the Phillipson and Adebo Commission that submitted its Report in 1952. I will return to the matters arising from the Report in the next section in this paper.

Nigerianization therefore fits into what David Dorward described as the "mixed dependency" that began in 1861 with the creation of a colony in Lagos.[5] To the men on the on the spot, history of Nigerian civil service dates back to March 1862 "when the British government declared its interest in the Port and Island of Lagos under the title of the settlement of Lagos. A government was constituted and provision was made for the various posts of Governor, Chief Magistrate, Colonial Secretary and Senior Military Officers. The Offices of Private Secretary to the Governor and Auditor for Public Accounts, Chief

4 See, Hakeem I. Tijani and Ashley Carter, "Decolonization," in *Africa and the Wider World*, eds. Hakeem I. Tijani, et. al. (Boston: Pearson Publisher, 2010).

5 David C. Dorward, *Annual Departmental Reports Relating to Nigeria and British Cameroons, 1887–1960* (West Yorkshire: Microfilm Academic Publishers, 2006), 4.

Clerk, Collector of Customs, Judge Gaoler and Registrar were established shortly afterwards."[6]

On another note, Nigerianization could be seen as a complex historical, constitutional, developmental plan, human resource development, and "modernization" of Nigeria by the British, that, however, transcends the colonial moment.[7] Nigeria as created from the union of the Colony and Protectorate of Lagos with the Protectorate of Southern Nigeria (the successor to the Niger Coast and Oil Rivers Protectorates) in 1906 and the subsequent amalgamation with the Protectorate of Northern Nigeria in 1914. This was the genesis or birth of the Colony and Protectorates of Nigeria later known as the Federal Republic of Nigeria. It is the beginning of the transition from military (pacification) administration to a civil administration in Nigeria. As a follow up to pre-1914, the British began consolidating and building upon the structure and institution for governance by establishing separate parallel technical departments in the component polities.

The policy of Indirect Rule therefore, cannot be exonerated from the formative era of Nigerian civil service structure. In many parts of the country, Indirect Rule was the ideal thing, except Lagos where direct administration was the order of the day. Anthony Kirk-Greene is right when he noted the limited number of British citizens willing to take up employment in the colonial service as a major factor for British experimentation with the two systems to manage and transform the polities.[8] Even when mosquitoes were no longer a major threat to lifespan of colonial officials, not many ventured into serving in the colonies.

At the top of civil administration was the Governor-General who was appointed by the Colonial Office. He was responsible for general administration of the country and reported to the Colonial Secretary, a Cabinet Minister and member of the British Parliament. The Governor-General was aided by

6 Ibid., 4–5.

7 To some scholars, it is the exploitation rather than development of Nigeria by the British. Studies in this category include Toyin Falola, ed., *Britain and Nigeria: Development or Underdevelopment?* (New Jersey, 1987); Hakeem Ibikunle Tijani, *Britain, Leftist Nationalists and the Transfer of Power in Nigeria, 1945–1965* (London, New York, 2005); Jeremiah I. Dibua, *Modernization and the Crisis of Development in Africa* (Ashgate Publishing, 2007).

8 See Anthony Kirk-Greene, *On Crown Service: A History of HM Colonial and Overseas Services, 1837–1997* (London: I.B. Tauris, 1999); Anthony Kirk-Greene, *Glimpses of Empire: A Corona Anthology* (London: *Glimpses of Empire*, 2001).

many officials in the execution of colonial policies, and the making of law and order throughout the colony and protectorates. The Chief Secretary in Lagos was actually in-charge of the civil service being the most senior officer after the Governor-General. The office holder was a seasoned colonial administrative officer who oversaw two divisions – Political and Technical. Departmental heads and professionals who ensured the smooth administration of the country assisted him. In addition, Lieutenant Governors, Residents Officers, District Officers were an essential part of the civil service. They were responsible for the implementation of policies, application of British justice, and effective resource mobilization within the regions, districts, and nocks and crannies of the country. In fact, this group constituted the police, judicial system, and technical staff, and in addition build the backbone of the emerging civil service. Sadly, they were mainly British officials, at least at the higher echelon of service. A few educated Nigerians that could have been appointed into the senior cadre were discriminated against during this period.

Despite the political unification in 1914, the Northern and Southern Provinces continued to maintain separate Agricultural, Education, Forestry, Land, Police, and Prison Services until well into the 1920s. No doubt, by this period Sir Lugard's "Dual Mandate" seems to have needed some rejuvenation for effective administrative execution of its goals. Hence, Sir Hugh Clifford,[9] his successor, continued the policy with the aim of increasing efficiency, and perhaps effective "exploitation" (to some scholars, modernization) of the resources.

His successor, Graeme Thomson (1925–1931) had similar plans for administration and the civil service structure when he assumed office in 1925. To him, decentralization was essential in view of the size of Nigeria relative to the number of trained civil servants. His successors, particularly Donald Cameron (1931–1935) and Bernard Burdillon (1935–1943), seemed to have the same idea. By 1937, the southern protectorates were divided into Eastern and Western Provinces, thus laying the foundation for the ultimate regional division of the country.[10] This was the situation until the end of World War II when further fragmentation took place. Under Governor Arthur Richard (1943–1948), each region had its civil service and was responsible for the training and development of human capacity within their region. The Secretariat in Lagos continued

9 Hugh Clifford, "United Nigeria," *Journal of the Royal African Studies* 21, no. 81 (1921): 1–14.

10 See, Jeremy J. White, *Central Administration in Nigeria, 1914–1951* (London: Irish Academic Press, 1981)

to wax stronger in terms of central government's civil service structure. The MacPherson Constitution of 1951[11] broadened the autonomy of the regional governments, increased local responsibility that consequently led to the proliferation of regional technical departments and civil service.

Nigerianization as decolonization (1948–1960)

Within a period of twelve years, 1948–1960, the colonial government restructured Nigeria through reforms in the civil service by creating the public service commission in 1954. Although regionalism dominated the activities of colonial restructuring or Nigerianization, efforts were made to satisfy demands from the central, eastern, northern, and western regions public service commissions to cater for the needs of the components within the polity. Contrary to existing historiography reform in the civil service and effort to consider professional Nigerians as equal to their British counterparts began in 1942.[12] The Walwyn Commission's major task was to review the admission of Africans into the senior or professional service, with a view to equal treatment with their British counterparts. The Commission was also charged with considering admission of Africans into sections other than the secretarial units. Except in the medical service, not much was accomplished in other sections of the civil service during this period.[13]

The issue of reform and integration of the colonial people into the colonial and overseas civil services was not limited to Nigeria.[14] In Nigeria, however, the event at Bristol Hotel in 1947,[15] and other embarrassing incidents of racial discrimination two years after the end of World War II, perhaps, gingered senior British officials to review how Nigerians could be pacified through civil service

11 Sir John Stuart Macpherson became governor in February 5, 1948. He was governor until October 1, 1954. He was later named Governor-General on October 1, 1954 and was in charge of Nigeria until June 15, 1955 when Sir James Wilson Robertson succeeded him as the governor-general. He occupied the position until November 16, 1960 when Dr. Nnamdi Azikiwe took over from him.

12 Olusanya, *The evolution of the Nigerian civil service.*

13 British National Archives (BNA), CO 537/5787, no. 74: CO, note of a meeting with Sir James Macpherson on the repercussions on the Nigerian civil service, the Positions of the secretariat and European interests, October 12, 1950.

14 Kirk-Greene, *On Crown Service*, 120–126.

15 BNA, CO 554/152/1, no 22: Bristol Hotel Incident – letter from G. Beresford Stooke to A. b. Cohen on the outcome of the Bristol Hotel Incident, April 1947.

reform. In the Gold Coast (Ghana), Sierra Leone, and The Gambia, nationalists' politics fanned unrest and demand for reforms was frequent. In 1945, the Harragin Commission was set up by Governor Richards to explore the question of integrating Africans into the senior echelon of the colonial civil service. Sir Walter Harragin and members of his commission were charged with examining the structure and conditions of the British West African colonies. Their terms of reference exclude casual or daily-paid staff. It included:

- the general standards of remuneration and superannuation payments;
- the relationship of the salaries and conditions of service of locally recruited and externally recruited officers;
- the machinery for adjusting remuneration to variations in the cost of living;
- the provision of suitable arrangements for consultation between the governments and organizations representing interests of staff on matters relating to salaries and conditions of services; and
- the provision, by means of a public service commission or otherwise, of suitable machinery, where this is not already in existence, for regulating the selection and promotion of candidates for posts, the filling of which is not subject to the approval of the Secretary of State.[16]

The commission spent 49 days in the Gold Coast, 12 days in Gambia, 24 days in Sierra Leone and 70 days in Nigeria. In all, 240 memoranda or letters were submitted and oral evidence taken from 256 witnesses (Gold Coast 114, Gambia 21, Sierra Leone 38, Nigeria 74 and London 9).[17] The report was submitted in September 1946. At the time of setting up the Harragin commission, the civil servants were generally unhappy about the rising cost of living, and failure of the colonial state to fulfill its war era promises. Even British mid-level officers believed that they have been unjustly treated. Their African counterparts were even more critical of the state of affairs in the service. They wondered why they had to contribute to the war efforts and not being compensated adequately. They wondered why there was no review of their salary relative to the cost of living. The allowance for junior African officers in 1944 did not stop a nationwide general strike in Nigeria in 1945; this seems a token, far short and too late to satisfy demands from African workers across board. Its major focus was to create an effective and efficient civil service in

16 Sir Walter Harragin, *Report* (London: HMSO, 1947), 5.

17 Bola Dauda, "Global Context of Public Service Reforms: A Review of Nigerian Reforms 1945–1988," *Politeia* 16, no. 1 (1997).

Ghana, Nigeria, the Gambia, and Sierra Leone. At the end of its evaluation of the civil service, it recommended structural reorganization of her Majesty's West African colonial civil service. The recommendation was the creation of senior and junior civil service that further discriminated against Africans/put Africans at disadvantage.

The Colonial Office was conscious about General repercussions of restructuring of the civil service in West Africa as in other colonies. At a meeting with the Governor (later Governor General), Sir John Macpherson the effects on the Nigerian civil service in relation to the position of the Secretariats' performance was front and center in the discussion. It is worth noting the following points of concern as the measures being taken were unfolding, and the attainment of self-governing status sooner was unambiguous. These are:

a) Changes in West Africa made necessary by the advance towards self-government would clearly affect the character of the unified Colonial Service and their effect would need to be closely watched.
b) The outcry in the Gold Coast about appointments to the posts of Secretaries to the new Ministries had brought to the fore an issue that was of concern to Nigeria also. The Secretary of State, as the recruiting agency and responsible for promotions, was vitally concerned in the issues raised by increasing Africanization of the Service. The principle of promotion on merit had to be upheld.
c) It would probably be necessary in West Africa to dispense with the Secretary of State's control of promotions below certain superscale posts, except when the Governor specifically asked for outside Recruitment (which would be either from inside the Colonial Office Service or without). At present posts with emoluments below £600 a year could be filled locally. This lower limit of £600 might be raised to a more appropriate level or alternatively there might be a list of posts, promotion or recruitment to which needed the Secretary of State's approval.
d) The progress of Nigerianization was of great interest to local politicians. In accepting the Report of the Commission on the subject in 1948, the Nigerian Government had agreed to the recommendation that 'no non-Nigerian should be recruited for any Government post except when no suitable and qualified Nigerian is available' and the position of the local African had in consequence to be constantly borne in mind.
e) There were very few Africans at present in high posts in Nigeria who could be considered for promotion to such posts as Heads of Departments. In this respect Dr. Manuwa of the Medical Department was a valuable exception.

f) It was possible that the West African territories would become more and more self-contained for staff as progress towards self-government went on. For the present, however, outside recruitment, especially for such posts as qualified Veterinary Officers and Agricultural Officers, was likely to be needed for some time, though African recruitment of lawyers and doctors should increase. It was, however, most valuable for Nigeria to have people with experience of other territories transferred on promotion.[18]

No doubt, the debate within Nigeria, particularly driven by the nationalist and labor leaders intensified, and the discriminatory distinctions made between Nigerian and British civil servants became more contentious. The Chief Secretary, H. M. Foot was charged with the task of finding a lasting solution to the issue of race relations in the civil service as well as general reforms that would ensure integration of Nigerians into the senior cadre. More importantly, the commission was saddled with the task of implementing Harragin report as per restructuring of the civil service to meet the evolving system of governance throughout the federation. The term, Nigerianization, actually gained momentum from this date.[19] Foot's commission (1948) gave birth to the creation of the Central Public Service Commission, the use of merit system for appointments into the senior and junior cadre, and the emergence of regional civil service commissions. It also marked the era of "Nigerian McCarthyism" whereby Nigerians trained behind the Iron Curtain were prohibited from employment in the civil service. In addition, the Central Public Service Commission was granted full powers to appoint, promote, dismiss, and discipline junior civil servants.[20] At independence, the body was renamed the Federal Civil Service Commission with authority to cover all civil service grades.[21]

An aftermath of the Foot Commission Report was the regionalization of the Nigerianization process. The three regions began to replace British colonial

---

18 BNA, CO 537/5787, no 74: CO note of a meeting with Sir John Macpherson, October 12, 1950.

19 See, Tijani, *Britain, Leftist Nationalists and the Transfer of Power.*

20 Hakeem Ibikunle Tijani, "McCarthyism in Colonial Nigeria: The Ban on the Employment of Communists," in *The Foundations of Nigeria,* ed. Adebayo Oyebade (Trenton: Africa World Press, 2003), 647–68; Hakeem Ibikunle Tijani, "Communists and the Nationalist Movement," in *Nigeria in the Twentieth Century*, ed. Toyin Falola (Durham: Carolina Academic Press, 2002), 293–313.

21 Muhammed Salisu, "Incentive Structure, Civil Service Efficiency and the Hidden Economy of Nigeria," *Working Paper No. 2001/86*, World Institute for Development Economics Research, United Nations University, 2001, 3.

civil servants with qualified Nigerians at different pace. Since the western and eastern regions were ahead of the North in western education, filling most of the positions in the civil service was not difficult at all. Although some southerners (from east and west) were employed in the north, the emerging restructuring soon become a stumbling block in their promotion and condition of service in a regionally based civil service commission established a few years afterwards. In addition, the emergence of regionally based nationalist parties and governments (Northern Peoples Congress, Action Group, and the National Congress of Nigerian Citizens) worsened/cemented the ethnic divide among Nigerians. The fear of southern domination of the civil service in the northern and central/ federal civil service was higher than in any other period. Nigerianization to the northerners was southern domination, pure and simple. To the North, getting qualified indigenes to occupy positions during the period was challenging, and a threat to their sovereignty in the polity. More so, unlike the northern region, the eastern and western regional executive councils was composed entirely of Nigerians.[22] In fact, the nationalist government of NPC preferred employment of "outsiders" such as the Arabs, Pakistanis, Indians, and anyone except their brethren from the south.[23] The point of convergence for all regions was that gradually, British officials gave way for professional Nigerians. Using example from western region, Adedeji remarked, "of the staff strength of 11,819 in June 1960, only 411 were expatriates."[24]

Training and investment in human development in Nigeria after the activities of the Foot Commission has no parallel in the history of British commitment to Nigerianization. Both Macpherson (the Governor) and Foot (the Secretary) were strategists and astute colonial administrators who chaperoned the process from the late 1940s to the late 1950s. As Martin Lynn rightly noted, "the process of constitutional consultation was accompanied by other measures to increase the role of Nigerians in the administration."[25] The Foot Commission that included Nnamdi Azikiwe, the leader of the NCNC, recommended the establishment of scholarships to be awarded to Nigerians as part of the training of qualified officers in the public service. In fact, by late 1948, 208 Nigerians were employed in the

22 BNA, CO 554/320: A. E. T. Benson to Mr. Lyttleton, September 9, 1953.

23 Olusanya, *The Evolution of Nigerian Civil Service.*

24 Adebayo Adedeji, "Federal and State Civil Service," *Quarterly Journal of Administration* V, no.1 (1970): 12.

25 Martin Lynn, *British Documents on the End of Empire: Nigeria, Part 1* (London: Her Majesty Stationary Publication, 2001), lv–lvi.

Tab. 1:

Nigeria Civil Service Reforms in Nigeria 1934–1959
Hunts Commission 1934
Walwyn Commission 1942
Harragin Commission 1945
Foot Commission 1948
Phillipson-Adebo Commission 1950
Gorsuch Commission 1954
Newns Commission 1959

senior cadre, and by 1951 the number had reached 597.[26] The establishment of the University College, Ibadan (to be discussed later) during the same year, and the pronouncement of the 1948 Education Ordinance are indications of the commitment of Macpherson and Foot in the process of Nigerianization. The Ordinance set up education boards, launched increased spending on education and gave Native Authority Councils throughout the country the right to levy education rates to pay for schools. This initiative, as surmised by Lynn "coinciding with the measures for mass education and the opening of University College, Ibadan, earlier that year, showed the degree to which the pre-war hesitations over the relationship between the Native Authority system and the educated Nigerian had been resolved; the long term future of Nigeria lay with the latter."[27]

Furthermore, the colonial government in 1950 set up a commission chaired by Sir Phillipson with Simeon Adebo as secretary to identify ways and means of realizing the objective of Nigerianization. Funds from the Colonial Development and Welfare Act came handy for training Nigerians who later occupied senior positions in Labour and Welfare, Foreign Service, Information, Education, and other government ministries and parastatals on both the federal and regional level. In the Labour Ministry for instance, Adio Moses and other Nigerians were trained to replace British officials.

In a letter to Mr. Lyttelton on September 9, 1953, Arthur Benson noted that the 1952 Phillipson and Adebo Report was germane for colonial office response to the urgency for a review of the public service similar to initiatives being undertaken in the Gold Coast colony during the same period. Four key points were noted in Benson's letter. These are:

26 Ibid, lvi.

27 Ibid, lvi.

I. Division of Nigerian Public Service into four.
II. Review of condition of service and the latitude for transfer, retirement, and promotion between/within the three regions and Lagos.
III. Creation of the Nigerian Public Service Commission directed by Sir Sydney Phillipson and Mr. Simeon Adebo.
IV. Creation of Regional Public Service.[28]

Benson's view confirmed the position of the nationalists and British officials position during the 1953 Lagos conference. It was resolved that the Centre and Regions should each have their own Public Service with the aspiration of developing their manpower at their pace. It was also decided that each legislature should have power to create new posts, abolish posts, set salaries, allowances, or condition of service, etc. The clause, however, was that the Governor General or Governor as the case may be, retained the veto power on such matters.[29]

In 1954, the colonial government set up another commission to look into the issue of discrimination in the civil service. The colonial government was not acquiescing of the racial discrimination in the civil service despite previous efforts. For instance, there were reports of British secretarial staff condescending and disrespect for their Nigerian senior officers. Thus, the Gorsuch Commission of 1954 was set up to review evidence of discriminatory practices and the structure of the colonial civil service. Upon the completion of its hearings, the Gorsuch Commission Report recommended the abolition of the senior and junior civil service structure in view of gross discrimination inherent in the system. It further recommended five-grade levels that remained up to the present day. The new structure includes a super scale, an administrative/professional scale, a sub-professional/technical cadre, a secretarial/clerical cadre, and a sub-clerical cadre. The new structure implies that officers' enlistment and promotion would be based on qualification, experience, and periodic review.

The government of Sir James Robertson (1955–1960) was concerned about the challenges of the recommendations of the Phillipson-Adebo Commission of 1952. It set up the Newns' Commission in 1959 to look into the implementation of its successes and challenges. It would seem that the envisaged transfer of power in the following year hinges on a perfect civil service structure. There was need to separate career civil servants from politicians who by now were in charge of ministries. There was the urgency to ensure that professionalism of the civil servants was respected without getting involved in party politicking.

28 BNA, CO 554/320: Benson to Lyttleton, September 9, 1953.
29 BNA, CO 554/320: Benson to Lyttleton.

The integration of departments into ministries in preparation for Nigeria's independence was therefore its major task. Secondly, it was charged with outlining Ministers' portfolios or responsibilities as an appendage to the functioning of the ministries. The position of permanent secretaries became a super scale in the new dispensation. The position became the highest level attainable by any career civil servant. The office of the permanent secretary was charged with the function of managing government expenditure and establishment matters. They were [and still are] accounting officers and chief executives of their various ministries.

Nigerianization and the Labour Department (Ministry) (1938–1960)

The establishment of the Labour Department in the colonies was pivotal to British "modernization" through training of local manpower for the running of the administration, and eventually the transfer of power. With the exception of Anthony Kirk-Greene's study of the colonial civil service, much is yet to be uncovered in relation to Nigerianization. As the following analysis will show, the Labour Department (Ministry) is germane to the dynamic and multidimensional nature of Nigerianization. It should be noted that previous studies hardly noticed events in the Labour Department, later Ministry, related to the idea of Nigerianization. I posit that to underscore the process, structure, and dividends of Nigerianization before 1960, we should revisit the activities of the organ responsible for training, skills empowerment, and industrial relations among emerging ministries during the period.

The process began in 1938 with the setting up of the Labour Department. Between 1939 and the late 1950s, labor officers, assistant labor officers, and exchange managers trained and mentored an African cadre of labor officers as part of a general education goal of increasing the number of African labor officers and sustaining the idea of Nigerianization. Some Nigerians were employed as labor officers-in-training and sent to undergo further education at the London School of Economics and Political Science. Upon completion of studies, they were appointed as assistant labor officers with a few becoming exchange officers by the mid- to late 1940s. In addition, by the early 1950s, some of them had become labor officers in charge of many policy matters including training and general education in other colonial government's departments.

It is worthy of note a few of the pioneers that shaped and modeled the kind of labor education that pervaded labor centers and many workshops or on-the-job training throughout the decolonization era on one hand and the caliber of Nigerians that later occupied middle level civil service cadre in the various Departments/Ministries.

To the Labour Commissioner E. A. Miller and his staff the expansion of possibilities for education and training of Nigerians was crucial to the success of the British efforts during the period. Thus, during 1946 fiscal year, training and appointment of industrial welfare officers and exchange managers became central to the fledging central civil service. The officers being trained were not for government offices alone. They were also aimed at filling positions in private companies such as the United African Company. The central theme of the training was called "sound industrial relations."[30] Within the Department of Labour, industrial welfare officers were appointed as first-line officers in charge of general welfare matters, while exchange officers were in charge of employment matters. They in turn were charged with training clerical cadre positions in the civil service, which was filled by increasing number of secondary school graduates throughout the country.

In March 1946, Miss L. B. Maslin was seconded from the United Kingdom to train staff for the Department in Lagos. Her previous credentials included a five-year instructor rank in His Majesty's Ministry of Labour and National Service in London. While the instructional mode was lecture, a considerable amount of seminal activities and experiential learning were adopted as part of the pedagogy and methodology throughout the course. Besides the lecture and theoretical training, great emphasis was placed on practicum and exercises at different locations. The six-month course also included industrial welfare officers from the United African Company (UAC) and the Nigerian Railways (NR), the leading employers of workers in the private and public sectors during the period.

Commissioner Cozen, who succeeded Miller in the Labour Department in 1950, continued training of Nigerians in Lagos Island, Lagos Mainland, and Apapa centers. Although the classes were in Lagos, they nonetheless attracted an average of two hundred lower cadres from the three regions. In addition, the Department of Labour (later renamed the Ministry of Labour in the same year) organized classes in the provincial areas in July 1950. The Ministry collaborated with union officials to ensure success of its goal of Nigerianization, and "sound industrial relations" as increasing number of Nigerians were being trained and employed in the civil service. The western and eastern regions were the first port of call. Toward the end of the year, major towns in the Northern region were added. Labor training centers in line with the Macpherson Constitution's delineation of Nigeria in 1950 became functional in Benin, Oyo, Ondo, and

30 Hakeem I. Tijani, "Britain and the Foundation of Anticommunist Policies in Nigeria, 1945–1960," *African and Asian Studies* 8 (2009): 47–66.

Warri provinces of the western region; in Calabar, Cameroons, Onitsha, and Owerri provinces in the eastern region; and in Plateau and Zaria provinces in the Northern Region. The same year, 202 Nigerians, mostly union members, were registered for courses organized by the Ministry. I should note that some Nigerians regarded training organized by the Ministry of Labour as a springboard for promotion. A good example is the itinerant members of the Train Guards' Union (a section of the Railway Workers' Union) members that took advantage of the opportunities in the provinces to participate whenever their schedule permited. In late 1950, five members of the Train Guards' Union were reported to have successfully completed one or two courses.[31]

University College, Ibadan, and its center for extra-mural studies in Nigerianization

The University College, Ibadan, was established in 1948 as an extension of the University of London, but more importantly, to serve Nigeria's rising demand for higher education as well as an agent for training of the needed work force as part of the Nigerianization effort. The cost of overseas education and scholarships in a post–World War II economy was becoming unbearable for the colonial government, and Nigerian nationalists and labor leaders welcomed the idea of an accredited college that would award or prepare Nigerians for baccalaureate degrees or diplomas. Since access to higher education was regarded as *sine qua non* to Nigerianization and decolonization, the University College was regarded as a stakeholder. The University College established in 1950, a continuing education center named Centre for Extra-Mural Studies.[32] Here, continuing education, certificate, diploma, and none-degree courses would be the foci throughout the decolonization era. It became a center were middle and lower cadre of civil servants were trained for effective performance on the job.

The task of training Nigerians at the Centre was given to Ayodele Matthew Tokunboh, its first director (1950–1957). Ayodele had been one of the early beneficiaries of British Colonial government scholarship scheme in late 1940. He had studied economics at the London School of Economics. After graduating

31 Hakeem I. Tijani, *Union Education in Nigeria: Labor, Empire, and Decolonization Since 1945* (New York: Palgrave Macmillan, 2012): 66.

32 Tijani, *Britain, leftist nationalists*, 58. A pioneering work relating to universities is that of Joseph Agbowuro, "Nigerianization and the Nigerian Universities," *Comparative Education* 12, no. 3 (1976): 243–254.

and returning to Nigeria in 1945, he had joined the Department of Labour from where he had been selected to study labor and industrial relations at Cornell University, Ithaca, New York. By 1949, he had risen to the rank of a labor officer in the Department of Labour. Hence, the choice of Tokunboh as the first director to oversee a center primarily dedicated to building the human capacity for civil service was not fortuitous.[33]

Between 1952 and 1959, the UCI Extra-Mural Centre became an important forum for disseminating the ideal "sound industrial relation," and the focal point for both the colonial state and the nationalist governments to seek and employ Nigerians for civil service positions. Training was not limited to the campus at Ibadan; rather, the Extra-Mural Centre became an itinerant or mobile center of education throughout the country. In 1952, the Department of Labour and the UCI Extra-Mural Centre pulled together and organized a week residential course at Enugu, the capital city of the eastern regional government. The annual report of the Department of Labour for 1952/53 noted that the attendance was impressive and a success.[34]

In August 1953 yet another course was introduced at Ibadan. It was a ten-day course tailored on trade union and industrial relations matters. By early 1956, it organized a weeklong residential course on trade union affairs on the UCI campus. With a record number of 122 attendants, it was another successful attempt at increasing the pool of Nigerians trained, skilled, and ready to assume positions in different government offices. A regular weekend course was also organized at regional centers throughout Nigeria beginning in 1958. Moreover, on the eve of independence in 1959, there was an increase in the activity of Labour Department-sponsored courses directed by the UCI Extra-Mural Centre. Additional weekend courses were organized at Aba, Benin, Ibadan, Lagos, Kaduna, and Port Harcourt, to mention a few.

One can argue that between 1956 and 1959, the process of Nigerianization anchored in the Ministry of Labour, with the Chief Secretary's oversight in the Governor-General's office, continued to gain more interest among British and Nigerian officials. In 1956, Francis Nwokedi was appointed to oversee the process, structure, and implementation of Nigerianization policy. He was until the

33 London Metropolitan University, North London, Trade Union Congress Collections, Trade Union Congress (TUC) colonial advisory committee file 1, 1948–1949, December 15, 1948: 2; file 2, 1948–1949, April 21, 1949: 6; Mss 292/file 966.3/4: Winterbottom to Curry, March 4, 1952.

34 Tijani, *Union Education in Nigeria*, 49

appointment, an assistant commissioner for labor in eastern region of Nigeria.[35] On the other hand, T. M. Yesufu was transferred to the UCI Extra-Mural Centre to direct labor and industrial relations programs as well as labor union education. In April 1956, a branch of the Marine Department known as the Seamen's Welfare and Employment Office was transferred to the Department of Labour for administrative purposes, and as part of the process of ensuring that Nigerian seamen began to occupy senior level positions in the sector.

Furthermore, three labor officers, two trades testing officers, and six assistant labour inspectors were appointed as part of the sustained labor education goal. Perhaps of more significance was the secondment of Miss. D. S. Johnson (former deputy chief inspector of Factories, UK) to the labor department to assist in implementing the Factories Act and training of labor inspectors. For nine months, Miss. Johnson organized technical training for inspecting staff throughout Nigeria.[36]

An interesting dimension was the increased investment in training schemes by both the government and foreign corporations. The majority of the larger industrial and commercial firms inaugurated and funded systemic training on the job, complementing the government's "Training in Workplace" program. They appointed permanent instructors at their various centers to ensure continuity and progress. Of note was the use of primary school teachers at the centers, partly because of the level of education of most workers and the better understanding of an effective pedagogy by this group of instructors for assuring trainees success. Trade Centers could be referred to as centers of excellence in the overall goal of the process of Nigerianization because they served, as a quick and short term educational centers where skills where hands-on training are carried out. Trade Centers gave opportunities to Nigerians who did not have the resources to attend conventional schools for credential or degree purpose. The training lasted between two and five years and was directed by resident instructors. Upon completion, Ministry of Labour and Welfare's Trade Testing officers conducted a Trade Test in preparation for the intermediate examination of the City and Guild of London. For the government, this was a win-win situation whereby investments in workers' education led to lifelong skills and expertise, and the zeal for Nigerianization remained on course.

35 He later spent greater part of his career in the Foreign Service of Nigeria. See section titled, Nigerianization and the making of the Foreign Service cadre for details.

36 See Tijani, *Union Education in Nigeria*: 70–71.

Nigerianization and the making of the Foreign Service Cadre

Like in the Labour Department, Nigerianization of the emerging foreign ministry was considered important to the success of Nigerianization. The issue of training Nigerians for diplomatic service and international affairs gained momentum in mid-1950s.The Cold War was central to training and development of Nigerians that would assume senior and middle level ranks in the Foreign or External Affairs Department. Machineries were set up in Lagos and Nigeria's office at the United Nations in New York. British Embassy officials in Washington DC and New York conducted liaison with United States embassies and officials. Beginning in 1957, Reginald Barrett, a Briton in charge of the Nigerian Liaison office in Washington DC was asked to train six mid-career Nigerians who later became Assistant Secretaries in the External Affairs Department on completion of their training. Additional forty Foreign Service cadets were selected to train in Washington DC and other British embassies in Europe. British and United States' officials in New York and Washington DC tutored them in international relations, protocol, and diplomatic procedures. All of them attended a compulsory course on issues in international relations organized by the School of Advanced International Studies, Johns Hopkins University, Baltimore, Maryland. Some of them later became senior officials in the ministry after independence.[37]

Many, if not all, the new Minister's and civil servants supported by Northern Peoples' Congress stalwarts shared the foreign policy goals of Abubakar Tafawa Balewa, the prime minister who espoused the policy of anti-communism in foreign relations colored under a non-neutrality policy.[38] While I have discussed the role of the Nigerian pioneer officers in the Foreign Department in another study,[39] it is worth noting the career of one of them, Anionwu. He studied at the Imperial Defense College, University of London where he was acclaimed to be a brilliant student among his peers. His tutors and the director of the College, Sir Robert Scott, for an officer position in the Ministry of External Affairs, later recommended him. Sir Scott recommended him first as a liaison officer for Balewa's government in London. On July 4, 1960, Sir Scott made no reservation when he recommended him for the position of a permanent under-secretary of

---

37 Anthony Kirk-Greene, "Diplomacy and Diplomats: The Formation of Foreign Service Cadres in Black Africa," in *Foreign relations of African states – Colston Paper No. 25*, ed. Kenneth Ingham (London: Butterworth, 1974), 298; Vernon Mckay, *Africa in world politics*, 2nd edition (Westport: Greenwood Press, 1974), 399–400.

38 Tijani, *Britain, Leftist Nationalists*, 91.

39 Tijani, *Britain, Leftists Nationalist.*

defence and external affairs. As Sir Scott eloquently remarked, "Anionwu would be a very good investment and well worth the trouble."[40] Anionwu later served as adviser to Balewa on defense and foreign affairs after independence. On the other hand, both Ifeagwu and Aig-Imoukhuede served at the Nigeria Permanent Mission to the United Nations.

Nigerianization of the Foreign Service Ministry was unique in a number of respects. It was pro-Western in its ideological orientation. It was aimed at concretizing anti-communist policies aimed at delaying or denying the eastern bloc any room in Nigeria, an idea unapologetically practiced in the Foreign Affairs Ministry. The Robertson/Balewa government was careful in the selection of Nigerians to be trained and appointed as foreign affairs officers. In fact, beginning in 1957, non-career party stalwarts were appointed or seconded to serve in various units of the External Affairs Ministry.

Conclusion

It could be concluded that human capital development is significant to the socio-economic development of a nation. Suffice it to say that an investment in human capital development is critical to polity-building in general and to development in particular. In addition, investment in this direction would enable the effective harnessing of the nation's human resource endowment and the optimal exploitation and utilization of other resources that propel growth and development. This paper, therefore, has reexamined decolonization in Nigeria emphasizing the process of Nigerianization and the sustenance and creation of new polities for development. It broadens the definition of decolonization emphasizing its multidimensional nature. It invalidates the existing view that Nigerianization started with the Foot Commission report of 1948 and posits that the idea, process and structure gained momentum after Foot's report. It argues that the development of the civil service not only predates 1948, but also was a key process in the overall decolonization of British rule ending in 1960. I argued that it actually began with the unfolding events in post-World War II era and particularly the 1948 declaration by Mr. Foot, the colonial secretary. The integration of Nigerians into various sections of the colonial departments, and later ministries, and overall administration of the colony and protectorates of Nigeria was part of the decolonization, "modernization" and western model of administration. Despite its challenges and foibles, civil/public service remained a major institutional organ of modern

40 BNA, FO 371/146831: Sir Robert Scott to foreign Office, July 4, 1960.

administration created by the British in Nigeria. Furthermore, the paper brings to fore, the significance of Department (Ministry) of Labour, the role of UCI Extra-Mural Unit, and the development of training schemes for foreign service cadets and officers as part of the general scheme of Nigerianization (decolonization) before 1960. In addition, the paper shows the confluence between the two major issues that confronted the colonial powers and the colonized during the twentieth century – Decolonization and the Cold War. It contends that efforts at developing the colonies manpower was central, although unintended, to decolonization. Yet, the element of Cold War ideological differences played a pivotal role in the process between 1945 and 1960 in Nigeria, as elsewhere, in former British colonies worldwide.

Appendix

Government (colonial) Training Schemes at the Height of Nigerianization

Department	*Type of trainee*	*Total number of persons trained* **1-4-56** *to* **31-3-57**	*Total number in training on* **31-3-57**
Agriculture	(i) Agricultural assistants and overseers	79	243
	(ii) Native administration agricultural workers	30	28
Antiquities	Museum technical assistants	–	1
Broadcasting	(i) Broadcasting officers (programs)	37	–
	(ii) Broadcasting officers (general and administrative duties)	6	–
	(iii) Junior technical staff (engineering) (at Yaba Technical Institute)	11	13
	(iv) Technical officers (at Yaba Technical Institute)	–	5
Cooperative	Cooperative inspectors	6	8

Department	*Type of trainee*	*Total number of persons trained 1-4-56 to 31-3-57*	*Total number in training on 31-3-57*
Commerce and Industries	(i) Handloom manipulators (including weaving and dyeing)	56	21
	(ii) Pottery and brick makers	78	38
Customs and Excise	(i) Probationary assistant water guard officers	38	18
	(ii) Maritime officers	19	–
Education	(i) Teaching training colleges: Female teachers	385	624
	(ii) Teacher training colleges: Male teachers	1,434	3,613
	(iii) Clerks' training centers and technical institutes: Post standard VI:	633	136
	(a) Fitter machinist (b) Motor-mechanics (c) Painters and decorators (d) Cabinet makers (e) Carpenters (f) Word machinists (g) Bricklayers (h) Sheet metal workers (i) Black smiths and welders (j) Coach builders (k) Electricians (l) Plumbers	214	1,377
	(iv) Technical institutes, Yaba: Junior Technical Staff (various courses)	221	1,033
	(v) Man O'War Bay Training Course in Leadership and Citizenship	257	43

(continued on next page)

Department	*Type of trainee*	***Total number of persons trained* 1-4-56 *to* 31-3-57**	***Total number in training on* 31-3-57**
Electricity Corporation of Nigeria	Artisan grade III (Linesmen, electrical fitters and cable joiners)	23	–
Fisheries Service	(i) Quartermaster (course in mechanized fishing, rudiment of seamanship and ability to handle little fishing boats)	4	17
	(ii) Artisan, grade III	1	4
	(iii) Assistant technical officer	2	2
Forestry	Forest assistants and forest guards	36	13
Information Service	(i) Process engraving	2	1
	(ii) Photographers	–	1
Inland Revenue	(i) Assessment clerks and clerical assistants	173	81
	(ii) Assistant executive officers	11	11
	(iii) Assessment officers	12	6
	(iv) Miscellaneous officers	2	2
Labor	(i) Assistant labor Inspectors	–	3
	(ii) Department training courses (overseas)	1	3
Land Marketing and Exports	Potential land officers	–	1
	(i) Accountancy courses (local and overseas)	1	3
	(ii) Weighting machines superintendents	–	1
	(iii) Produce inspectors training scheme (overseas)	1	–
Medical	(i) Laboratory technical assistants	18	–

Department	*Type of trainee*	*Total number of persons trained 1-4-56 to 31-3-57*	*Total number in training on 31-3-57*
	(ii) Nurses and midwives	335	488
	(iii) Chemists and druggists	147	113
	(iv) Sanitary inspectors and overseers	117	43
	(v) Dispensary attendants	16	17
	(vi) Dental technicians	–	25
	(vii) Assistant physiotherapist	2	2
	(viii) X-ray technicians	3	10
Meteorological Services	Meteorologist observers	29	25
Nigeria Magazine	(i) Training in story writing	1	1
	(ii) Photographers	2	2
Nigerian Ports Authority	(i) Marine cadets (technical apprentices engineering)	–	29
	(ii) Apprentice craftsmen and operators	–	232
	(iii) Management cadets	–	7
	(iv) Administrative assistants	–	7
	(v) Accountants	–	6
Nigerian Railway Corporation	(i) Probationary traffic staff-in-training (initial course)	200	126
	(ii) Goods guards (initial course)	104	–
	(iii) Traffic assistants-in-training	5	23
	(iv) Probationary telecommunications staff-in-training	10	18
	(v) Trade apprentices (civil engineering)	–	63

(*continued on next page*)

Department	*Type of trainee*	***Total number of persons trained* 1-4-56 *to* 31-3-57**	***Total number in training on* 31-3-57**
	(vi) Signal apprentices (civil engineering)	–	12
	(vii) Permanent way apprentices	–	54
	(viii) Technical staff-in-training	–	26
	(ix) Trade apprentices (mechanical engineering)	67	686
	(x) Technical assistants-in-training	1	13
	(xi) Accounting assistants-in-training	3	5
	(xii) Staff assistants-in- training (administration)	–	5
	(xiii) Stores assistants-in-training	–	4
	(xiv) Junior technical staff (printing)	–	17
Posts and Telegraphs	(i) Aeronautical wireless operators	44	–
	(ii) Police wireless operators	25	–
	(iii) Cable jointers	52	–
	(iv) Technicians subscribers apparatus maintenance	49	–
	(v) Technical officers-in-training	131	161
	(vi) Technicians teleprinter maintenance	12	–
	(vii) Workshop apprentices	29	–
	(viii) Supervising officers' course for senior technicians	43	–
	(ix) Assistant Instructors' Course	24	–

Department	*Type of trainee*	*Total number of persons trained 1-4-56 to 31-3-57*	*Total number in training on 31-3-57*
Printing and Stationery	(i) Compositors, machinists, and book-binders	31	118
	(ii) Typist	–	6
	(iii) Typewriters mechanics	–	19
Prisons	(i) Government wardens	113	31
	(ii) Native Authority wardens	–	41
Public Works	(i) Road overseers	58	22
	(ii) Accountant-in-training	–	1
	(iii) Civil engineering assistants	2	44
	(iv) Mechanical engineering assistant	–	11
	(v) Architecture engineering assistants	–	3
	(vi) Electrical engineering assistants	–	2

Source: Tijani, Hakeem Ibikunle, *Union Education in Nigeria: Labor, Empire and Decolonization since 1945* (New York/London: Palgrave Macmillan, 2012): 109–111

Archives

British National Archives

London Metropolitan University Archives, North London.

Literature

Adedeji, Adebayo. "Federal and State civil service." *Quarterly Journal of Administration* V, no. 1 (1970): 7–32.

Agbowuro, Joseph. "Nigerianization and the Nigerian Universities." *Comparative Education* 12, no. 3, (1976): 243–254.

Aluko, Olajide. "Politics of Decolonization in British West Africa 1945–1960." In *History of West Africa* 2, edited by J. F. Ade Ajayi and Michael Crowder. London: Columbia University Press, 1974.

Bamgbose, Adele. J. "The Nigerian Civil Service: Past and Present." *ASCON – Journal of Management* 12, no. 1, 2 (1993): 31–44.

Clifford, Hugh. "United Nigeria." *Journal of the Royal African Studies* 21, no. 81 (1921): 1–14.

Dauda, Bola. "Global Context of Public Service Reforms: A Review of Nigerian Reforms 1945–1988." *Politeia* 16, no. 1 (1997): 20–46.

Dibua, Jeremiah I. *Modernization and the Crisis of Development in Africa.* Aldershot: Ashgate Publishing, 2007.

Dorward, David C. *Annual Departmental Reports Relating to Nigeria and British Cameroons, 1887–1960.* West Yorkshire: Microfilm Academic Publishers, 2006.

Falola, Toyin, ed. *Britain and Nigeria: Development or Underdevelopment?* New Jersey: Zed Books, 1987.

Fieldhouse, David K. *Merchant Capital and Economic Decolonization: The United Africa Company, 1929–1987.* Oxford: Clarendon Press, 1994. In *The Journal of African History*, vol. 38, no. 3 (1997): 514–515.

Fieldhouse, Roger. "Cold War and Colonial Conflicts in British West African Adult Education, 1947–1953." *History of Education Quarterly* 24, no. 3 (1984): 359–371.

Harragin, Walter Sir. *Report.* London: HMSO, 1947.

Kirk-Greene, Anthony. "Diplomacy and Diplomats: The formation of foreign Service Cadres in Black Africa." In *Foreign relations of African states – Colston Paper* no. 25, edited by Kenneth Ingham. London: Butterworth, 1974.

Kirk-Greene, Anthony. *On Crown Service: A History of HM Colonial and Overseas Services, 1837–1997.* London: I.B. Tauris, 1999.

Kirk-Greene, Anthony. *Glimpses of Empire: A Corona Anthology.* London: I.B. Tauris, 2001.

Lynn, Martin. *British Documents on the End of Empire: Nigeria,* Part 1. London: Her Majesty Stationary Publication, 2001.

Mckay, Vernon. *Africa in World Politics,* 2nd edition. Westport: Greenwoord Publisher Group, 1974.

Nwosu, Henry N. *Political Authority and the Nigerian Civil Service.* Enugu: Fourth Dimension Pub., 1985.

Olopade, Dayo. "The Nigerian Civil Service and Change." *ASCON: Journal of Management* 8, no. 1, 2 (1989): 96–103.

Olusanya, Gabriel O. *The Evolution of the Nigerian Civil Service 1861–1960.* Lagos: University of Lagos, 1975.

Salisu, Muhammed. "Incentive Structure, Civil Service Efficiency and the Hidden Economy of Nigeria." *Working Paper No. 2001/86.* Helsinki: World Institute for Development Economics Research, United Nations University, 2001.

Tijani, Hakeem I. "Communists and the Nationalist Movement." In *Nigeria in the Twentieth Century*, edited by Toyin Falola, 203–313. Durham: Carolina Academic Press, 2002.

Tijani, Hakeem I. "McCarthyism in Colonial Nigeria: The Ban on the Employment of Communists." In *The Foundations of Nigeria*, edited by Adebayo Oyebade, 647–668. Trenton: Africa World Press, 2003.

Tijani, Hakeem I. *Britain, Leftist Nationalists and the Transfer of Power in Nigeria, 1945–1965.* London: Routledge, 2005.

Tijani, Hakeem I. "Britain and the Foundation of Anticommunist Policies in Nigeria, 1945–1960." *African and Asian Studies* 8 (2009): 47–66.

Tijani, Hakeem I. *Union Education in Nigeria: Labor, Empire and Decolonization since 1945.* New York: Palgrave Macmillan, 2012.

Tijani, Hakeem I., and Ashley Carter. "Decolonization." In *Africa and the Wider World*, edited by Hakeem I. Tijani, Raphael C. Njoku, and Tiffany F. Jones. 146–185. Boston: Pearson Publisher, 2010.

White, Jeremy J. *Central Administration in Nigeria, 1914–1951.* London: Irish Academic Press, 1981.

Young, C. "Decolonization in Africa." In *Colonialism in Africa 1870–1960,* edited by L.H. Gann and P. Duignan. 450–502. Cambridge: Cambridge University Press, 1970.

Ting-Hong Wong[1]

The Effects of Decolonization on Colonial Governance: A Case Study of the Polytechnic in Colonial Hong Kong

Abstract The rapid emergence of post-colonial polities after 1960 led to the swift dismantling of the major colonial empires. Yet individual, minor colonies continued to exist even under British and French authority. The contribution shows how decolonization in multiple ways also provided a crucial background for the re-definition of colonial educational policies. The British Crown Colony of Hong Kong serves as an example. As a study in the micro-politics of educational institution building during decolonization, the author opens an otherwise often-ignored trans-colonial perspective on the founding of a Polytechnic Institution in Hong Kong during the early 1960s. He shows how the strategies implied by the main protagonists were informed by personal experiences with the reform of educational institutions gathered in different colonial and decolonizing contexts.

Keywords: Hong Kong Polytechnic, Hong Kong, Singapore, trans-colonialism, higher education

Decolonization was by no means merely a political revolution; for when dependencies were striding towards independence, massive education reforms were routinely being carried out to facilitate and smoothen the transformation. The entwined relations between decolonization and school education have intrigued many historians and inspired them to produce large number of scholarly works. Researchers have discovered that when power transferal was underway, ruling authorities in many (ex)-dependencies founded universities to groom new elites for the (soon-to-be) self-governing territories.[2] They have also chronicled how political leaders in many newly independent countries nationalized the colonial educational institutions in order to root out the empire's lingering influences

1 The research project for this article was funded by the National Science Council of Taiwan (project numbers 98-2410-H-001-060-MY2 and 105-2410-H-001-040-MY2).

2 Ogechi E. Anyanwu, "Challenging the Status Quo: Alan Pifer and Higher Education Reform in Colonial Nigeria," *History of Education* 42, no. 1 (2013): 70–91; A. J. Stockwell, "'The Crucible of the Malayan Union': The University and the Making of a New Malaya, 1938–1961," *Modern Asian Studies* 43, no. 5 (2009): 1149–1187.

and to align the school system with the agenda of the national government.[3] Studies also document how during the transitional period, many state authorities, with the view of turning the populace into productive and patriotic citizens, attempted actively to popularize education and carry out curriculum reform.[4] These valuable scholarly works have shed light on the decolonization/education nexuses and deepened our understanding of the impacts of power transferal on the school system.

Notwithstanding these contributions, the existing research has one serious limitation since researchers have so far focused only on the cases in late-colonial and early-post-colonial settings. The literature, as a result, overlooks the ramifications of decolonization on education in territories still under imperial domination. This bias in focus is costly because empires sometimes, if not often, dismantle in protracted and uneven ways. With some territories gaining independence earlier and others within the same empire remaining dependencies much longer, changes occasioned by the decolonized regions – for instance, the metropolitan powers' shifts of perspectives and priorities and the diaspora occasioned by power transferal – are bound to affect the territories still under metropolitan control. Thus, historians' fixation on late-colonial and early-post-colonial milieus blinds us from these trans-colonial currents. It hinders us from comprehending more thoroughly the declining empires' metamorphoses and their resultant impacts on governance in remaining dependencies. To take a first step to overcome this limitation, I examine in this article the struggle over the establishment of the polytechnic in colonial Hong Kong during the 1960s and 1970s.

---

3 Apollos O. Nwauwa, *Imperialism, Academe and Nationalism: Britain and University Education for African, 1860–1960* (London: Frank Cass, 1997).

4 Joseph W. Elder, "The Decolonization of Educational Culture: The Case of India," *Comparative Education Review* 15, no. 3 (1971): 288–95; John Holford, "Mass Education and Community Development in the British Colonies, 1940–1960: A Study in the Politics of Community Education," *International Journal of Lifelong Education* 7, no. 3 (1988): 163–183; Kate Skinner, "Who Knew the Minds of the People? Specialist Knowledge and Developmentalist Authoritarianism in Postcolonial Ghana," *The Journal of Imperial and Commonwealth History* 39, no. 2 (2011): 297–323; Ting-Hong Wong, *Hegemonies Compared: State Formation and Chinese School Politics in Postwar Singapore and Hong Kong* (New York: Routledge, 2002); Ting-Hong Wong and Michael W. Apple, "Rethinking the Education/State Formation Connection: Pedagogic Reform in Singapore, 1945–1965," *Comparative Education Review* 46, no. 2 (2002): 182–210.

Hong Kong is an ideal case to explore the ramifications of decolonization on education in an empire's yet to be decolonized territories. As negotiations between London and Beijing over the colony's future did not begin until the early 1980s, Hong Kong's power transferal commenced much later than in most other British possessions. When the colonial authorities started planning for the founding of the Hong Kong Polytechnic (HKP) in the mid-1960s, the tiny territory was still securely under the Union Jack, though the British Empire had already been more than half disassembled. As Hong Kong continued to be British ruled, its proposed polytechnic, like all education establishments in overseas territories, was still exploitable by agencies from other regions of the British Commonwealth. For instance, the polytechnic in Hong Kong could provide teaching and administrative staff in technical education in the United Kingdom and the Dominions – Australia, New Zealand, and Canada, all dominated by Whites – with opportunities for employment and career advancement. In addition, business corporations in Britain could use the fledging poly to influence a new generation of manufacturers, technicians, and professionals in Hong Kong and to bolster the marketability of British equipment and products overseas. In the heyday of decolonization, however, such external agents should have realized that the institution would have to be insulated from the colony's political vicissitudes in order to prolong its exploitability. This is because in many late-colonial and early-post-colonial settings, agents from outside had suffered miserably from decolonization. When power was transferred, many national governments – which gained power through championing an anti-colonial cause – ruthlessly nationalized the education systems, localized their staffing, expelled the expatriates, and curbed unwanted outside interference in the school systems.[5] Having witnessed and experienced such tribulations, the external powers were keen to shield the colonial institutions from political uncertainties in the remaining colonies. The ways in which decolonization was taking place elsewhere, thus, predisposed them to prefer that the educational establishments

5 One of the most well-known instances of this is the case of the Singapore Polytechnic – an institution founded in 1954 under the British. After coming into power in 1959 the People's Action Party led by Lee Kuan Yew overhauled the Polytechnic and expelled many of its expatriate staff. For this event in Singapore, see BW (file of The British Council, Public Records Office, Kew) 91/1072 and CO (file of Colonial Office, Public Records Office, Kew) 1030/923. For state interferences in higher education in other late-colonial or early-post-colonial settings, see Nwauwa, *Imperialism, Academe and Nationalism*.

in yet to be decolonized territories be as autonomous from the local colonial state as possible.

Hong Kong is useful for exploring the effects of power transferal on education in the remaining suzerainties also because it, being the last major dependency of the British Empire, received some servicemen from the ex-colonies who were looking for "second careers" elsewhere within the empire.[6] As illustrated by S. F. Bailey – a seasoned officer from decolonized Kenya who became the Secretary of the Hong Kong University Grants Committee when the colony's polytechnic was being founded – in this article's later sections, these displaced officers harbored outlooks colored by transfer of power and its resultant disruptions they had personally gone through. And their experiences and connections were much broader than those of the tiny colony's incumbent officers. Furthermore, being newcomers to Hong Kong, the relocated servicemen felt less constrained by social ties in the small territory. They, hence, could be freer to pursue their agendas and impose their preferences. This diaspora from decolonized territories could interrupt the balance of power within the colonial state and modify the processes and outcomes of struggles over Hong Kong's higher education.

This paper will explicate this argument. I contend that the above-mentioned impacts set forth by the British Empire's dissolution shaped the polytechnic's administrative form in colonial Hong Kong, making it more autonomous than its metropolitan equivalents. Since the HKP was established following the model of polytechnics in Britain, I will start by outlining the UK's system of higher education in the next section. Doing so is to contextualize the struggle over the founding of Hong Kong's polytechnic against a larger background.

Colonialism and higher education governance

The HKP was a vocational training institution modelled after the UK's polytechnics, which in Britain belonged to the service sector in postsecondary education. In the UK, tertiary education consisted of two parts, namely, the autonomous and the service sectors. The former was made up chiefly of the universities, whose proclaimed mission was to preserve and extend knowledge free from undue interference from economic and political powers; the latter comprised vocational-based institutions, such as polytechnics and technical colleges,

6 Anthony Kirk-Greene, "Decolonization: The Ultimate Diaspora," *Journal of Contemporary History* 36, no. 1 (2001): 135.

which were expected to fulfil the manpower demands of the state and the economy. These two types of establishments were governed differently.

The autonomous sector in Britain was under the University Grants Committee (UGC), an advisory body composed largely of unofficial members. Through the UGC, the universities relayed to the state their needs, financial and otherwise; and the government informed the academies of its policies and priorities. The UGC's mediations spared the schools excessive state interference and enhanced their independence. Moreover, the universities' autonomy was protected by the 'block grant' principle, through which state funding under general categories was allocated to the academies for an extended period of usually three years. This rule allowed universities flexibility in pursuing relatively long-term academic plans.[7] In sharp contrast, the service sector faced much stricter state surveillance. It was directly overseen by the Local Educational Authorities (LEAs) – the state bureaucracies also taking charge of primary and secondary education. The LEAs monitored closely the curriculum, personnel, and other matters of their constituent institutions; and they allocated funding to the academies yearly and under more restrictive rules. This form of governance was to ensure service sector schools were accountable to the public and responsive to the state and industry.[8]

When the HKP was being founded from the mid-1960s to the early 1970s, its planners aimed at constructing a postsecondary institution providing programs in areas such as garment production, management, accounting, engineering, and public administration. This school, like its counterparts in England, was meant to be a service sector academy. The HKP, nevertheless, ended up being governed in a form divergent from its British peers'. When it was formally inaugurated in 1972, it joined an expanded University Grants Committee of Hong Kong (UGCHK), renamed the University and Polytechnic Grants Committee (UPGC) – instead of being under the Education Department (ED), the colonial state's educational bureaucracy – and received state funding through the block grant rule.[9] The UGKHK, modelled after the UGC in the UK, was established in

7 Michael Shattock, *The UGC and the Management of British Universities* (Bristol, Pennsylvania: Open University Press, 1994), 1–6.

8 John Carswell, *Government and the Universities in Britain: Program and Performance, 1960–1980* (London: Cambridge University Press, 1985); John Pratt, *The Polytechnic Experiment* (GB: Open University Press, 1997), 9–12. About the genesis of the binary system in the UK, see C. D. Godwin, "The Origin of the Binary System," *History of Education* 27, no. 2 (1998): 171–91, and Michael Shattock, *Making Policy in British Higher Education, 1945–2011* (Berkshire: Open University Press, 2012), 9–102.

9 R. C. Griffiths, "Hong Kong University and Polytechnic Grants Committee," *Higher Education* 13, no. 5 (October, 1984): 545–552.

1965.[10] Like its forebear in England, it was a buffer protecting the independence of the autonomous sector.[11] It is mysterious how the HKP, presumably a service sector institution, crossed the binary line and came under an administrative system for the independent division.

In this article, I attempt to disentangle this anomaly of educational governance in colonial Hong Kong. I contend that the HKP could cross the binary line because an autonomous HKP could better protect itself against hostilities from the local political arena. This concern was a very significant one for the agencies from outside in the 1960s and 1970s. This is because, as mentioned above, when the founding of the HKP was underway, the British Empire had already undergone two decades' of decolonization; and to protect their interests, external actors took pre-emptive actions to make educational institutions in the remaining dependences at least partially autonomous from the colonial state.[12] Powers from outside were able to influence the HKP's form of governance because since Hong Kong was still a colony, its system of policy-making in higher education was penetrable by external forces. For instance, in 1968 the UGCHK, one of the major implementers of the polytechnic project, was dominated by non-local members – with its Chairman being a Scottish sojourner and six of its other nine members being academics in England and Australia.[13] The expatriate-controlled UGCHK gave external agents leeway to tamper with

---

10 *The Financing of Universities in Hong Kong: A Report Submitted to His Excellency the Governor* (Hong Kong: The Government Printer, 1965).

11 *University Grants Committee, Hong Kong, Report, October 1965 to June 1968* (Hong Kong: The Government Printer, 1968), 2–3.

12 Shielding the institution from Hong Kong's political uncertainty, of course, was not the only reason that a polytechnic not subordinate to the colonial state was preferred. External agencies also wanted the HKP to be UGCHK-affiliated because a semi-autonomous polytechnic would give its expatriate employees higher status and spare them the hassles of dealing with the educational bureaucracy. Ting-Hong Wong, "Crossing the Binary Line: the Founding of Polytechnic in Colonial Hong Kong," *History of Education* 43, no. 4 (2014): 524–541.

13 With another UGCHK member being R. C. Griffiths, the Deputy Secretary of UGC in England, the committee only had two Hong Kong-based members. *University Grants Committee, Hong Kong, Special Report, 1965 to 1976* (Hong Kong: The Government Printer, 1976), 53. Filling the UGCHK mainly with outsiders was recommended by Edward Hale, the UGC Secretary in the UK from 1951 to 1957, who maintained that as Hong Kong had only two universities, members drawn from local academics were unlikely to advise allocation of funding in higher education impartially. *The Financing of Universities in Hong Kong*, 17–8.

the polytechnic's development. Relying on the fact that the UGCHK Secretary at that time was a shrewd, ambitious, and well-connected serviceman relocated from the decolonized Kenya, the agencies from outside had leverage to influence higher education in Hong Kong and steer the polytechnic into the autonomous sector.

The external forces' maneuvrings, nevertheless, did not go unchallenged. The Director of Education (DofE), the head of Hong Kong's colonial educational bureaucracy, was adamant in curbing the institution's defection in order to safeguard his territory and power. With actors from within the colony and outside harboring different preferences for the HKP's mode of administration, the polytechnic's form of governance depended on the two sides' strategies and the support they could muster.

The prelude: The polytechnic proposed

When Hong Kong was undergoing a vibrant process of industrialization in the mid-1960s, it had very limited facilities for postsecondary technical education. In the academic year 1963–1964, technical training at the tertiary level was available only in the Hong Kong Technical College (HKTC) and Hong Kong University (HKU). The HKTC, operated by the Education Department, offered various types of programs in commerce, engineering, and other areas and enrolled 9,980 students. Only 730 (about 7 %) of these students, however, attended full-time courses – the postsecondary level programs that required entrants to have completed secondary education; the rest were enrolled in day-release or part-time evening classes that required lower academic qualifications.[14] The HKU had a Faculty of Engineering, but in the mid-1960s it produced only 25 mechanical engineers and 40 electrical engineers annually.[15] This situation worried both local industrialists and the colonial authorities. Many manufacturers blamed the government for not training enough craftsmen, technicians, and other technical personnel.[16]

---

14 *Hong Kong Education Department, Annual Report, 1963–1964* (Hong Kong: The Hong Kong Government, 1964), 2–3, 38; *Hong Kong Technical College, Prospectus, 1967–1968* (Hong Kong: Hong Kong Technical College, 1968), 2–3.

15 SCHE Minutes, October 26, 1967, 146/5/32. Hong Kong Government Records Service (HKRS), Hong Kong.

16 'Hong Kong's Progress is More by Accident than by Training', *Hong Kong Standard*, November 29, 1967.

Amid these criticisms, the Special Committee on Higher Education (SCHE) – a consultative body for manpower training – commissioned scholars to investigate demands for high-level manpower in Hong Kong.[17] Using data from censuses, the SCHE-sponsored research projected that the total shortfall of high-level manpower in 1971 would be 31,800. It also warned that such a shortage could not be resolved merely by expanding existing institutions.[18] Later, another SCHE-delegated survey concluded that the colony's school system had supplied the economy with very little high-level manpower. It encouraged expanding technical education at the tertiary level.[19] This advocacy was echoed by the UGCHK. In 1967 a UGCHK paper revealed that in 1965, when the territory had 9,800 students passing the School Certificate Examinations – the qualification for postsecondary schooling – only 3,000 of them had secured places for full-time higher education. It projected that the number of School Certificate passes would grow to 21,000 in 1971 and then to 30,000 in 1976. Unless more institutions were founded, the paper warned, the proportion of School Certificate holders able to continue full-time education would definitely drop, and a huge number of frustrated students might precipitate political unrest.[20] It was at this juncture that the idea of a polytechnic was introduced.

Within days, several UGCHK members endorsed the belief that there was a gap in tertiary education that needed to be filled. They recommended developing technical and commercial postsecondary programs up to and perhaps including the level of pass degree.[21] R. C. Griffiths, who was a UGCHK member as well as the Deputy Secretary of the UGC in the UK, proposed founding a polytechnic in Hong Kong. He suggested that since the major deficiency in qualified manpower appeared to be technicians, the top priority was for a multi-disciplinary institution offering an array of postsecondary courses to complement those of the universities. With the UK's binary system in mind, perhaps, he concluded that the polytechnic should remain a government responsibility.[22]

17 146/5/32, Background Note; SCHE, undated, HKRS 482/2/6/3; Members of the SCHE (1966, 1967).
18 Interim Report of SCHE, attached to SCHE paper No. 11, January 1967, HKRS 146/5/32.
19 Press release, August 21, 1968, HKRS 457/3/49.
20 "The Future Pattern of Higher Education in Hong Kong," UGC paper, April 6, 1967, HKRS 482/2/10.
21 "Future Patterns of Higher Education in Hong Kong, Comments on the Preliminary Paper," UGCHK paper 116, May 13, 1967, HKRS 482/2/10.
22 Griffiths to Herries, May 16, 1967, HKRS 482/2/10.

In June 1967 Michael Herries, the UGCHK Chairman who was also the head of a leading British firm in the colony, informed David Trench, the Hong Kong Governor, that the future development of higher education lay in full-time technical studies programs below the honors degree level and generally outside universities. He also reported that the UGCHK proposed founding a polytechnic – a large, non-residential, and urban-centered institution that would eventually enroll more students than the universities. He stated that whether the institution should operate under the ED or have a measure of autonomy was an issue for further discussion.[23] A few months later Herries urged Trench to set up a planning board for the polytechnic as soon as possible.[24]

External agencies take the initiative

Immediately after the project was proposed, overseas members of the UGCHK – whose views had been skewed by the experiences of state intervention in higher education in other ex-British overseas outposts and the metropolis – expressed concern that the proposed polytechnic would be under the local colonial state. N. S. Bayliss, a chemist from the University of Western Australia, held that the proposed institution should have some degree of autonomy and not be under the ED.[25] A. G. Lehmann, a scholar in French Studies at the University of Reading, warned Hong Kong to avoid state interference in educational institutions that were not branches of the civil service.[26] M. J. Wise of the London School of Economics and Political Science stressed that the polytechnic in Hong Kong should not be ED-governed.[27]

In October 1967 the impetus to make the proposed polytechnic independent from the colonial educational bureaucracy gained more momentum because S. F. Bailey, a prominent serviceman recruited from outside, replaced Kenneth Topley – an Administrative Officer seconded from the Colonial Secretariat – as the UGCHK's Secretary.[28] Bailey had had a highly successful career in Kenya. There, he had headed a number of departments and ascended to the position of Under-Secretary. He left Kenya in 1965, two years after the territory became independent; and he was made a Commander of the Most Excellent Order

23 Herries to Trench, June 16, 1967, HKRS 482/2/11/1.

24 Herries to Trench, September 7, 1967, HKRS 482/2/11/1.

25 Bayliss to Topley, September 12, 1967, HKRS 482/2/11/1.

26 Lehmann to Topley, September 19, 1967, HKRS 482/2/11/1.

27 Wise to Topley, September 19, 1967, HKRS 482/2/11/1.

28 *University Grants Committee, Hong Kong, Report, October 1965 to June 1968*, 8–9.

of the British Empire (CBE) in the same year. Before assuming the UGCHK Secretaryship, Bailey worked at the Science Research Council of the UK for two years.[29] Unlike his predecessor – Topley, a 'local' colonial officer spending almost his entire career in Hong Kong[30] – Bailey had wider horizons and better external connections. Records in the archives imply that he considered himself superior to his colleagues in Hong Kong, whom he found too 'parochial.' Moreover, arriving as a midcareer serviceman with a glamorous record behind him, he faced less constraint from ties with his new colleagues within the Hong Kong colonial bureaucracy, had confidence in exercising his own judgment and imposing his preference, and, probably, aspired to expand his jurisdiction in the colony. Furthermore, with his own career having been disrupted by the turmoil of decolonization in Kenya, Bailey was no doubt cognizant of the threat of power transferal and predisposed to shield the institution he helped build from possible political vicissitudes in Hong Kong.[31] These considerations ought to have inclined him to prefer that the HKP be autonomous and UGCHK-affiliated.

The UGCHK actively solicited support from both within and outside Hong Kong for the polytechnic project after Bailey arrived. In November 1967 Herries secured the SCHE's unanimous endorsement that an institution should be launched as soon as possible to train manpower at the level between the universities and the HKTC.[32] In July 1968 Bailey made an overture to the Council of the Technical Education and Training for Overseas Countries (CTETOC), an advisory body of the Ministry of Overseas Development (MOD) in the UK.[33] Frederick Pedler, the Director of Unilever, a leading British industrial firm, then chaired the Council. Pledging to help developing countries to produce middle-level manpower for economic growth, the CTETOC had assisted a number of Commonwealth territories to found technical training institutions.[34] Moreover,

29 *Staff List: Hong Kong Government, part 3* (Hong Kong: Government Printer, 1970), 7; *The British Imperial Calendar and Civil Service List* (London: Her Majesty's Stationery Office, 1966), col. 637; and Anthony H. M. Kirk-Greene (ed.), *A Biographical Dictionary of British Colonial Service, 1939–1966* (London: Hans Zell Publishers, 1991), 18.

30 *Staff List: Hong Kong Government, part 4* (Hong Kong: Government Printer, 1966), 94.

31 For the upheavals in Kenya during decolonization, see Daniel Branch, *Defeating Mau Mau, Creating Kenya: Counterinsurgency, Civil War, and Decolonization* (New York: Cambridge University Press, 2009).

32 SCHE Minutes, November 8, 1967, HKRS 146/5/32.

33 Bailey to the Personnel Manager, Unilever Ltd., July 4, 1968, HKRS 482/2/11/1.

34 Council for Technical Education and Training in Overseas Countries, drafted on March 15, 1962; and Moult to Bailey, July 19, 1968. Both in HKRS 482/2/11/1. For the

in the summer of 1968 the UGCHK actively sought assistance from the MOD and the Commonwealth Office (CO) for the polytechnic project.[35] During the deliberation process, it was suggested that the proposed polytechnic would help London perpetuate its influence in the Far East after the impending military withdrawal from east of Suez, familiarize young engineers in Hong Kong with British equipment, and facilitate trade promotion in the long term.[36]

The UGCHK's moves aroused many other external agents' interest in the polytechnic project. For instance, Norman Hunt, a member of the Working Party on Management Education and Training in Developing Countries, another consultative body of the MOD, expressed great interest in the plan and offered his support.[37] Hunt proclaimed that a greater involvement of the British in management education would strengthen the UK's position in the Far East.[38] The UGCHK's 'diplomatic onslaught' made many external agencies realize their stakes in the proposed institution in Hong Kong and built up useful connections that could be mobilized later when the Committee battled for the polytechnic.

With these supports from outside, Bailey advised Trench to install a planning board for the polytechnic at the earliest possible date.[39] Between late 1968 and early 1969, academics and politicians in the colony continued to lobby for expanding technical training at the tertiary level.[40] These pressures prompted the Governor to convene seven high-level officers – including W. D. Gregg, the

---

history of CTETOC, see Frederick Pedler, "Universities and Polytechnics in Africa", *Africa: Journal of the International African Institute* 42, no. 4 (October 1972): 263–274.

35 Polytechnic – meeting with Commonwealth Office and Ministry of Overseas Development, July 26, 1968; Extract from minutes of meeting in London on August 7, 1968. Both from HKRS 482/2/11/1.

36 Selection of Projects for Possible Additional Expenditure Overseas in the Non-Military Field, drafted by W. S. Carter, Hong Kong Department, Commonwealth Office; Carter to Trench, October 7, 1968. Both in FCO (file of Foreign and Commonwealth Office, Public Records Office, Kew) 40/90.

37 HKRS 482/2/11/1, Bailey to Morgan, Colonial Secretariat, Hong Kong, October 4, 1968.

38 General note by Professor Hunt on his visit to the Far East, September 1968, Public Records Office, Kew (PRO) BW (file of The British Council) 91/1072 and CO (file of Colonial Office) BW 91/487.

39 Polytechnic, supplementary brief for HE the Governor, October 3, 1968, HKRS 482/2/11/1.

40 Stewart to Bill, October 18, 1968, HKRS 482/2/11/1; "Councillors to Ask Questions at Legco," *South China Morning Post*, December 2, 1968; and "More Technical Courses," *Hong Kong Standard*, January 6, 1969.

Director of Education (DofE), Albert Rodiques (the SCHE Chairman), Herries, and Bailey – to discuss the polytechnic project in Government House in January 1969. The meeting kicked off the struggle between the colonial education bureaucrats and state actors more responsive to external forces over the poly's administrative form.

Sensing that the proposed polytechnic might perhaps not be under the ED, Gregg denounced the necessity of such an academy. He maintained that the problem of manpower training at the postsecondary level could be resolved by developing the HKTC's upper-level courses and at the same time moving its lower-level programs to the new Morrison Hill Technical Institute (MHTI). This recommendation was only partially accommodated, however. The conference resolved that the HKTC should be upgraded into a college of technology, as suggested by Gregg, and then merged with another college of technology – a new institution launched simultaneously when the HKTC was being overhauled. The two schools would then together become the polytechnic. The meeting decided to put the proposal to the Executive Council for approval. It also resolved that the UGCHK Secretary might serve as the secretary of the polytechnic's planning board. Finally, the conference seemed to prefer an UGCHK-controlled poly: its minutes recorded that the Secretariat of that Committee might be the best administrative link between the two component colleges and the government.[41]

The conflict escalates

With this progress on the project, the tension between the UGCHK and the ED mounted. On January 28, 1969, just a week after the Government House meeting, Bailey wrote to J. M. Rowlands of the Colonial Secretariat, reiterating the necessity of making the UGCHK the intermediary between the polytechnic and the government.[42] He held that the future poly should play an important role in providing part-time and sub-degree courses, and that curbing the poly from changing into a university would be crucial in ensuring the availability of such programs. Through their experiences with the LEAs, Bailey continued, many technical institutions in the UK reckoned the educational bureaucracy was hindering their performance and had become adamant about being transformed

41 Note on meeting about polytechnic at Government House on January 20, 1969, HKRS 482/2/11/2.

42 Bailey to Rowlands, January 28, 1969, HKRS 482/2/11/2.

into universities. Bailey argued that such undesirable scenario could be prevented in Hong Kong if the poly was UGCHK-controlled.[43]

Bailey's view met with rebuttals from the DofE. In a letter to the Colonial Secretariat, Gregg averred that the proposed colleges should remain government institutions staffed by civil servants. He stressed that the present HKTC received a great deal of support from the ED on matters including the handling of buildings, equipment, and around 1,000 staff. He doubted the UGCHK was ready to take over these tasks. Gregg also remarked that in the process of setting up the MHTI he had realized that close liaison between the HKTC and the MHTI – both directly under the ED – would facilitate better coordination and planning. If vocational education was fragmented by two different administrations, cautioned Gregg, cooperation among institutions would be difficult.[44]

Bailey fought back swiftly, reminding the DofE that the Government House meeting had determined that the polytechnic would be a relatively independent institution consisting of two technical colleges. He reasserted that an UGCHK-controlled poly would prevent its isolation from the universities and ensure a balanced allocation of resources in tertiary education.[45] Later, Bailey sought to delink the polytechnic from the ED by sabotaging the 'two-college plan' – the proposal that the new academy should be formed through merging two colleges, one of them being upgraded from the ED-controlled HKTC. He went so far as to write to Jack Canning – the new DofE a few months later – reminding him that they had agreed before that a unitary and larger polytechnic could attract a principal of higher caliber and that the double-college idea should be ditched. Bailey told Canning that the goal now was a single poly – an independent institution connected with the ED only informally.[46]

Bailey's aggressive posture alerted Griffiths, simultaneously a UGCHK member and the Secretary of the UGK in the UK. He cautioned that if the polytechnic was UGCHK-governed, it would be difficult to hold off for long the installation of honors degrees, major research, and higher degrees – changes that would amount to the founding of a new university. Griffiths contended that UGC-type governance was not necessarily best for an academy providing essentially vocational education, for it would be ineffective in checking the ambition

43 Proposed polytechnic, explanatory note, by UGCHK, January 16, 1969, HKRS 482/2/11/2.

44 Gregg to Rowlands, January 27, 1969, HKRS 482/2/11/2.

45 Note, by Bailey, February 5, 1969, HKRS 482/2/11/2.

46 Note: Association of Department of Education with Polytechnic, S. F. Bailey, February 10, 1969; Bailey to Canning, February 14, 1969. Both in HKRS 482/2/11/2.

of the institution and preventing it from abandoning the sub-degree and part-time programs. He warned people to be more careful before pronouncing that the poly must not be a direct governmental responsibility.[47]

This backing from Griffiths notwithstanding, the DofE's hankering for the polytechnic suffered setbacks both within the colony and outside shortly afterwards. In a meeting of the Legislative Council on March 13, S. Y. Chung, an industrialist who had constantly called for stronger linkages between the school system and industry expressed his disappointment over the HKTC's administration. He declared the new college of technology should be an autonomous establishment under an independent board of governors.[48] A few days later, students of the HKTC accused the DofE for failing to resolve a chronic shortage of teaching staff and proclaimed that their school would have no future if it remained ED-governed.[49] These calls for checking the ED's role in technical education reverberated outside the colony: After a trip to Hong Kong, Gordon Watts, Technical Advisor to the MOD in the UK, proclaimed that the proposed polytechnic should be UGCHK-affiliated and that an ED-linked poly would not be free enough to do pioneering work in technical education at the advanced level.[50]

Amidst these contestations, the UGCHK convened in Hong Kong in March 1969. Shortly afterwards, a memorandum suggesting that the poly should be subject to roughly the same financial and administrative autonomy as the universities was submitted by the Committee to the Executive Council.[51] On April 1, the Executive Council concurred that the scheme should proceed. The Polytechnic Planning Committee (PPC) was installed shortly thereafter. P. Y. Tang, an American-educated industrialist whom Bailey gauged as espousing an UGCHK-affiliated poly, was appointed the PPC Chairman.[52] The PPC had 10 other members – including Bailey (who was also made the PPC Secretary), five government officials (the DofE being one of them), three local industrialists, and a senior

47 Griffith to Bailey, February 28, 1969, HKRS 482/2/11/2.

48 Speech by Dr. S. Y. Chung on 13th March 1969, Budget Debate, HKRS 482/2/11/2.

49 "HK Tech Wants Reforms" and "Students' Grounds for a 'Divorce'," both in *Hong Kong Standard*, March 22, 1969; "To See Technical Education Expert", *South China Morning Post*, March 22, 1969.

50 Proposed Hong Kong Polytechnic, Memorandum for Dr. G. Watts, by Norman Hunt, March 1969, PRO-BW 91/487.

51 Memorandum for Executive Council, the Development of Higher Vocational Education in Hong Kong, for discussion on April 1, 1969, PRO-BW 91/488.

52 *Bailey to Gavin, May 16, 1969, HKRS 482/2/11/3.*

administrator of a leading British firm. The Government aimed at enrolling up to 4,000 full-time and 20,000 part-time students in an institution governed by the Polytechnic Board by 1974.[53] The PPC swiftly instituted five subcommittees to found the school.[54]

The confrontation widens

After installing the PPC, both the UGCHK and the ED sought to enlist more supporters, and more parties involved themselves in the contestation. On May 21, Hunt wrote to Herries, reminding him to ensure that the poly would be under the UGCHK.[55] Later, Malcolm Gavin, the Principal of the Chelsea College of Science and Technology and a UGCHK member, told Herries that since England was establishing 30 new polytechnics, principals of high caliber were at a premium. He attested that making Hong Kong's polytechnic autonomous and giving its principal the status of vice-chancellor would be crucial to lure the right person.[56]

Almost at the same time, Tang, the PPC Chairman, contacted Pedler, the CTETOC head, asking for general advice as well as help in staff recruitment.[57] Pedler promised that his Council would assist the project in all possible ways.[58] At a CTETOC meeting in London a few months later, Tang and Bailey were advised that good candidates for positions were more likely to be attracted if the poly were semi-autonomous, that a principal could perform more effectively if he were not a civil servant, and that the institution would operate more smoothly if it was unitary and under one administration and a single director.[59] Moreover, under the auspices of the CTETOC and PPC, John Marsh, the Director-General of the British Institute of Management in the UK, visited Hong Kong in late October 1969. Marsh advocated that the polytechnic have a high degree of

53 The Development of High Level Vocational Education in Hong Kong, the Polytechnic Planning Committee, attached to Tang to Pedler, June 6 1969, PRO-BW 81/487.

54 Bailey to Lehman, July 5, 1969, PRO-BW 81/487.

55 Hunt to Herries, May 21, 1969, HKRS 482/2/11/3.

56 Gavin to Herries, June 25, 1969, HKRS 482/2/11/3.

57 Tang to Pedler, June 6, 1969, PRO-BW 91/487.

58 Pedler to Tang, July 19, 1969, PRO-BW 91/487.

59 Note of a meeting held with the Chairman and Secretary of the Hong Kong Polytechnic Planning Committee, September 9, 1969, The Council for Technical Education and Training for Overseas Countries, PRO-BW 91/487.

independence, with active participation by industry and commerce in its governing body.[60]

These maneuvres of the UGCHK, the PPC, and CTETOC provoked challenges from the ED. Canning, the new DofE, argued that the poly should fall completely under the ED and be overseen by a Deputy Director of Education who would attend to technical education at all levels. At the eleventh meeting of the PPC, the DofE refused to endorse empowering the polytechnic to employ its own staff, as he regarded such authority should belong to the ED. Canning's position was at odds with the stances of all the unofficial members of the PPC – three industrialists and a senior manager of a leading British firm – as they worried that the salary scale of a poly under the ED would be too rigid to entice quality applicants, that the rules for civil servants would block the staff from undertaking external consultancy work, and that the principal would have no power over staff recruitment. The DofE, however, did have a supporter inside the PPC in Philip Hadden-Cave, the Deputy Financial Secretary. Hadden-Cave, according to Bailey, regretted that the principle of block grant had been adopted for the two universities and wanted the powers the Financial Secretary now had over the HKTC to be extended to the new institution.[61]

Late 1969 witnessed an immense boost to Canning; for the Governor, who had heretofore preferred an UGCHK-linked polytechnic, suddenly defected and sided with the colonial education bureaucracy. At a meeting with several CTETOC members in London in December, Trench expressed his concern that a highly autonomous polytechnic might defy colonial state's control and declared his preference for an ED-governed poly.[62] Trench's defection, some CTETOC members later discovered, arose from his distrust of Tang, whom the Governor deemed pro-American. Tang had been trying to recruit the polytechnic's director from the US. Sources also disclosed that he went so far as to prepare to sponsor the director's salary from personal means should the emolument of a director hired from the US exceed the salary allowed by the Hong Kong government's fixed scale. Since Tang, who now chaired the PPC, would under normal circumstances become head of the polytechnic board – its

60 Report by John Marsh on his 5-Day visit to Hong Kong as a member of the Council for Technical Education and Training in Overseas Countries – 27th October/1st November 1969, PRO-BW 91/487.

61 Bailey to Lehman; July 5, 1969, HKRS 482/2/11/3.

62 Hong Kong Polytechnic, note of a discussion with H.E. The Governor, the Council for Technical and Training For Overseas Countries, December 31, 1969, PRO-BW 91/487.

future governing body – Trench strenuously opposed the institution's becoming too independent.[63]

The UGCHK's campaign was also fettered because some PPC members from the government, though they did not hold that the polytechnic should be under the ED, had reservations about entrusting the school to the UGCHK. Bailey surmised this stance stemmed from these officials' unfamiliarity with the UGC system and the block grant principle.[64] Moreover, after the Governor pledged to support the ED, the officials might consider siding with the UGCHK to be injudicious. Thus, when the PPC Interim Report was finalized in late 1969, the Committee, though agreeing that the poly should be quasi-independent, recommended that the school's finances should be provided from public funds voted by the Legislative Council instead of through the UGCHK's block grant rule.[65]

These setbacks galvanized reactions from the UGCHK and its proponents both outside and inside the colony. In December 1969, Bayliss, a UGCHK member from Australia, expressed his concern that higher education in Hong Kong would be fragmented. Invoking the example of West Australia, in which a single advisory body covered both the universities and the institute of technology, he suggested the colony form a single committee dealing with both the universities and the polytechnic.[66] Three months later, in March 1970, Kenneth Marshall of the CTETOC, persuaded Trench to empower the UGCHK also to oversee the polytechnic when visiting Hong Kong.[67] Moreover, Bailey sought to dispel the officials' suspicion of the UGC-type system and block grant principle.[68] These efforts, however, failed to stop the official ratification of the PPC Interim Report, which did not entrust the poly to the UGCHK.

Stalemate broken

In January 1970 the PPC Interim Report was submitted to the government. After approval by the Executive and the Legislative Councils, the government disclosed

63 Visit of Mr. Kenneth Marshall to Hong Kong, 15–17 March 1970, BW 91/488; Bailey to Herries, March 10, 1970, HKRS 482/2/11/3.

64 Progress Report, Polytechnic Planning Committee, August 21, 1969, HKRS 482/2/11/3.

65 General Principles and their Application, Polytechnic Planning Committee, attached to Tang to Trench, August 22, 1969, PRO-BW 91/487.

66 Bayliss to Herries, December 19, 1969, HKRS 482/2/11/3.

67 Visit of Mr. Kenneth Marshall to Hong Kong, 15–17 March 1970, PRO-BW 91/488.

68 Bailey to Clinton, March 18, 1970, HKRS 482/2/11/3.

in early April that it would take steps towards setting up a polytechnic. The colonial administration also announced that immediate action should be taken to recruit a director for the planned academy.[69] Meanwhile, Tang's behavior continued to suggest he was not a reliable watchman of British interests. In May 1970 Tang was found cutting his UK visit 'indecently short' in order to lengthen his US tour. Bailey learned that Tang would visit Lowell, Massachusetts – known as "the cradle of industrial revolution in America" – as well as the Massachusetts Institute of Technology, Tang's alma mater. He believed Tang would use this trip to look for candidates for the director's post.[70] Consequently, the Governor continued to curtail the poly's independence. In January 1971 the draft Polytechnic Ordinance, which contained a provision empowering the Governor-in-Council to issue directions to the polytechnic board, was passed by the PPC.[71]

Beginning in early 1971, exponents of an ED-controlled polytechnic suffered a big blow; for at that time London had already announced Trench, their most powerful backer, would be replaced as Hong Kong's Governor before the end of the year. More importantly, in early April Crawford Murray MacLehose, the Governor-Designate, had asked the CTETOC – which had been supporting the UGCHK throughout – to brief him on Hong Kong's technical education.[72] These developments rekindled the UGCHK's hopes and weakened the ED's position. The government officials on the PPC, except the DofE perhaps, now considered that throwing their weight behind the outgoing Governor would be imprudent. Hence, on April 20, Bailey reported to the UGCHK members that the PPC had already agreed on drafting a final report that would recommend that the polytechnic come under a reconstituted UGCHK, renamed the University and Polytechnic Grants Committee (UPGC).[73]

Two months later, in June 1971, the ED's campaign was further debilitated when Tang suddenly died after a stroke, and S. Y. Chung, a Ph.D. in Engineering Science from the University of Sheffield, swiftly took over as Acting Chairman of the PPC. With the removal of the irritant spurring Trench to keep a tight rein on the polytechnic, and the PPC now being safely controlled by a British-educated

69 Proposed Hong Kong Polytechnic, the UGC, April 10, 1970; Polytechnic for Hong Kong, Draft Press, PPC. Both in HKRS 482/2/11/3.

70 Bailey to Collins, the CTETOC Secretary, May 22, 1970, HKRS 482/2/11/3.

71 Polytechnic Legislation – Directions by Governor-in-Council, note by S. F. Bailey, January 9, 1971, HKRS 482/2/11/4.

72 MacLehose to Collins, April 6, 1971, PRO-BW 91/488.

73 University Grants Committee (Hong Kong) Meeting in London on Tuesday, April 27, 1971, April 20, 1971, paper no. 322/8, HKRS 482/2/11/4.

industrialist,[74] the outgoing Governor had less reason to support the DofE and mitigate the poly's independence.

In July 1971 the Legislative Council passed the Polytechnic Ordinance – the legislation stipulating the purposes, structure and governance of the institution. The statute officially named the establishment the Hong Kong Polytechnic (HKP) and made provision for the formation of a Board of Governors.[75] In the same month the PPC's Final Report submitted to the Governor suggested inaugurating the UPGC and applying the block grant method to the HKP. The document proposed that after the Board was appointed, the land, building, equipment, and all other assets of the HKTC be transferred to the Board.[76] In September Charles Old, formerly principal of colleges of technology in Rotterham and Wolverhampton, became Principal of the HKP.[77]

The polytechnic project made further strides after MacLehose became the new Governor of Hong Kong in November 1971. In February 1972 the Government accepted the recommendations of the PPC's Final Report. As a result, the HKP would be established and the UGCHK would be transformed and renamed the UPGC.[78] In May 1972 the UPGC was formed and the polytechnic's Board of Governors was installed.[79] In the same month the UPGC decided that "normal block grant" procedures would be applied to the HKP in August 1974. About three months later, on August 1, 1972, an UPGC-affiliated HKP was officially inaugurated.[80] A vocational-based polytechnic now came under a form of governance for autonomous academies.

74 About Chung's backgrounds, especially his connection with the British, see HKRS 545/1/135.

75 Hong Kong Polytechnic Ordinance, 1971, PRO-BW 91/488. It should be noted that the government still did not allow the polytechnic to have the same level of autonomy as the universities, as the Ordinance empowered the Governor-in-Council to give orders to the Board when he thought fit.

76 *Final Report of the Polytechnic Planning Committee* (Hong Kong: Government Printer, 1971).

77 Hong Kong Polytechnic, University Grants Committee (Hong Kong) paper no. 328/9, September 29, 1971, HKRS 482/2/11/4.

78 "Polytechnic Plans Advance," *South China Morning Post*, February 11, 1972.

79 "Sir Kenneth Joins Committee," *Hong Kong Standard*, May 13, 1972; *Hong Kong Polytechnic, Annual Report, 1972/73* (Hong Kong: Libra Press Ltd., 1973), 1.

80 *University and Polytechnic Grants Committee, Report for the Period July 1972 to June 1974* (Hong Kong, the Government Printer, 1973), 23.

Recapitulation and implications

Over the past several decades, many scholars have been researching the effects of decolonization on education. The resultant literature, though insightful and valuable, concentrates almost exclusively on cases in late-colonial and early-post-colonial settings. This bias of historians has been costly, as it has prevented researchers from examining the effects of power transferal on school education in remaining colonies and impeded a more complete understanding of the metamorphoses of dissolving empires To take a first step to address this inadequacy, I use the historical case of the polytechnic in British Hong Kong to illuminate the impacts of decolonization on education governance in territories still under metropolitan domination.

When the Hong Kong Polytechnic was inaugurated in 1972, it was put under an administrative form that granted it more autonomy than its counterparts in the UK. The HKP was able to secure a high level of independence because of two dynamics set forth by decolonization within the British Empire. First, after witnessing or personally suffering from sovereignty changes in other ex-colonies, many external agencies with stakes in remaining dependencies' educational institutions realized that such establishments had to be ensured against uncertainties occasioned by local politics. This predisposition drove the agencies from outside to make the schools concerned autonomous from the local colonial state. Second, the empire's dissolution forced many colonial officers to leave the decolonized regions and seek 'second careers' in the yet-to-be decolonized territories. This diaspora brought into many servicemen with outlooks that had been colored by power transferals they had gone through. Moreover, the experiences, competence, and networks of these incoming servicemen differed vastly with those of the incumbent officers in the territories they were moving into. This diaspora of officers triggered by decolonization altered the power balance within the state and modified the process and outcome of politics of higher education in the remaining dependencies. In the article, I also highlight that the external agencies had leeway to impose their preferences because the mechanism of decision-making in education in the yet-to-be decolonized territories remained colonial and thus penetrable by powers in the metropolis as well as other dominant regions of the empire. The findings of this article hint that historians of imperial history should pay due attention to the impacts of power transferal on territories still under metropolitan control in order to understand more thoroughly the metamorphoses of empires' dissolution.

Appendix

Abbreviations

CBE	Commander of the Most Excellent Order of the British Empire
CO	Commonwealth Office
CTETOC	Council of the Technical Education and Training for Overseas Countries
DofE	The Director of Education
ED	Education Department
HKP	Hong Kong Polytechnic
HKTC	Hong Kong Technical College
HKU	Hong Kong University
LEAs	Local Educational Authorities
MHTI	Morrison Hill Technical Institute
MOD	Ministry of Overseas Development
PPC	Polytechnic Planning Committee
SCHE	Special Committee on Higher Education
UGC	University Grants Committee (of England)
UGCHK	University Grants Committee of Hong Kong
UPGC	University and Polytechnic Grants Committee

Archives

Hong Kong Government Records Service

Public Records Office, Kew/England

Literature

Anyanwu, Ogechi E. "Challenging the Status Quo: Alan Pifer and Higher Education Reform in Colonial Nigeria." *History of Education* 42, no. 1 (2013): 70–91.

Branch, Daniel. *Defeating Mau Mau, Creating Kenya: Counterinsurgency, Civil War, and Decolonization*. New York: Cambridge University Press, 2009.

Carswell, John. *Government and the Universities in Britain: Program and Performance, 1960 -1980.* London: Cambridge University Press, 1985.

Elder, Joseph W. "The Decolonization of Educational Culture: The Case of India." *Comparative Education Review* 15, no. 3 (1971): 288–295.

Final Report of the Polytechnic Planning Committee (Hong Kong: Government Printer, 1971).

Godwin, C. D. "The Origin of the Binary System." *History of Education* 27, no. 2 (1998): 171–91.

Griffiths, Robert C. "Hong Kong University and Polytechnic Grants Committee." *Higher Education* 13, no. 5 (October, 1984): 545–552.

Holford, John. "Mass Education and Community Development in the British Colonies, 1940–1960: A Study in the Politics of Community Education." *International Journal of Lifelong Education* 7, no. 3 (1988): 163–183.

Hong Kong Education Department, Annual Report, 1963–1964. Hong Kong: The Hong Kong Government, 1964.

Hong Kong Government, part 3. Hong Kong: Government Printer, 1970.

Hong Kong Government. part 4. Hong Kong: Government Printer, 1966.

Hong Kong Polytechnic, Annual Report, 1972/73. Hong Kong: Libra Press Ltd., 1973.

Hong Kong Technical College, Prospectus, 1967–1968. Hong Kong: Hong Kong Technical College, 1968.

Kirk-Greene, Anthony H. M. (ed.), *A Biographical Dictionary of British Colonial Service, 1939–1966.* London: Hans Zell Publishers, 1991.

Kirk-Greene, Anthony H. M. "Decolonization: The Ultimate Diaspora." *Journal of Contemporary History* 36, no. 1 (2001): 135.

Nwauwa, Apollos O. *Imperialism, Academe and Nationalism: Britain and University Education for African, 1860–1960.* London: Frank Cass, 1997.

Pedler, Frederick. "Universities and Polytechnics in Africa." *Africa: Journal of the International African Institute* 42, no. 4 (October 1972): 263–274.

"Polytechnic Plans Advance." *South China Morning Post.* February 11, 1972.

Pratt, John. *The Polytechnic Experiment 1965–1992.* Bristol & Buckingham: Open University Press, 1997.

Shattock, Michael. *The UGC and the Management of British Universities.* Bristol, Pennsylvania: Open University Press, 1994.

Shattock, Michael. *Making Policy in British Higher Education, 1945–2011.* Berkshire: Open University Press, 2012.

"Sir Kenneth Joins Committee." *Hong Kong Standard*, May 13, 1972.

Skinner, Kate. "Who Knew the Minds of the People? Specialist Knowledge and Developmentalist Authoritarianism in Postcolonial Ghana." *The Journal of Imperial and Commonwealth History* 39, no. 2 (2011): 297–323.

Stockwell, Anthony. J. "'The Crucible of the Malayan Union': The University and the Making of a New Malaya, 1938–1961." *Modern Asian Studies* 43, no. 5 (2009): 1149–1187.

The British Imperial Calendar and Civil Service List. London: Her Majesty's Stationery Office, 1966.

The Financing of Universities in Hong Kong: A Report Submitted to His Excellency the Governor. Hong Kong: The Government Printer, 1965.

University and Polytechnic Grants Committee, Report for the Period July 1972 to June 1974. Hong Kong: The Government Printer, 1973.

University Grants Committee, Hong Kong, Report, October 1965 to June 1968. Hong Kong: The Government Printer, 1968.

University Grants Committee. Hong Kong, Special Report, 1965 to 1976. Hong Kong: The Government Printer, 1976.

Wong, Ting-Hong. *Hegemonies Compared: State Formation and Chinese School Politics in Postwar Singapore and Hong Kong*. New York: Routledge, 2002.

Wong, Ting-Hong. "Crossing the Binary Line: The Founding of Polytechnic in Colonial Hong Kong." *History of Education* 43, no. 4 (2014): 524–541.

Wong, Ting-Hong, and Michael W. Apple. "Rethinking the Education/State Formation Connection: Pedagogic Reform in Singapore, 1945–1965." *Comparative Education Review* 46, no. 2 (2002): 182–210.

Sónia Vaz Borges

Delineating Youth between the Old and the New. The Youth Magazine *Blufo* during the Liberation Struggle in Guinea-Bissau (1966–1973)

Abstract The fall of the French and English colonial empires and their tremendous impact in world politics have also diverted attention from the latest processes of decolonization, particularly those of the Spanish and Portuguese last dominions. The chapter addresses a model case of a liberation struggle accompanied by a whole set of educational strategies: Guinea-Bissau. The analysis of the characteristics and impact of the Guinean liberation front's magazine *Blufo*, a novel militant and educational initiative aimed at 'youths', addresses the question of how the process of mobilization against colonial rule both used and transformed elements of traditional local cultures. Whereas the very name of the magazine referred to local notions of transitioning to adulthood, the idea of an age-related 'youth' as a clearly defined period was clearly a rupture in the local environment. By using and actualizing traditional notions about growing-up, independence fighters were transforming some aspects of this cultural resource. The involvement of the Brazilian educator Paulo Freire as a reference in many initiatives in Guinea-Bissau opens a perspective in which South-South-cooperation and mutual observation are paramount.

Keywords: Guinea-Bissau, youth magazines, Paulo Freire, South-South Cooperation, indigenous culture

Schooling is not simply about learning, for pedagogy is intrinsically linked to the ideological concerns of the state – be it colonial or independent.[1] Under normal circumstances education is partly a result of contextual factors, it is directly related with the society where it develops, and it is considered an important tool for development and social-individual transformation.

A fair number of studies about education in Africa tend to be implicitly divided in three main chronological periods – pre-colonial, colonial, and post-colonial. This chronological division contributes to advance the idea that during and after the colonial period Africans had given not develop of gave any contribution of

1 Lesley A. Sharp, *The Sacrificed Generation. Youth, History, and the Colonized Mind in Madagascar* (California: University of California, 2002), 75.

how education in their colonized territories was being organized. Of course, this perspective neglects the specific contributions advanced by Africans while at the same time reproduces the idea of an African inferiority or only as passive education receptacles. Paulo Freire in his book *Cartas à Guiné-Bissau. Registo de uma experiência em Processo*[2] (1977), and in his lecture *Amílcar Cabral. O pedagogo da revolução* (1985) reveals how his knowledge, experience and his involvement in the PAIGC[3] liberation struggle in Guinea Bissau as well as the educational initiatives developed in the territory after independence informed his thoughts and writings on revolutionary education.

The present article, is part of an extensive research on revolutionary education,[4] that occurred between 1963 and 1978, in Guinea Bissau under the leadership of PAIGC. During the liberation struggle in Guinea Bissau and following the directives defined during PAIGC's underground Congress in the region of Cassacá in Guinea Bissau in 1963, a network of schools was developed inside the Guinean territory in areas then defined as *Zonas/Areas Libertadas* (Liberated Zones/Areas) as well as in the neighboring countries, namely Guinea Conakry and Senegal. According to PAIGC school year report from 1971/1972, the newly created educational structure included 164 schools, 258 teachers and 14,531 students with grades from pre-school to 6th grade.[5] The educational concept underlying these underground schools was understood to form *Educação Militante* (Militant Education).[6]

Militant education, as a product of the liberation struggle, can be defined as a committed, engaged and conscious anti-colonial and decolonizing principle focused on an ample concept of liberation, and was to be a central part of and Africanized curriculum which at the same time reflected Party objectives. Rooted and supported by the realities and necessities of the community in struggle,

---

2 The English title is *Pedagogy in Process: The Letters to Guinea-Bissau.*

3 The initials PAIGC stays for *Partido Africano para a Independência da Guinea Bissau e Cabo Verde* (African Party for the Independence of Guinea Bissau and Cape Verde), that between the years of 1960–1973, developed in the colonized territory today Guinea Bissau, a armed and ideological struggle against Portuguese colonial occupation.

4 Sónia Borges, *Militant Education. Liberation Struggle, Consciousness and the Underground Educational Structures in Guinea Bissau. 1963–1978* (Berlin: Peter Lang, 2018) (in press).

5 PAIGC, Reconstrução Nacional, *Quadros Formados pelo P.A.I.G.C Desde o Início da Luta*, 1972, 5.

6 PAIGC, Comissariado de Estado da Educação Nacional, *Educação, Tarefa de Toda a Sociedade*, 1978, Républica da Guiné-Bissau.

militant education, in combination with technical and professional training, had as its aim the transformation of individual as well as the collective behavior. Pupils/students were supposed to be guided toward the development of his/her Self as a liberated African 'citizen' whose work was to give his/her conscious contribution for the sustainable development of the newly independent and liberated country, integrated in the international system of states. For the practice of such objectives, PAIGC militants and trained teachers developed a diversity of school materials, such as a new school curriculum, novel school regulations, manuals and magazines and additional educational programs for adults.[7]

In this contribution, I focus on a particular educational instrument developed and directed by PAIGC teachers and students: *Blufo. Orgão dos Pioneiros do PAIGC*, appeared between 1966 and 1973, was a magazine published by the Party extraterritorial boarding school, the *Escola Piloto* that was functioning in Guinea Conakry in cooperation with the PAIGC's youth organization *Pioneiros do Partido.*[8] Its prime objective was to function as a complementary educational instrument that would also contribute to the ongoing PAIGC process for an anti-colonial and post-colonial education. Firstly, I will explore through oral testimonies the reasons behind the publication. Then, through a selection of issues I will present some of the content of the magazine, relating them with the Party objectives. Finally, I will shortly analyze the tensions raised by the magazine on traditional and modern concepts of youth, and influence of the magazine in the liberation struggle context and in the decolonization process.

The context, the making and the main contents of the PAIGC youth magazine *Blufo. Orgão dos Pioneiros do Partido*

The name *Blufo* took its inspiration from the tradition of the largest ethnic group in Guinea-Bissau, the *Balanta*. *Blufo*[9] means the young person who has

7 These materials correspond to a set of unpublished documents located in different archives. Between them are seminar reports produced during the PAIGC teacher training courses, like "Para a reorganização e melhoria do trabalho Brigadas de Acção Política", February 1971. 7, the lesson manuscript "História de África. Lições feitas no Centro de aperfeiçoamento de professores em 1966", 60, or the school regulation "Regulamento Interno dos Internatos das Regiões Libertadas." 1971: Publicação do Serviço de Reconstrução Nacional/Ensino, n.d. 7.

8 The *Pioneiros do Partido* (Party Pionners) was a youth organization created by PAIGC in the year of 1966. This organization directed to PAIGC pupils was designed for every student that attended the Party schools within the ages between of 10 to 15 years old.

9 The word *Blufo* corresponds to one of the stadiums to achieve adulthood.

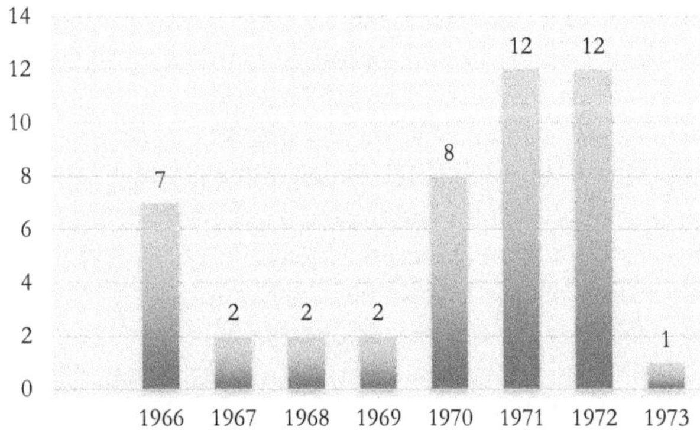

Fig. 1: *Blufo* Youth Magazine 1966–1973: Number of issues per year. Source: Own elaboration based on *Blufo* youth magazine analysis.

not yet done the traditional ritual passage from child to adulthood – the circumcision. In the traditional culture circumcision described the threshold to the world of adults, ready to live in and contribute to society as responsible persons. PAIGC's choice of this traditional expression as the title of their youth magazine symbolizes one central aspect of their concept of militant education, namely the "transformation of individual and collective behaviors."[10]

Between 1966 and 1973 PAIGC published a total of 47 issues of the *Blufo* youth magazine (see Fig. 1). The foldable A5 paper format was printed at the PAIGC Party headquarters in Guinea Conakry. In collaboration between *Escola Piloto* and PAIGC *Rádio Libertação*, a radio programme was broadcasted under the same name, *Blufo*. For this program, students' talks, traditional songs, readings and direct warnings and reminders were recorded and then broadcast on the daily or weekly radio program.[11]

10 PAIGC, *Educação tarefa de toda a sociedade,* 12.

11 Interview with Maria Amélia Araújo, director of PAIGC Radio – *Rádio Libertação*, September 26, 2013. Maria Amélia Araújo, Angolan of Capeverdean origin, joined the PAIGC liberation struggle together with her husband José Eduardo Araújo (responsible for the PAIGC's justice department), after the clandestine escape from Portugal of a group of African students in 1961. During the struggle, between 1962 to 1966 she worked in the Secretariat's information section in Conakry, and in 1966 she trained as a radio broadcaster in the former Soviet Union and became a producer and a speaker for the Rádio Libertação.

Ana Maria Cabral,[12] PAIGC militant, teacher and responsible for *Blufo*, together with other collaborators, revealed that the primary objective of *Blufo* was thus to encourage PAIGC pupils and members of the Party Pioneers to read, to enlarge their worldview, knowledge and understanding, and to expand the pupils' knowledge about PAIGC's struggle at national and international levels. Under the moto "Blufo should be read by all students", the editorial line of the magazine, got its inspiration from teachers traveling abroad and their contact with other pedagogical material produced in other territories.

Inspired by articles, stories found in magazines and books found in bookshops in Senegal-Dakar or in Cuba, text would be translated from different languages (French, Spanish, English) to Portuguese, and games, crosswords, riddles, images, names and some themes would be adapted to the local realities. At the same time, it was also included in the magazine editorial, traditional stories, poems of African writers, local and international news about the struggle, visit reports, celebrations, or mail exchange between schools. According to the testimony of Ana Maria Cabral, the French books *Quest qui c'est* and collection *Le monde merveilleux,* that she found during her travels to Dakar, had a major influence *Blufo* articles, as her memories unveiled while during the interview she skimmed through a compilation of all the magazine publications:

> Then I found a book in Dakar. The title is 'Quest qui c'est' with lots of information for young people. There was also another (book), 'Le monde est tout merveilleux', something like that. I have done translations. (some of the text titles). "How was the life of the first men on the earth", "The amazing world". All this was translated. I found this (stories) a fantastic thing. And more, "In the endless sky", so to talk about the stars, the wind what it was the rain and the snow, and afterwards we would discuss it, "The art of

12 Born in 1940 in Canxungo – Guinea Bissau, Ana Maria de Foss de Sá Cabral, traveled with her parents to Angola-Uíge. There she studied in a boarding school in Luanda. After her father's assassination in 1955, the family traveled to Lisbon, where she continued her studies while working as at the *Caixa dos Operários Metalurgicos*.
In Lisbon, she got in contact with the organizations of *Casa dos Estudantes do Império* and *Centro de Estudos Africanos*. In 1963, she traveled to Prague-Czechoslovakia, where she studied Philosophy with a fellowship offered by the Czech (government) to PAIGC militants. There she was vice-president of *União Geral dos Estudantes da África Negra sob Dominação Colonial Portuguesa* - UGEAN (The General Union of Students from Black Africa under Portuguese Colonial Domination). In 1966 she joined PAIGC in Guinea Conakry, where she worked as a teacher at *Escola Piloto* during the years 1966–1971. In May of the same year, she married Amílcar Lopes Cabral, PAIGC's General Secretary. Ana Maria Cabral was one of the persons responsible for the publication of PAIGC's youth magazine *Blufo. Orgão dos Pioneiro*.

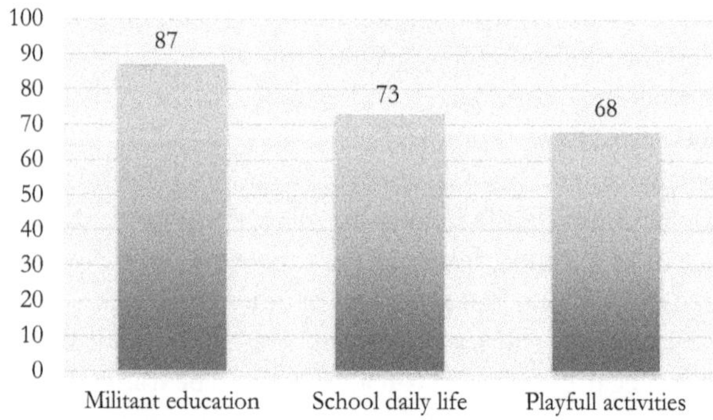

Fig. 2: Distribution of themes according to title entries on *Blufo* magazine. Source: Own elaboration based on *Blufo* youth magazine analysis.

> food conservation", "Modern techniques of conservation", cold conservation. (also texts) about women. I translated several things from this book 'Qu'est qui c'est'. Let me see if is there anything else, "On our planet earth", to explain what was a volcano, a seismograph, an earthquake, a fountain. [...] I translated, I adapted, about people around the world, about the Indians. All this to explain that there were other people in the world and not just people of Guinea Bissau. (Other themes like) The calabaceira,[13] the eucalyptus, the palm tree. I was translating and adapting (the stories from) this book, which was a very interesting book that I found when I went to a bookstore in Dakar. And found formidable to enrich our newspaper Blufo.

The broad range of topics approached in the magazine can roughly be divided in three groups according to their title, content and number of entries throughout 47 publications (see Fig. 2). The first group approached themes related with the Party militant education, which included articles related with history and culture of Guinea Bissau and Cape Verde, history of colonialism, history of the PAIGC liberation struggle and the news reports of internationalism of the struggles for liberation, such as the exchanges between the youth group Party Pioneers on the national level and with other Pioneers countries such as the USSR and the GDR; it includes also international visits that the school received; the visit of International Union of Students (UIE) representatives; or the United Nations Organization (ONU) observers in 1972 received particular attention. Militant education also included articles related with the Party anniversaries, important battles from the liberation struggle, or more international subjects and

13 African baobab's fruit.

celebrations of the Workers and Womens Day. Articles in this category were more about explaining to pupils, members of the Party Pioneers, and other readers the Party organization, principles and struggle – its reasons and objectives.

The second group, corresponds to the school's daily life, and here its included themes such as the student-teacher relationship (congratulations and farewell), school year results, end of the school year; students holiday reports; or mail exchanges between schools. The third group corresponds to the more playful activities, such as the crossword and observational games, with the objective for instance to encourage students to think in a more playful manner about history, local fruits, rivers, national locations and territorial divisions. It also had its educative side, by including in this third group articles related to deciphering nature and its elements already explained by Ana Maria Cabral, to which we can add articles about Soviet satellites sent to the moon, or the first man on Earth. In addition, there was also the presence of fables (local and international) in the magazine. The objective attached to them was to transmit an educative, behavioral and moral character.

The presence of these three thematic groups in the magazine, gave the Party the opportunity to explore themes that were not fully approached in the lessons published on the school manual produced by the Party. An important aspect of *Blufo* magazine, was the opportunity that it gave to students to participate in their own educational process. Although teachers were the first and main coordinators of the magazine, students actively participated in the magazine through correspondence between schools, sharing their experiences when travelling abroad, or simple by contributing with drawings that would illustrate the text in the magazine (see Fig. 3).

The Figure 3, represents one of the examples of the pupil participation in the magazine. On the top left of the image is the Party Pioneers emblem, followed by the title and the drawing made by the school pupil Albino N'Deque. The text that serves as descriptive of the drawing says, "The Portuguese colonialist days are numbered in our land, from where they will be shamefully expelled." The drawing serve as a representation of how "pupils" understood the struggle and its outcomes, especially the end of the colonial regime. The draw also reflects situation of political and anti-colonial education that PAIGC was developing in the territory and how pupils interpreted a translated the message and learnings in their drawings.

Fig. 3: First Page of *Blufo* youth magazine n. 39 from December 1972. Source: Archive Fundação Amílcar Cabral.

The magazine as a decolonization instrument during the PAIGC's liberation struggle: Selected issues

To understand colonialism and the colonizer's work, one must understand it in its diverse dimensions:

> "the colonizer not only seized land, but also minds. If colonialism's influence had been merely the control of land that would have required only one form of resistance, but

> when information is also colonized, it is essential that resistance must interrogate issues related to education, information and intellectual transformations."[14]

This process of decolonizing the minds was an important step in the liberation struggle, here understood as a social and political phenomenon that I define as an individual-collective process-response of people who, becoming conscious of racialization, dehumanization, oppression and exploitation through which they are subjugated under colonial-oppressive government inside and outside their 'country', organize themselves to dismantle/destroy the institutions and practices to which they are subjugated, employing for this end any means at their disposal – whether violent acts, such as the armed guerilla struggle, or nonviolent acts, such as strikes, education projects and programs, or cultural and civil resistance, or any combination thereof.

Therefore, political education in the sense of understanding the political, social, economic, and psychological characteristics of colonialism and the process of dismantling it was transversal and by no means confined to schools. It is not unexpected that political education as an important aspect of the PAIGC political education, was heavily present in the articles in the youth magazine. Frantz Fanon, whose writings inspired many of the protagonists of the decolonization movement, had defended in "The Wretched of the Earth" the need for "political teaching" as an integral part of the decolonization process:

> The greatest task before us is to understand at each moment what is happening in our country. We ought not to cultivate the exceptional or to seek for a hero, who is another form of leader. We ought to uplift the people; we must develop their brains, fill them with ideas, change them and make them into human beings. We once more come up against that obsession of ours –which we would like to see shared by all African politicians – about the need for effort to be well informed, for work which is enlightened and freed from its historic intellectual darkness. To hold a responsible position in an underdeveloped country is to know that in the end everything depends on the education of the masses, on the raising of the level of thought, and on what we are too quick to call "political teaching".[15]

In the following, I shall focus in three aspects about the presence of direct Party-political teachings present in *Blufo* magazine. They are, the political education of the Party Pioneers; followed by the gender equity policy defended by the Party; and last the internationalism of the liberation struggle.

14 George J. Sefa and Arlo Kempf, *Anti-Colonialism and Education. The Politics of Resistance* (Rotterdam: Sense Publishers, 2006), ix.

15 Frantz Fanon, *The Wretched of the Earth* (New York: Grove Press, 1963), 197.

a) The political education of the PAIGC Party Pioneers

In the year of 1966 and simultaneously with the inauguration of the boarding school Escola Piloto, PAIGC created the youth organization named Pioneiros do Partido. The goals behind the creation of this group that what was defined as an "organization of vanguard" for youth between the ages of 10 and 15 years old who had concluded the first year of primary education, was according to their statutes Estatutos do Pioneiro do Partido,[16] to contribute to a good education for children, based and acting on the principles of the Party. Other goals included the reinforcement of the children's love for the Guinean and Capeverdean people, their dedication to the struggle, the respect for the family and schools, and the student "fondness for justice, work, progress, and liberty."[17]

These goals and the activities designed around these key words, had the aim to make all members of this youth organization as "worthy militants" of the Party and "conscious citizens" with great responsibilities in the future construction of the country and the "uncompromising defense of the conquest of the revolution."[18] It was under the slogan "Education – Work – Struggle" and the salutation "By the PAIGC, strength, light, and guidance for our nation",[19] that the Party started to train what he would consider to be "the best sons" of the nation, namely the pioneer and militant student.

Considered to become the vanguard of the struggle, the pioneers characteristic included the love for "justice, work, progress and freedom"; to be a good student that seek to be better through the everyday activities, disciplined, responsible and organized and "a good friend of his comrades [that] seeks friendship every day with all the children of his school, of his land and of the world."[20] With the *Blufo* publication in the same year, the youth magazine became an important extracurricular instrument for the training of the PAIGC Pioneers. The first number of *Blufo* youth magazine from 1966 opened with the following, statement:

> "Long life to National Liberation
> With the creation of the newspaper 'Blufo', the youth of our country contributes to the achievement of a great objective of our Party. 'Blufo' is a newspaper of the P.A.I.G.C pioneers. It will be the voice of our Youth guided by our great Party that courageously launched itself in the national liberation struggle of our people in Guinea and in

16 Translation: Statutes of the Party Pioneers.

17 Ibid.

18 Ibid.

19 Ibid.

20 PAIGC, *O nosso livro 4ª classe* (Uppsala: Wretmans Boytryckeri AB, n.d.), 20.

> Cape Verde. We pay a big tribute to our Party, to our brave people and to our heroic combatants, that after three years of hard fighting against the enemy, achieved great victories. We are confident that our brave people, guided by our Party, will soon have its total and complete independence.
> Long life to PAIGC, vanguards of our people in the national liberation struggle!
> Long life to the people of Guinea and Cape Verde!
> Death to the Portuguese colonialists!"

The statement is clear with regard to whom PAIGC's struggle for independence was directed to: The objective was to prepare the future generation of the free and independent country and integrate a new generation in Party principles and politics. One important aspect present in this article and one of PAIGC's political education principles was the difference that the text draws between Portuguese people and Portuguese colonialists. The last phrase "Death to the Portuguese colonialists!" is a clear example of PAIGC political education and lines out against whom the struggle was fought. The phrase makes also clear that the ultimate goal of the struggle was for the "total and complete independence."

The language may be considered today as inappropriate for a youth magazine. However, it's important to contextualize such wording in the reality of daily life and the objectives and process of the struggle. Maria da Boal,[21] director of PAIGC *Escola Piloto* in Conakry (1969–1974), points to the importance of the presence of the political education aspect in PAIGC's developed learning/teaching instruments such as *Blufo*:

> Constantly we received the news that the comrade went [to the front] and stayed [died]. And so, there was this environment of living the struggle, and the will to be free. It was

21 Born in 1934 in Tarrafal – Santiago – Cape Verde. Maria da Luz Boal, daughter of Cape Verdean small businessmen, attended primary school in Tarrafal, and moved to São Vicente Island to continue the preparatory studies, and later to Portugal to finish secondary school. Between 1956 and1961, she studied History and Philosophy in Coimbra and Lisbon. In 1961, together with her husband the Angolan medicine student Manuel Boal, she joined the group that clandestinely left Portugal. In the same year, she moved to Dakar where she at the same time that she worked at the PAIGC's office attended the course Propaedeutic and African History for two years at Dakar University. She participated in the elaboration of the PAIGC's school manuals. In 1969, she was nominated by Amílcar Cabral as the Director of *Escola Piloto*, where she kept her position until 1974. Between 1966 and1973, she was one of the persons responsible for the organization of the Teacher Course in Conakry. After the independence, she was the General Director of National Education in Bissau. During the *coup d' Etat* she moved to Cape Verde, where she continued to work in the educational area. Today she is retired and lives in Cape Verde.

Fig. 4: Cover of *Blufo* youth magazine n. 33 from November 1971.

so strong that those kids would draw the airplane, the rifle, the bombings. That was their world. […] We were politicians in that situation, it was difficult not to be. A child who comes from the liberated areas, who hears the bombings, you have to explain why there were bombings about colonialism, that he didn't see but that he was feeling.[22] You had to explain why the people decide to fight to be free from colonial oppression. Politics was so evident, that they had to know and understand.[23]

22 View Fig. 3, referring to a draw made by a student portraying the scene of a village bombing. The draw help to make clear Lilica Boal statement over how the war impacted the student routines and learnings.

23 Interview with Maria da Luz Boal, September 12, 2013.

Political education based in anti-colonial and decolonizing principles for, as it was called, conscientization continued all through the magazine's history. A further central aspect of this direct political education consisted in clear definitions of the organizational frame within which independence could be achieved. The PAIGC and its affiliated organizations embodied the collective purposes, as propagated in a special number of *Blufo* dedicated to the work and duties of the youth organization Party Pioneers, as the following texts reveals.

> Our emblem
> Do you know for example what is the meaning of our emblem? Here on the side is the emblem of the Pioneers, so you can see well how it is. In the center is written P.A.I.G.C with red letters. It is the name of our Party. Our salutation says: "For the P.A.I.G.C strength, light and guide of our people." It also says STUDY, WORK and STRUGGLE. It says STUDY, because you, Party Pioneer, must be studious, so that later you can build useful and beautiful things in our land, and defend them from the enemies of our people; it says WORK, because only working close to our people you can build tomorrow our land; it says STRUGGLE, because we the pioneers, should be interested in the struggle of our people and be ready to fight and defend everything that our people is achieving with the sacrifice of many heroes. You can also see the torch that burns with a red flame and that represents our national liberation struggle; the red star represents the Party that is the guide of our People; the yellow background symbolizes the African sun and the unity of our struggle in Africa; and finally the green palm tree leaves represent the natural wealth of Guinea and the shell or the sea flower represents Cape Verde. But is not enough to know the meaning of the emblem to really be a Pioneer. It's still necessary that we became an example in each moment, to our comrades, in the school, in study, in the street, in the tabanca (village) and in each place we are. [...] I promise, to study each day with more attention. Work each day with more will. Always fight with courage. To always deserve the title of the Pioneer of our Party. In the vanguard of the youth of our country. To give my contribution for the realization, of our party program, in the service of the national liberation, and the construction of peace, progress and happiness, of our people in Guinea and Cape Verde.[24]

Training conscious pupils who would become adults for "service of the national liberation, and the construction of peace, progress and happiness" was certainly the central concern in these statements. The first activity, studying, is salient here due to the direct interpellation to "you, party Pioneer". This partial focus on school attendants or students and the description of the results of their study – to "build useful and beautiful things in our land" – shows a strong image of youth and the future of the country. Both the act of schooling youth and the purpose

24 "O nosso emblema," *Blufo. Orgão dos Pioneiros do Partido*, July, 1967, 1–2.

of participating in a rather developmental future shifted the characterization of youth and the nature of the hitherto dominating form of religious schooling.

b) Gender equity political education in PAIGC policies

Both international women's day, the 8th of March and the contribution of women in the liberation struggle were often celebrated in the *Blufo* youth magazine. Titles such as "The women of Komo" reflecting the role of women in the Komo battle in March 1964; or articles on the ocassion of the 8th of March of 1967, 1969, 1970 and 1971 (under the title "Open letter to the women of our land"), or an article from 1968 with the title "We and the Soviet women", are referring to gender equity as a central element of the struggle for liberation.

> "The teacher also said that today every woman of our land must thank our Party, because it wants to end women's exploitation. Women in our land were exploited three times; by her parents, by the tradition and also by the colonialist. But there are several women in our land who understand what the Party wants, they understand that our land can advance only if everybody, men and women, work. Only with the work of all of us can our land develop. Today we find women in our liberated areas as militiamen, nurses, working in production (farmers), in teaching, as party officials, political commissars, etc. All these women do any of the work that the Party had given to them. This shows that the women of our land have already understood that the party wants them to be free."[25]

Gender equity was an important PAIGC policy as expressed in its directives from early 1960s:

> "Defend the rights of women, respect and make others respect them (whether as children, young girls or adults), but persuade the women of our country that their liberation must be their own achievement on the basis of their work, dedication to the Party, self-respect, personality and decisiveness toward everything that can act against their dignity."[26]

In practice the principle was being applied in the Party structures under the stipulation that at least two of the five members elected councils – village, sector, regional – should be women.[27]

25 "Felicitemos Todas as mulheres do Nosso Partido," *Blufo. Orgão dos Pioneiros do Partido*, January–June, 1968, 6.

26 PAIGC, "Palavras de Ordem," 1960s.

27 For more information about the role of women in PAIGC liberation struggle, Stephanie Urdgang, *Fighting Two Colonialism. Women in Guine-Bissau* (New York: Monthly Review Press, 1979), describes her visit to PAIGC liberated areas in Guinea Bissau,

The integration of such issues in the magazine, intended to create early awareness in the pupils' minds about the social structure they were living in, breaks the notions of inferiority of women, and explores several forms that oppression can have. The emancipation of women as essential to total liberation was one aspect of PAIGC political education.

c) Understanding the internationalism of the liberation struggle

During the late 1950s, 60s, and 70s the world was faced with dozens of African liberation and independence movements, with Africans claiming the sovereignty over their countries and lives. Several other African, as well as European, Asian and Latin American countries supported the liberation struggle. Socialist and non-socialist countries such as the German Democratic Republic, the Soviet Union, Romania, Bulgaria, Czechoslovakia, Hungary, and Sweden as well as Cuba, the Peoples Republic of China, Guinea Conakry, Senegal, Ghana, and Tanzania were part of the group of *países amigos* (friend countries) that supported the PAIGC's liberation struggle. It was also during this period that the Organization of Africa Unity (OUA) was created in Addis Ababa in 1963.

Internationalism, understood from a Marxist perspective, would mean "working whole- heartedly for the development of the revolutionary movement and the revolutionary struggle in *one's own* country, and supporting (by propaganda, sympathy, and material aid) *this struggle,* this, and *only this,* line, in *every* country without exception."[28] This constituted a further central aspect of PAIGC political education.

The presentation of the activities carried out in different countries in the magazine – from Amílcar Cabral or the Party Pioneers' visits abroad, the reception of international visitors to the struggle as the case of the special UN group in 1972, the international support received from Cuban doctors, or the Swedish publication of the PAIGC school manual, the group of woman that went to Ghana to study nursing, or a letter from old students studying abroad intended to make pupils conscious not just about the international network of the liberation struggle, but about understanding the international dimension itself. To conceive of colonialism, oppression and exploitation as being phenomena in

---

and her reflections and the interviews she had conducted with women during her visit to the territory.

28 Karl Marx and Friedrich Engels, "*Manifesto of the Communist Party*," Marxist Internet Archive, accessed November 16, 2016. https://www.marxists.org/archive/marx/works/download/pdf/Manifesto.pdf.

a broader sense together with the importance of collective work against them became a third departure from more traditional frames.

Blufo, the tensions between traditional and modern concepts of youth and its contributions for decolonization and "intellectual transformation"

By placing schools and a political education program as an integral part of its liberation project PAIGC organized according to its principle of cultural resistance[29] a more specific resistance front *i.e.* the education front. With the creation of *Blufo* youth magazine PAIGC created one important resistance and intellectual instrument whose goal was to achieve this "intellectual transformation".

As already mentioned, the word *Blufo* in traditional Balanta culture corresponds to one of the stadiums to achieve adulthood. In Guinea Bissau in the *Nhacra* and *Khuntoé*, one can identify several stages inside the *Blufo* category, namely the *Mpum*; *Nguadj*, *Mpebé*, *Fur*, *Nkuman*, *Nhghaé*. Only after the passage from these categories, the initiated assumes the social category of Tchõ (advanced *Blufo*). The circumcision occurs in a third grade called *Ntan-an*, where the circumcised youth after a period of time in the bushes where the youth pass through a period of assuming responsibilities.[30] According to the Balanta group, there is no specific age of when such rituals should occur, and an individual can be a *Blufo* until it's decided (personally and collectively) that such ritual should occur.

PAIGC created the Party Pioneers based on a western definition of youth as a transition from dependence to independence, and defined this group as people within the age range from 10 to 15 years old. In relation with education in the context of the struggle, this definition brought to the territory an idea of 'youth' that somehow was in conflict with African traditional values, that according to the African Youth Charter where 'youth' means "every person between the ages of 15 and 35 years old,"[31] an age range that is in complete dissonance with PAIGC Party Pioneers statutes, but in consonance with traditional Balanta principles. This tension between the African traditional and western modern concept of 'youth', according to teacher and student testimonies and

29 Amílcar Cabral, *Análise de alguns tipos de resistência* (Lisboa: Seara Nova, 1974).

30 Mário A. R. Cissoko, *Povo e Escola nos reinos felupes e noutras regiões da margem direita do Rio Cacheu*. Bissau: Agencia Sueca para o Desenvolvimento Internacional (ASDI), 1994, 16, accessed November 16, 2016.

31 African Union Commission, "African Youth Charter," accessed November 16, 2016, http://www.un.org/en/africa/osaa/pdf/au/african_youth_charter_2006.pdf.

experiences, was more visible in the daily school life, when the boarding school regulation and teacher expectation of behaviors from their students clashed with the students' traditional life in the villages under traditional values and practices.

Born from the special conditions of PAIGC liberation struggle and the necessity to give to offer to PAIGC students the opportunity to expand their horizons through reading and to know more about the process of the struggle for liberation through news reports, but also according to Ana Maria Cabral to, "help these young people the best we could, give as much as we had so they could face the reality more prepared and understand" the future and the goals of the struggle, *Blufo* can be considered a unique example of this practice in the context of the liberation struggles against Portuguese colonial regime, and it is likely to be a unique example in the history of education in the African continent during the anti-colonial struggle.

Written for and by the pupils and youth with ages between 10 and 15 years old, the magazine was received with great enthusiasm. However, testimonies report that the interest for the magazine superseded the group to whom it was directed. The adult population also became interested in the magazine and started to follow the publication, as Ana Maria Cabral described:

> "Later we came to find out that Blufo was the newspaper most read by all combatants (and that) they had learned to read (through Blufo). Imagine that for adults was Libertação,[32] but this (referring to Blufo) was the one everybody liked because it had stories, it had riddles, poems, it had a bit of everything. [...] The demand for Blufo was tremendous!"

The fact that *Blufo* surpassed the group of pupils for whom it was designed made it into a bridge between traditional and modern concepts of 'youth'. In the light that adults used the youth magazine as an instrument to teach and learn the skills of reading and writing, PAIGC's policies and practices in their mobilizing nature open the field for modes of organization and interaction that emerged in many contexts at that time and became epitomized as "The Pedagogy of the oppressed" following Paulo Freire's words.

32 *Libertação – Unidade e Luta* (Liberation – Unity and Struggle) was a PAIGC newspaper, written in Portuguese for PAIGC combatants. It stated to be published from 1960 onwards, being the last traced edition from 1971. In total 121 numbers were published during this period. After independence, the newspaper was substituted by the magazine *Nô Pintcha* (1975) and *O Militante* (The Militant) published between 1977 and 1979.

In the same way that the PAIGC militant teachers decided to start the publication in 1966 and followed its publication for eight years despite the difficulties imposed by the war, January of 1973, the same month of the assassination of Amílcar Cabral marked the end of *Blufo* publication. The war situation that emerged with Cabral's death and the emergency to gain independence on the political and armed field, left very few available time for teachers and students to continue to work on the publication. Between the period that marked the recognition of Guinea- Bissau independence by the Portuguese regime, and transfer of PAIGC government and educational structure form Conakry to Bissau, the several challenges that militants faced during the country reconstruction and finally the military coup in 1980, didn't make it possible for teachers to return to the publication of *Blufo*.

Today, and due to the partially destruction of PAIGC archives organized still during the struggle, and the lack of enough material, besides the interviews with those who produced or were influenced by the magazine, it is impossible to have a quantitative idea of the impact of *Blufo*. To today, there is no knowledge of how many copies of each issue of the magazine were made during the eight years existence and therefore no information about how many copies circulated. Nonetheless, in the process of decolonization of the minds and "intellectual transformation," meaning one engaging and promote activities of creating and consciously using various strategies to liberate oneself, *Blufo* for the wide range of news that it approached, the new themes that it introduced throughout its articles, the focus on restoring and creation of values, but especially by its high political content, made *Blufo* an important decolonization instrument during the struggle.

By the subjects it approached and as immediate product of the struggle, the teachers and students who were directly attached to *Blufo* through the magazine were able to create this extra-curricular pedagogical material developed and use it toward decolonization in the context of revolutionary education.

Interviews

Interview with Ana Maria Cabral, September 5, 2013.

Interview with Maria da Luz Boal, September 12, 2013.

Interview with Maria Amélia Araújo, September 26, 2013.

Literature

African Union Commission. African Youth Charter. Accessed November 16, 2016. http://www.un.org/en/africa/osaa/pdf/au/african_youth_charter_2006.pdf.

Borges, Sónia Vaz. *Militant Education, Liberation Struggle, Consciousness. The PAIGC Education in Guinea Bissau 1963–1978*. Frankfurt: Peter Lang, 2019.

Blufo. Orgão dos Pioneiros do Partido, 1966–1973.

Cabral, Amílcar. *Análise de alguns tipos de resistência*. Lisbon: Seara Nova, 1974.

Cissoko, Mário A. R. *Povo e Escola. Os Reinos Felupes e Noutras regiões da Margem Direita do Rio Cacheu*. Bissau: Agência Sueca para o Desenvolvimento Internacional, 1994.

Fanon, Frantz. *The Wretched of the Earth*. New York: Grove Press, 1963.

Freire, Paulo. *Cartas à Guiné-Bissau. Registo de uma experiência em processo*. Lisbon: Moraes Editores, 1978.

Freire, Paulo. *The Pedagogy of the Oppressed*. New York: Bloomsbury, 2000.

Freire, Paulo. Amílcar Cabral. O Pedagogo da Revolução. Accessed November 18, 2016. http://forumeja.org.br/files/amilcar.pdf.

Marx, Karl, and Friederich Engels. Manifesto of the Communist Party. Marxist Internet Archive. Accessed November 16, 2016. https://www.marxists.org/archive/marx/works/download/pdf/Manifesto.pdf.

PAIGC. *Palavras de Ordem*. N.d. (1960s).

PAIGC. *Estatutos dos Pioneiros do Partido*. n.d.

PAIGC. *O nosso livro 4ª classe*. Uppsala: Wretmans Boytryckeri AB, n.d.

PAIGC. *Reconstrução Nacional, Quadros Formados pelo P.A.I.G.C Desde o Início da Luta*. n.d., 1972.

PAIGC. *Comissariado de Estado da Educação Nacional, Educação, Tarefa de Toda a Sociedade*. Républica da Guiné-Bissau: n.d., 1978.

Sefa, George J., and Arlo Kempf. *Anti-Colonialism and Education. The Politics of Resistance*. Rotterdam: Sense Publishers, 2006.

Sharp, Lesley A. *The Sacrificed Generation. Youth, History, and the Colonized Mind in Madagascar*. California: University of California, 2002.

Urdgang, Stephanie. *Fighting Two Colonialisms. Women in Guinea-Bissau*. New York: Monthly Review Press, 1979.

Tim Kaiser, Ingrid Miethe, Alexandra Piepiorka

Educational Transfers as Means of Decolonization in Vietnam and Mozambique

Abstract Decolonization took place in the broader context of the Cold War and the existence of specific socialist entanglements throughout the world. In their comparative analysis of educational transfers within the socialist world in the era of decolonization, the authors present the establishment of a specific type of institution: the worker-peasant complementary education. Following their establishment and dissemination in post-colonial Vietnam and Mozambique, their discussion focuses on the crucial issue of the production of new forms of dependency, now within the socialist world-system, during decolonization. Their study offers surprising results: Applying a meticulously empirical approach, the authors can demonstrate that transfers were mostly locally activated and far from being imposed from the outside. The authors argue that local actors led the process all along, adapted the imported type of institutions to local needs and brought about genuine educational hybrids. By challenging the notion of new dependencies, the authors argue that these cases of educational transfers come close to an idea of 'true decolonization'.

Keywords: Vietnam, Mozambique, educational transfer, socialist cooperation, workers' faculty

Introduction

Decolonization can be understood as the process of gaining formal independence by overseas colonial territories that were formerly under the rule of an imperial power.[1] But "decolonization did not just end with the transfer of political power to formerly colonized peoples. It was a process of political, social, economic and cultural transformation."[2] This process has often been described either from the viewpoint of the colonial powers or from the perspective of former colonies as nationalist narratives that include anti-colonial struggles and the subsequent building of independent states. In the latter case, "methodological nationalism"[3]

1 John Springhall, *Decolonization since 1945: The Collapse of European Overseas Empires* (Houndmills, Basingstoke, Hampshire, New York: Palgrave, 2001), 2.

2 Leslie James and Elisabeth Leake, "Introduction," in *Decolonization and the Cold War: Negotiating independence*, ed. Leslie James and Elisabeth Leake (London: Bloomsbury Academic, 2015), 3.

3 Roger Dale and Susan L. Robertson, "Beyond Methodological 'isms' in Comparative Education in an Era of Globalization," in *International Handbook of Comparative*

was and is often amplified by the desire of politicians and scientists in the former colonies to portray the post-independence construction of states as a largely independent, national affair.[4]

Yet, during the open-ended processes of decolonization, governments of the newly independent states aiming at building efficient state structures often turned to other countries in their search for inspiration and examples for how to create and run a modern state. In many cases, the model that was followed was chosen based on a number of factors, such as the newly independent state's leadership's ideological world view, historical and post-colonial[5] international relations of the respective country, or the willingness of other countries to provide guidance and resources for post-colonial development without infringing too much on national sovereignty often won at a high price in the struggle for independence.[6] Thus, decolonization and the construction of independent states drew on and resulted in complex transfer processes, including transfers of educational policies and institutions. However, such educational transfers[7] and their role in the creation of newly independent states remain largely unexplored so far. Especially educational transfers between the "Second" (the Soviet Union (USSR) and other European socialist countries) and countries of the "Third World" following a socialist development path remain under-researched and those studies

---

Education, ed. Robert Cowen and Andreas M. Kazamias (Dordrecht: Springer Netherlands, 2009), 1113–1128.

4 Springhall, *Decolonization;* Dietmar Rothermund, *The Routledge Companion to Decolonization* (London, New York: Routledge, 2006); Martin Shipway, *Decolonization and Its Impact: A Comparative Approach to the End of the Colonial Empires* (Malden/Mass.: Blackwell Pub, 2008).

5 We use the term "post-colonial" here to refer to the historic period that immediately followed the end of colonialism in the respective countries. See also Michael Crossley and Leon Tikly, "Postcolonial perspectives and comparative and international research in education: a critical introduction," *Comparative Education* 40, no. 2 (2004): 147–156.

6 Ragna Boden, "Jakarta, 1965: Zur Rolle kommunistischer Parteien in der Dritten Welt," in *Die Sowjetunion und die Dritte Welt, Band 99*, ed. Andreas Hilger (München: Oldenbourg Wissenschaftsverlag, 2009), 132; Odd A. Westad, *The Global Cold War: Third World Interventions and the Making of Our Times* (Cambridge, New York: Cambridge University Press, 2005).

7 Educational transfers are commonly understood as "the movement of educational ideas, institutions or practices across national borders." Jason Beech, "The Theme of Educational Transfer in Comparative Education: a view over time," *Research in Comparative and International Education* 1, no. 1 (2006): 2.

that exist largely focus on bilateral international relations and cooperation or on projects in countries of the "Second World".[8]

To provide examples of educational transfers and their impact in the early post-colonial history, we focus on the history of particular educational institutions, the Worker-Peasant Complementary Education Schools of the Democratic Republic of Vietnam (DRV) and the FACOTRAV of the People's Republic of Mozambique (PRM), as well as the transfer processes associated with their establishment.[9] These institutions embodied a very specific combination of goals: to quickly prepare workers and peasants for entry into higher education, and to contribute to the creation of a well-trained intelligentsia for the new states. This

---

8 Martin Aust, "Russland und die Sowjetunion in der Globalgeschichte," in *Globalisierung imperial und sozialistisch: Russland und die Sowjetunion in der Globalgeschichte 1851–1991*, ed. Martin Aust (Frankfurt am Main: Campus Frankfurt/New York, 2013), 13–38; Ragna Boden, "Globalisierung sowjetisch: Der Kulturtransfer in die Dritte Welt," in *Globalisierung imperial und sozialistisch: Russland und die Sowjetunion in der Globalgeschichte 1851–1991*, ed. Martin Aust (Frankfurt am Main: Campus Frankfurt/New York, 2013), 425–42; Andreas Hilger, "Sowjetunion, Staatssozialismus und Dritte Welt 1945–1991," in *Die Sowjetunion und die Dritte Welt*, ed. Andreas Hilger (München: Oldenbourg Wissenschaftsverlag, 2009), 7–17.
Studies focusing on such transfers include for example: Tom G. Griffiths and Euridice Charon Cardona, "Education for Social Transformation: Soviet University Education Aid in the Cold War Capitalist World-System," *European Education* 47, no. 3 (2015): 226–241; Tom G. Griffiths and Zsuzsa Millei, ed., *Logics of Socialist Education: Engaging with Crisis, Insecurity and Uncertainty* (Dordrecht, New York: Springer, 2013); Constantin Katsakioris, "Soviet Lessons for Arab Modernization: Soviet Educational Aid to Arab Countries after 1956," *Journal of Modern European History* 8, no. 1 (2010): 85–106; Jane Schuch, *Mosambik im pädagogischen Raum der DDR: Eine bildanalytische Studie zur "Schule der Freundschaft" in Stassfurt* (Wiesbaden: Springer, 2013); Gita Steiner-Khamsi and Ines Stolpe, *Educational Import: Local Encounters with Global Forces in Mongolia* (New York: Palgrave Macmillan, 2006); Brigitte Studer, *The Transnational World of the Cominternians* (Houndmills, Basingstoke, Hampshire: Palgrave Macmillan, 2015).

9 This paper is part of the research project "Globalization of an educational idea: Workers' Faculties in Cuba, Mozambique and Vietnam" carried out at the University of Gießen under the leadership of Prof. Ingrid Miethe. It is funded by the German Research Foundation (Deutsche Forschungsgemeinschaft, DFG) as projects MI 667/7-1 and MI 667/7-2. The case studies rely on data gathered during archival research and interviews in Vietnam (note that the exact spelling of Vietnamese documents is replicated here even when the original does not include diacritics) and Mozambique, complementing this material with research in archives of the former German Democratic Republic and interviews with former Eastern German educational experts working in Mozambique.

selection of cases covers a time span from the mid-1950s to the late 1980s as well as two very different cultural contexts. Both cases, however, share that the respective institutions were established during a period of post-colonial state building shortly after achieving independence. Both institutions' also have in common that their origins lie in complex transfer processes that can ultimately be traced back to the institution of the so called Soviet Workers' Faculty, an early result of the Russian Revolution of 1917.

The question of power relations between countries involved in educational transfers has received wide attention in the field of comparative education. For example, Phillips and Ochs have provided a model that describes a continuum between two extremes. On one end of the continuum one finds transfers that are voluntarily driven by independent countries and in which foreign ideas are introduced by general influence. On the other end, they locate transfers "imposed" by an occupying force on a dependent country.[10] Educational transfers can thus be the results of dependency or subordination or might lead to new dependencies. Employing them as a means of decolonization seems in this light to constitute a rather ambiguous strategy. However, we argue that in the cases presented here, educational transfers indeed served as means of building independent states.[11] They worked in this way first by becoming part and parcel of the very creation of educational systems of newly independent countries; and second by contributing to the training of a new, national intelligentsia supporting the building of independent states.

---

10 Kimberly Ochs and David Phillips, "Processes of Educational Borrowing in Historical Context," in *Educational Policy Borrowing: Historical Perspectives,* ed. David Phillips and Kimberly Ochs (Didcot: Symposium, 2004), 7–24.

11 This does of course not mean that the creation of the Vietnamese and Mozambican institutions were not connected to internal conflicts over the development of these newly independent states. However, in this text we are concerned with inter-state power relations between the actors and states involved in the transfer processes, not with power struggles or conflicting interests within the respective societies. Furthermore, compared to, for example, the creation of Worker-and-Peasant-Faculties in the GDR, such conflicts played a minor role in the creation of the Vietnamese and Mozambican institutions. Ingrid Miethe, *Bildung und soziale Ungleichheit in der DDR: Möglichkeiten und Grenzen einer gegenprivilegierenden Bildungspolitik* (Opladen, Farmington Hills: Verlag Barbara Budrich, 2007). See the interplay of the creation of the respective institutions, power struggles, and conflicts within these societies. Ingrid Miethe, Tim Kaiser, Tobias Kriele, and Alexandra Piepiorka, *Globalisation of an Educational Idea: Workers' Faculties in Eastern Germany, Vietnam, Cuba and Mozambique* (Berlin, Boston: De Gruyter Oldenbourg, 2019).

Educational transfers for decolonization and state building: Case studies of Vietnam and Mozambique

As stated in the introduction, transfer processes that hark back to the Soviet Rabfak (short for Rabochiy fakultet, Workers' Faculty) played an important role in the history of both the Vietnamese Worker-Peasant Complementary Education Schools and the Mozambican FACOTRAV. The Rabfak itself was invented in 1919 in Soviet Russia and was widespread in the Soviet Union until 1941. The post-revolutionary educational reform of 1918 allowed every citizen from the age of 16 access to university without the need for any formal qualification. As a result, many students failed in university and better preparation became necessary. In this context, the Rabfak's function was to prepare workers and peasants for university entrance.[12] However, the entrance of workers into higher education was not an end in itself, but the Rabfak was intended to play a political role within the university and wider society as well. Therefore, a very specific set of three goals was combined in one institution: First, "making over" the higher education institutions; second, to train new cadres of specialists; and third, to create a new Soviet intelligentsia.[13] It was this specific combination of goals that set the Rabfak apart from other educational institutions.

The first Rabfak was founded at the institute for economics "G. V. Plechanov" in Moscow. From September 1920 on Rabfaks were founded all over Soviet Russia and other Soviet Republics.[14] Up to 1930, Rabfaks could be part of a university as well as of a factory. After 1930 the system was restructured so that all Rabfaks had to be assigned to a university. At the same time the number of Rabfaks and their students increased: In the 1932/33 academic year 339,517 students were enrolled in 1,025 Rabfaks.[15] Thereafter numbers decreased and by the beginning of World War II in the Soviet Union (1941) the Rabfaks were closed. However, during a long period from the end of World War II until the 1980s, educational

12 Harley D. Balzer, "Workers' Faculties and the Development of Science Cadres in the First Decade of Soviet Power," in *The Social Direction of the Public Sciences: Causes and Consequences of Co-operation between Scientists and Non-Scientific Groups*, ed. Stuart Blume et al. (Dordrecht: Springer Netherlands, 1987), 193–211; Katunceva, N. M., *Rol' rabočich fakul'tetov v formirovanii kadrov narodnoj intelligencii v SSSR [The Role of the Workers' Faculty in the Creation of the People's Cadres Intelligentsia]* (Moscow, 1966); Fredrika M. Tandler, "*The Workers' Faculty (Rabfak) System in the USSR*," (PhD diss., Columbia University, 1955).

13 Tandler, "The Workers' Faculty," 317.

14 Ibid., 48–55.

15 Katunceva, *The Role*, 68–71.

transfers led to the establishment of institutions that drew on the Rabfak model in European, Asian, African, and American countries.[16] Notably, the People's Republic of China (PRC) and the German Democratic Republic (GDR) created institutions that built on the Rabfak model and which subsequently became models for other countries. The Chinese institutions became important for the creation of the Worker-Peasant Complementary Education Schools of the DRV, while the German Workers'-and-Peasants'-Faculty influenced the Mozambican FACOTRAV.

Educating Worker-Peasant Cadres: The Worker-Peasant Complementary Education Schools in the Democratic Republic of Vietnam

The Worker-Peasant Complementary Education Schools (Trường Bổ túc văn hóa công nông, W-P Schools) of the DRV were part of educational policies that aimed at enabling workers and peasants to enter higher education and thereby contribute to the building of an independent, socialist state. As will be shown below, both the Soviet Rabfak and the Chinese Worker-Peasant Accelerated Middle Schools, which in turn resulted from educational transfers between these two countries, influenced the creation of the respective Vietnamese institutions.

Faced with the legacy of colonial education,[17] educational campaigns for general and popular education which spanned the entire country, started shortly after the declaration of the independent DRV in September 1945 by the anti-colonial movement Việt Minh. These were promoted by the new leadership as a means of building an independent state and a new society, and quickly led to rising educational levels in the areas under the control of the Việt Minh during the anti-colonial war against France and the French-sponsored State of Vietnam between 1946 and 1954.[18]

16 John Connelly, *Captive University: The Sovietization of East German, Czech and Polish Higher Education, 1945–1956* (Chapel Hill: University of North Carolina Press, 2000); Tim Kaiser, Tobias Kriele, Ingrid Miethe, and Alexandra Piepiorka, "Educational Transfers in Postcolonial Contexts: Preliminary Results From Comparative Research on Workers' Faculties in Vietnam, Cuba, and Mozambique," *European Education* 47, no. 3 (2015): 242–259; Miethe, *Bildung und soziale Ungleichheit.*

17 By 1945, when Vietnam was declared an independent country, about 95 % of its population was illiterate. Alexander Woodside, "The Triumphs and Failures of Mass Education in Vietnam," *Pacific Affairs* 56, no. 3 (1983): 404.

18 Woodside, "The Triumphs," 405–406; Kim Ngoc Bao Ninh, *A World Transformed: The Politics of Culture in Revolutionary Vietnam, 1945–1965* (Ann Arbor: University of

From the beginning, the USSR and the PRC served as reference countries for the design of the Việt Minh's educational policies.[19] Corresponding educational transfers in many instances resulted from the experiences high-ranking Vietnamese revolutionaries had gained in these countries. Hồ Chí Minh, for example, had studied at the Comintern-run International Lenin School in Moscow and had worked as an instructor at both the Communist University for the Toilers of the East and its successor, the Scientific Institute for the Study of National and Colonial Problems, in the 1930s (both of these were Comintern institutions, too).[20] At the same time as Hồ Chí Minh, Nguyễn Khánh Toàn, who became Deputy Minister for Education in the DRV in 1946, was also working at the Scientific Institute.[21] Nguyễn Khánh Toàn had already started studying in the USSR in 1930, and joined the Chinese communists in Yenan[22] in 1939.[23] In their writings both Hồ Chí Minh and Nguyễn Khánh Toàn promoted the application of the educational experiences of the USSR and the PRC in the DRV.[24]

After the 1954 peace settlement and the division of Vietnam into two separate political entities the DRV was faced with the task of training cadres for the newly established state in the North. To make access to education more widely available and to prepare workers and peasants for new positions in an independent socialist state, an adult education program had already been created in the late 1940s under the name Complementary Education. It aimed at improving

---

Michigan Press, 2002); Thaveeporn Vasavakul, "*Schools and Politics in South and North Việt Nam: A Comparative Study of State Apparatus, State Policy, and State Power (1945–1965)*" (PhD diss., Cornell University, 1994).

19 See for example the folder *Tài liệu giới thiệu về tổ chức và kinh nghiệm ngành giáo dục ở Liên Xo và Trung Quốc năm 1951* Ministry of Education Fonds, Folder 4206, Vietnam National Archives Centre 3 (VNAC3), Hanoi.

20 Sophie Quinn-Judge, *Ho Chi Minh: The Missing Years 1919–1941* (London: Hurst & Co., 2003), 202–218.

21 Ibid., 218.

22 On educational policies of the Chinese Communist Party in Yenan see: Peter J. Seyboldt, *Yenan Education and the Chinese Revolution, 1937–1945* (PhD diss., Harvard University, 1969).

23 Nguyễn Thanh Tú. *GS. Nguyễn Khánh Toàn: Nhà kiến trúc sư trong giai đoạn đầu của nền giáo dục cách mạng*, accessed March 8, 2009, http://100years.vnu.edu.vn/BTDHQGHN/Vietnamese/C1778/c1779/2006/05/n7775/.

24 Respective works include for example Hồ Chí Minh's (written under his pen-name Trần Lực): Trần Lực, *Mấy kinh nghiệm Trung-Quốc mà chúng ta nên học* (Hà Nội: Nhà Xuất bản Sư thật, 1958); Trần Lực, "Cần công, kiệm học," *Giáo dục Nhân dân*, No. 6 (March, 1958): 31–32; Nguyễn Khánh Toàn. *Giáo dục dân chủ mới*. Bộ quốc gia giáo-dục, 1947.

the work skills of adults as well as carrying out political education; furthermore it was to supply cadres and workers for the state.[25] Despite such measures, only small numbers of people with worker or peasant background entered higher education after 1954, leaving the leadership of the ruling Vietnamese Workers' Party (VWP) disappointed with the class composition of those who were to become "core cadres" of the socialist state. In response, Worker-Peasant Complementary Education Schools (W-P Schools) were created as fast-track institutions preparing adult workers and peasants for higher education. Intended to close the gap that continued to exist between the educational level of cadres with worker-peasant background and the level required to enter universities or mid-level colleges, these institutions aimed at two goals: giving workers and peasants access to higher education, as well as at placing a group of "core" worker-peasant students in higher education institutions who would subsequently fill high-level positions instrumental to the construction of the socialist state. As the W-P Schools were administratively located within the Complementary Education system, they also formed an administrative link between popular adult education and higher education.[26]

The first of these institutions, The Central Worker-Peasant Complementary Education School (Central W-P School) started operating in Hanoi in 1956 with 584 students.[27] This first group of students graduated already after six months during which the students had completed a program equivalent to three years in the general education system, indicating that they had a relatively high educational level prior to entering the school.[28] In total, about 7,000 students graduated from the Central W-P School between 1956 and 1964. Many of them came to hold important positions in the state and the party after they had completed

25 Ninh, *A World Transformed*, 223–227.

26 Ban Bí thư khóa II, *Thông tri số 82-TT/TW về việc chọn học sinh thành phần công nông để học bổ túc cấp tốc về văn hoá*, 21.12.1955, accessed August 31, 2016, http://dangcongsan.vn/cpv/Modules/News/NewsDetail.aspx?co_id=28340670&cn_id=490786; Bộ Giáo dục, *Nghị định 43-NĐ thành lập trường bổ túc văn hóa cộng đồng [sic! công nông]*, 23.01.1956, accessed August 31, 2016, http://thuvienphapluat.vn/archive/Nghi-dinh/Nghi-dinh-43-ND-thanh-lap-truong-bo-tuc-van-hoa-cong-dong-vb22858t11.aspx.

27 Bộ Giáo dục, Nha Binh Dân học vụ, Trường Bổ túc văn hóa công nông, *Báo cáo 3 thang (3-4-5) ve tinh hinh hoc-sinh TBTVHCN*, VNAC3, Ministry of Education Fonds, Folder 5239, paginated 80–85.

28 Bộ Giáo dục, Vu giao duc cap III. *Số 3379/GD3. Tờ trình Bộ Giáo dục, Báo cáo tổng kết kinh nghiêm các chu trương cua Bộ Giáo dục về trường Bổ túc công nông*, 15.09.1964, VNAC3, Ministry of Education Fonds, Folder 4054, paginated 1–9.

their university studies. The most prominent graduate served as Prime Minister of the Socialist Republic of Vietnam from 1997 to 2006.[29]

While the Central W-P School was a quite successful institution in terms of number of graduates, the class composition of its student body did not conform to the goals initially formulated as a very large percentage of the students had formerly worked in administrative positions and/or came from a petty bourgeois background.[30] While it is unlikely that the numbers of workers and peasants were kept low on purpose, the urban location of the school as well as the admission criteria requiring an educational level equivalent to grade four of the general education system in fact worked to the disadvantage of workers and peasants, whose educational levels at the time were generally far lower.[31]

The Central Committee of the VWP seems to have been aware that the specific design and mission of the Central W-P School in practice removed it from the goal of Complementary Education to enable workers and peasants to run the new state[32]; and starting in 1959, a network of 8 provincial W-P Schools was set up throughout the DRV. These schools were to supply graduates primarily to vocational higher middle schools. The number of provincial Worker-Peasant Complementary Education Schools grew rapidly: by 1961 the total number of W-P Schools (including the Central W-P School) was 14. In total, the schools had 8,000 students in 1962.[33]

---

29 Ban Liên lạc Trường Bổ túc văn hóa công – nông trung ương và Trường Phổ thông lao động trung ương, *Thông tin về một số giáo viên, cán bộ nhân viên và học viên: Phụ bản cuốn: Một ngội trường cách mạng* (Hanoi: Nhà xuất bản giáo dục, 2005); Oanh, K, "Gặp mặt gần 1000 cựu học sinh bổ túc công nông," in *ViệtBáo.vn*, accessed November 14, 2013, http://vietbao.vn/Giao-duc/Gap-mat-gan-1000-cuu-hoc-sinh-bo-tuc-cong-nong/20503189/202.

30 Bộ Giáo dục, Vu giao duc cap III. *Số 3379/GD3.*

31 Out of a total of 62,000 people classified as technical and regular workers in the DRV, only about 17 % fulfilled this criteria in 1959. The educational level of peasants was generally even lower. *Đê cương đào tạo, bơi dương cán bộ giáo viên B.T.V.H., 1960,* VNAC3, Ministry of Education Fonds, Folder 1916, paginated 9–20.

32 Đang Lao Dong Viet Nam, Ban chap hanh trung uong, *So 93-NQ/TW. Nghi quyet vê viêc tăng cương lanh đao công tac bô tuc văn hoa cho can bô, công nhân, nông dân nhăm dây manh cach mang xa hôi chu nghia ơ miên Băc va dâu tranh thông nhât nươc nha,* 02.12.1959, VNAC3, Ministry of Education Fonds, Folder 3858, paginated 24–30.

33 Bộ Giáo dục, Bổ túc văn hóa, *Báo cáo chất lương các trường BTVH công nông và những đề nghị nham năng cao chất lượng những trường này,* 26.05.1962, VNAC3, Ministry of Education Fonds, Folder 3996, paginated 1–6.

The establishment of the provincial schools followed three arguments: First, for the construction of socialism larger numbers of mid-level technical cadres were required as quick as possible.[34] Secondly, the number of students from among workers and peasants had remained lower than expected in the Central W-P School.[35] Thirdly, implementation of the class-line regarding cadre training as well as regarding vocational middle schools and universities should be strengthened.[36] The differences between the provincial schools and the Central W-P School highlight problems encountered while trying to establish the institutions of the new state on the basis of the masses of workers and peasants with very low levels of education: On one hand more students of these schools had a worker-peasant background or were actual workers and peasants prior to entering the schools. On the other hand, the bulk of these students were clearly not expected to move on to universities, but to vocational middle schools. Their prospects to rise to high level positions in the party and the state were thereby much more constricted than those of Central W-P School graduates. Additionally, even the lower educational levels required to enter the provincial W-P Schools as well as the education provided there proved too ambitious for many applicants and students.[37]

The Vietnamese attempt to open fast-track channels for workers and peasants into higher education was short-lived, as all but one of the W-P Schools had been closed again by 1964. The advantages of preparing a group of adult workers and peasants on a short-track for entry into higher education in dedicated schools was now regarded as being outweighed by the difficulties associated with this policy, especially in light of the large numbers of people with worker-peasant background who were now graduating from the general education system.[38]

---

34 Bo Giao Duc, *Số 380 NĐ, Nghị định v/v thành lập các TBTVHCN*, 22.07.1959, VNAC3, Ministry of Education Fonds, Folder 1261, paginated 1.

35 Bộ Giáo dục, *Nghị định 334*, 07.09.1959, VNAC3, Ministry of Education Fonds, Folder 3860, paginated 51–53; Bộ Giáo dục, Văn phòng, *Số 291/KH, Bổ súng thông tư 23 TT/GD*, 29.09.1959, VNAC3, Ministry of Education Fonds, Folder 3860, paginated 66–67.

36 Bo Giao duc, Van phong, *So 1237/KH, v/v mo cac Truong Su pham va BTVH cong-nong o dia phuong*, 16.06.1959, VNAC3, Ministry of Education Fonds, Folder 3859, paginated 1.

37 Bộ Giáo dục, Bổ túc văn hóa, *Báo cáo chất lương;* Bộ Giáo dục, Vụ Bổ túc văn hóa, *Tờ trinh Bộ Giáo dục về chất lương các trường Bổ túc văn hóa công nông*, 31.05.1962, VNAC3, Ministry of Education Fonds, Folder 3996, paginated 7–14.

38 Bộ Giáo dục, Vụ Giáo dục cấp III, *Ph/ Hương mới đối với trường BTVH*, VNAC3, Ministry of Education Fonds, Folder 4054, paginated 10–14.

Experiences of both the USSR and the PRC were influential in the creation of the W-P Schools, reflecting the above described general orientations towards the educational policies of these countries. Nguyễn Duy Quý claims that the idea for the Central W-P School had been brought to the DRV by Hồ Chí Minh from the USSR.[39] While the general idea of the Rabfak was certainly known to Vietnamese educators who had spent time at universities in the USSR in the 1920s and 1930s[40], it was a study tour to the PRC by Vice-Minister for Education Nguyễn Khánh Toàn[41] in September 1954 that provided information on the concrete design of similar institutions in the PRC and initiated the establishment of the W-P Central School. Yet, what Nguyễn Khánh Toàn saw when visiting the PRC in 1954 was in turn a reflection of the Soviet educational system.[42] In 1951, a Chinese version of Workers' Faculties, the Worker-Peasant Accelerated Middle Schools[43], had been established and were the subject of Nguyễn Khánh Toàn's report on his study tour in the PRC.[44] These schools served as a stepping stone in the transfer of the Soviet Workers' Faculty to the DRV and as a result, the concrete institutional design of the Vietnamese W-P Schools was much closer to that of the Chinese schools. First of all, like the Chinese institutions, the Vietnamese W-P Schools were *schools*, not *faculties*. Yet, as they were not attached to a

39 Interview 27.07.2011, Nguyễn Duy Quý was a teacher at the Central W-P School and later became one of the most prominent social scientists in Vietnam. Ban Liên lạc, *Thông tin*, 25–26.

40 For example, Nguyễn Khánh Toàn made an explicit reference to the Rabfak in a text about the DRV's education system in the 1950s.

Nguyễn Khánh Toàn, "Успехи культурного строительства в Демократической Республике Вьетнам," in *Демократическая Республика Вьетнам 1945–1960*, ed. A. A. Guber and Nguyễn Khánh Toàn (Moscow: Izdatel'stvo Vostočnoj literatury, 1960), 194.

41 At that time, Nguyễn Khánh Toàn was also the highest ranking VWP member in the Ministry of Education.

42 Ninh, *A World*, 211.

43 Erik E. Christy, "Influence of the Soviet Union on Chinese Higher Educational and Scientific Development: 1920–1950," (PhD diss., University of Oregon, 1986), 1128–1143; Suzanne Pepper, *Radicalism and education reform in 20th-century China: The search for an ideal development model* (Cambridge [England], New York: Cambridge University Press, 2000), 183–189; Robert Taylor, *China's intellectual dilemma: Politics and university enrolment, 1949–1978* (Vancouver: University of British Columbia Press, 1981), 16–39.

44 Nguyen Khanh Toan, *Bao cao trung Trung uong Dang ve ket qua nghien cuu mot so van de giao duc o Trung Quoc*. N.d., VNAC3, Office of the Premier Fonds, 1945–1954, ML 02, Folder 2871, paginated 37–80.

university, as the Chinese Worker-Peasant Accelerated Middle Schools were attached to universities, the Vietnamese W-P Schools were also not simply a copy of the institutional design of the Chinese schools. While in the USSR Rabfaks had at some point been an integral part of higher education institutions and in the PRC some institutional linkage between the schools and the universities still existed, no administrative ties to higher education existed in the DRV. In the DRV, the W-P Schools were much closer connected to the popular education efforts than in the PRC, as they came under the administration of the Ministry of Education's department for Popular Education and later under the department for Complementary Education, while in the PRC the schools were administratively located in the Ministry of Higher Education.

Despite the traceable influence of Soviet and Chinese institutions, the transfer process was initiated by Vietnamese actors, most visibly Nguyễn Khánh Toàn, who actively pursued an interest in the educational systems and experiences of these countries. Given a shared ideological orientation as well as the personal relations they had with these countries, it is unsurprising that Vietnamese decision makers deemed solutions from these educational systems as suitable to the problems they identified at home when faced with the task to build a new education system and a new state. Yet, rather than copying wholesale foreign models, the W-P Schools were fitted into the existing institutional setting and, after an initial phase of experimentation, to local conditions such as the educational levels of Vietnamese workers and peasants. After the initial transfer led to the creation of the Central W-P School, the subsequent creation of the provincial W-P Schools and the eventual closure of the schools took place in response to experiences gained within the DRV, not with reference to the development of the respective Soviet or Chinese institutions.

Educating former liberation fighters: The FACOTRAV in the People's Republic of Mozambique

Transfer processes also led to the creation of the Faculty for Former Combatants and Vanguard Workers (*Faculdade para Antigos Combatentes e Trabalhadores de Vanguarda*, FACOTRAV) in Mozambique. Although as described in detail below the transfer processes were very different from those in the above case of Vietnam, the goals of the FACOTRAV were similar to that of the W-P Schools. The FACOTRAV's intended function was to quickly provide adults with education equivalent to secondary school in the framework of the university. Its target group consisted of former combatants of the independence movement and select workers who were delegated by their workplaces. Additional requirements were an educational level of six years and five years of either professional experience or participation in the independence movement.[45] The FACOTRAV was supposed to contribute to the construction of an independent, socialist Mozambique, and the quick training of urgently needed Mozambican cadres was portrayed as a "decisive factor in the economic and social development" of the country.[46]

Throughout the independence struggle (1964–1974) education had been considered to be a priority issue for FRELIMO independence movement.[47] In the areas under its control, literacy campaigns were carried out and primary schools for the liberation fighters and their children were created from 1965 onwards. This rudimentary schooling system was sustained by a considerable influx of foreign teacher. These included for example teachers from the GDR who came in the framework of agreements with the East German Solidarity Committee[48], but also individuals from non-socialist countries. Furthermore, a secondary school (*Instituto Moçambicano*) offered higher education for Mozambicans in Dar-es-Salaam (Tanzania) and selected activist were sent abroad for further studies, preferably but not exclusively to countries with a socialist orientation.[49]

Shortly after independence was achieved in 1975, the FRELIMO government was challenged by the *Resistência Nacional Moçambicana* (RENAMO) resulting

45 *O que é o Curso Pré-Universitário da Faculdade de Antigos Combatentes e Trabalhadores de Vanguarda*? (Maputo, Universidade Eduardo Mondlane, November 1985), 9. AHM (Arquivo Histórico de Moçambique), documentation Ganhão, box 16, not paginated.

46 *Curriculum do Curso Pré-Universitário da Faculdade para Antigos Combatentes e Trabalhadores de Vanguarda* (Maputo, Universidade Eduardo Mondlane, November 1985), 3. AHM, documentation Ganhão, box 16, not paginated.

47 Anton Johnston, "The Mozambican State and Education," in *Education and Social Transition in the Third World*, ed. Martin Carnoy and Joel Samoff (Princeton, Oxford: Princeton University Press, 1990), 279–282; Eduardo Mondlane, *Kampf um Mosambik* (Frankfurt: März Verlag, 1970), 80–103, 241–249.

48 Jason Verber, "True to the Politics of Frelimo? Teaching Socialism at the Schule der Freundschaft, 1981–1990," in *Comrades of Color: East Germany in the Cold War World*, ed. Quinn Slobodian (Oxford, New York: Berghahn Books, 2015), 193.

49 Michael Cross, *An Unfulfilled Promise: Transforming Schools in Mozambique* (Addis Adaba: Organisation for Social Science Research in Eastern and Southern Africa, 2011), 49–55; Buendía Miguel Gómez, *Educação Moçambicana. História de um processo: 1962–1984* (Maputo: Livraria Universitária, 1999), 91–161; Anton Johnston, *Study, Produce, and Combat! Education and the Mozambican State 1962–1984* (Stockholm: Institute of International Education, University of Stockholm, 1989), 68–84; Salvador André Zawangoni, *A FRELIMO e a Formação do Homem Novo (1964–1974 e 1975–1982)* (Maputo: CEDEDIMA - Central Impressora e Editora de Maputo, 2007), 36–86.

in an armed conflict that reflected Cold War dynamics and severely inhibited the Mozambican state-building process.[50] In addition to this war-situation, the FRELIMO government was faced with the departure of skilled personnel as 200,000 Portuguese citizens left the country after the foundation of the independent state.[51] This amounted to 90 % of Mozambique's technical cadres.[52] Furthermore, less than 10 % of the African population of Mozambique had achieved literacy under the colonial education system.[53] Given this extremely difficult situation in the early years of independence, the government initially employed 5,000 foreign cooperators from Eastern and Western countries to alleviate the shortage of personnel in all sectors of the society.[54]

Especially after independence had been achieved, the government's policies were oriented towards the development paths of the USSR and the GDR, as well as the Tanzanian variant of self-reliance.[55] The gradual integration of the People's Republic of Mozambique into the socialist "Second World" was on one hand pursued on ideological grounds, as the FRELIMO declared itself to be a socialist party in 1977.[56] But, additionally, this orientation also reflected the FRELIMO's experience during the independence war against Portugal, when the FRELIMO had built reliable political ties with supportive allies such as the GDR, USSR, Cuba, or Tanzania, which all but the latter firmly belonged to the socialist camp.[57]

---

50 Sayaka Funada-Classen, *The Origins of War in Mozambique: A History of Unity and Division* (Oxford: African Minds, 2013).

51 José P. Castiano, *Das Bildungssystem in Mosambik (1974–1996): Entwicklung, Probleme und Konsequenzen* (Hamburg: Institut für Afrika-Kunde, 1997), 35.

52 Barbara Barnes, "Education for Socialism in Mozambique," *Comparative Education Review* 26, no. 3 (1982): 406.

53 Castiano, *Das Bildungssystem*, 84; Johnston, "The Mozambican State," 275; Rainer Grajek, *Berichte aus dem Morgengrauen: Als Entwicklungshelfer der DDR in Mosambik* (Grossbothen: Bücherwerkstatt & Verlag Ute Vallentin, 2005), 21.

54 James H. Mittelman, *Underdevelopment and the Transition to Socialism: Mozambique and Tanzania* (New York: Academic Press, 1981), 114.

55 Cross, *An Unfulfilled Promise*, 70–71.

56 Informationsstelle Südliches Afrika – issa. *Dokumente des 3. Kongresses der FRELIMO.* (Bonn: issa, 1978), 215–225.

57 Mittelman, *Underdevelopment*, 37–38; António da Costa Gaspar, "Frente Diplomática," in *História da Luta de Libertação Nacional, Volume 1*, ed. Joel das Neves Tembe (Maputo: Ministério dos Combatentes, Direcção Nacional de História, 2014), 87–188; Dalila Cabrita Mateus, *A Luta pela Independência. A Formação das Elites Fundadoras da FRELIMO, MPLA e PAIGC* (Mem Martins: Editorial Inquérito, 2006),124, 127–138; Matthias Voss, ed., *Wir haben Spuren hinterlassen!: Die DDR in Mosambik: Erlebnisse,*

Reflecting this orientation the post-colonial educational reforms drew on models from the USSR and the GDR, in addition to the experiences from the "liberated zones" of the anti-colonial war.[58] Such tendencies were also visible in the higher education sector, whose task was now to train revolutionary cadres for construction of the state as quickly as possible.[59] Faced with the lack of qualified personnel, the University Eduardo Mondlane (UEM) had to rely on numerous foreign cooperators to carry out this task.[60] Among lecturers from socialist countries, Soviet, German, and Cuban cooperators formed the largest groups.[61] Between 1976 and 1989, a total of 115 lecturers from the GDR worked at UEM.[62] It was exactly this period that saw the founding process of the FACOTRAV.

Already in 1976 the FRELIMO central committee had considered the establishment of courses to prepare combatants, workers, and peasants at UEM.[63] To

---

Erfahrungen und Erkenntnisse aus drei Jahrzehnten. Die DDR und die Dritte Welt Bd. 6. (Münster: Lit, 2005).

58 Castiano, *Das Bildungssystem*, 108; Cross, *An unfulfilled promise*, 67–70; Mathias Tullner, "Die Zusammenarbeit der DDR und Mosambiks auf dem Gebiet der Bildung und die Tätigkeit der Bildungsexperten in Mosambik," in *Wir haben Spuren hinterlassen!: Die DDR in Mosambik: Erlebnisse, Erfahrungen und Erkenntnisse aus drei Jahrzehnten*, ed. Matthias Voss (Münster: Lit, 2005), 397–399.

59 Castiano, *Das Bildungssystem*, 108–109, 112; Cross, *An Unfulfilled Promise*: 77–79; Domingos J. Langa, "Understanding the Role of Public Universities in Mozambique: The case of the Eduardo Mondlane University (UEM)," (Master Educationis, MEd, University of the Western Cape, 2013), 57–58.

60 In 1979 cooperators provided around 80 % of UEM's teaching staff. Langa, "Understanding," 57–58. By 1982 75 % of UEM's lecturers were still recruited from abroad. Castiano, *Das Bildungssystem*, 102.

61 Of the 242 registered foreign lecturers at UEM between 1980 and 1983, 61 were from the USSR, 39 from the GDR, and 25 from Cuba. Abteilung Lehrkörper der UEM, "Abschlußbericht über die Tätigkeiten der Abteilung für Angelegenheiten des Lehrkörpers im Jahre 1983," Januar 1984, in *AV-Mitteilung der Botschaft Maputo, Kulturattaché an die Abt. OZA, Sektor OA II vom 14.02.1984*, Bundesarchiv (BArch), DR3, II. Schicht, 1539, not paginated.

62 Holger Hegewald, "Berlin, Maputo und zurück - Dozent an der Eduardo-Mondlane-Universität 1989–1990," in *Wir haben Spuren hinterlassen!: Die DDR in Mosambik: Erlebnisse, Erfahrungen und Erkenntnisse aus drei Jahrzehnten*, ed. Matthias Voss (Münster: Lit, 2005), 471.

63 FRELIMO, Comité Central, *Documentos da 8 sessão do Comité Central da Frelimo* (Maputo: Departamento de Informação e Propaganda, 1976), 107. The 3rd Party congress of FRELIMO stipulated the concrete establishment of such courses in 1978. See Gómez, *Educação*, 310; FRELIMO, "Ökonomische und soziale Direktiven," in

implement this plan, delegations of the Ministry of Education were to search for suitable models in foreign countries. For example, in 1977 Minister for Education Graça Machel went on a trip to Cuba were she visited a Worker-Peasant Faculty (*Facultade Obrera Campesina*, FOC) and received information on the FOC-System.[64] In 1979, a UEM delegation met the former director of a Workers'-and-Peasants'-Faculty (Arbeiter-und-Bauern-Fakultät, ABF) in the GDR.[65] Also of importance for the educational transfer was the work carried out at UEM that prepared the establishment of the predecessor courses and subsequently of the FACOTRAV. The actual designing of the FACOTRAV took place at UEM from 1978 onwards and was carried out by a small international team of lecturers and foreign experts on educational policies. The first concept for the FACOTRAV was worked out in a joint effort by the Mozambican-Portuguese director of the Faculty of Economics, a Chilean educator, an advisor from the GDR, and Mozambican as well as foreign lecturers.[66]

This process initially led to the creation of university preparatory courses that were offered at the Faculty for Economics of UEM from September 1979 on.[67] Before the FACOTRAV itself was established further planning took place at UEM as well as at the Ministry of Education, and again delegations visited the GDR.[68] During one such visit, a request to dispatch further GDR cadres

---

Dokumente des 3. Kongresses der FRELIMO, ed. Informationsstelle Südliches Afrika – issa (Bonn: issa, 1978), 187.

64 Patrocínio Silva, *Relatório: Ensino Superior. Visita da Delegação do MEC à Republica Socialista de Cuba* (Maputo: Ministério da Educação e Cultura (MEC), 04.07.1977), 3–5, 11–12, 19. AHM, documentation Ganhão, box 29, not paginated.

65 Auslandsvertretung des Ministeriums für Auswärtige Angelegenheiten der DDR (MfAA), III. Sekretär der AV Maputo, *Vermerk über ein Gespräch mit Carmen Vaz, verantwortlicher Sekretär des Zentrums für Auslandsverbindungen der Universität Maputo am 11.06.1979*, Maputo. PAAA (Politisches Archiv des Auswärtigen Amtes in Berlin), MfAA ZR 2949, 81, not paginated.

66 Interview with the former director of FACOTRAV's predecessor courses, Fernando Jorge Cardoso, 24.02.2014 in Lisbon. Interview with former lecturer at FACOTRAV, Helmut Dora, 03.02.2014 in Rostock.

67 *Informação. Assunto: Ponto da Situação do 1° Curso de Gestão de Empresas*, Maputo, UEM, Faculdade de Economia, Curso de Gestão de Empresas, July 1981, AHM, documentation Ganhão, box 55, not paginated; *O primeiro curso de gestão de empresa. Rascunho do informe para o partido Frelimo*, April 1982, AHM, documentation Ganhão, box 55, not paginated.

68 Strobel, *Bericht zur Einrichtung einer ABF-ähnlichen Einrichtung an der UEM*, 1981, BArch, DR3, II. Schicht, 1540, not paginated.

specifically for collaboration in "Worker-and-Peasant-Courses" was presented to the GDR Minister for Higher and Technical Education by his Mozambican counterpart.[69] In the end, discussions revolved around the question whether to establish subject-specific preparatory courses at respective faculties, or to create a single distinct faculty that would prepare students for all kinds of subjects.[70] The latter option followed the Eastern German ABF model and was supported by the East German advisors.[71] In the end the decision was taken by the rector of UEM, Dr. Fernando do Reis Ganhão, who opted for creating a separate faculty.[72]

The FACOTRAV was established as a separate faculty at UEM in 1983, providing general university preparatory education in three branches.[73] This final design of the FACOTRAV was approved during the fourth party congress (April 1983) by president Samora Machel, who presented the founding of the faculty as contribution of the FRELIMO party to the "political, technical, scientific and cultural" training of cadres, workers, peasants and former combatants.[74] The new faculty was administratively assigned to the "Sub-System for Adult Education", in which it formed a separate role of accelerated pre-university adult education.[75] As the FACOTRAV drew on the experiences of the then abolished preparatory courses, a number of these courses' particularities were carried over to the faculty, highlighting the specific roots of the FACOTRAV. First of all, the FACOTRAV absorbed a highly internationalized academic staff from the courses.[76] Secondly, the curriculum and pedagogic concept were also taken over.

69 Prof. Dr. Nast, *Gespräch mit Minister Machel [mit Minister für Hoch- und Fachschulwesen Böhme] vom 29.10.1981*, BArch, DR3, II. Schicht, B 1560, 3, not paginated.

70 Prof. Dr. R. Schlauch, *Halbjahresbericht I/1981 [*Gruppe der DDR-Lehrkräfte an der UEM*] – Bereich Gesellschaftswissenschaften*, Maputo, 10.06.1981.BArch, DR3, II. Schicht, 1540, not paginated (here pages 6–7).

71 Signature indecipherable, *Halbjahresbericht I/1983*, July 1983, BArch, DR 3, II. Schicht, 1540, not paginated (here pages 4–5).

72 Interview with the former director of FACOTRAV's predecessor courses, Fernando Jorge Cardoso, 24.02.2014 in Lisbon.

73 *O que é o Curso Pré-Universitário?*

74 Signature indecipherable, *Halbjahresbericht I/1983*, July 1983, BArch, DR 3, II. Schicht, 1540, not paginated (here pages 3).

75 República Popular de Moçambique, Assembleia Popular, "Lei no. 4/83 de 23 de Março," in *Boletim da República*, Vol. 1, no. 12: 13–21, http://www.iese.ac.mz/lib/PPI/IESE-PPI/documentos_educacao.html; Brazão Mazula, *Educação, Cultura e Ideologia em Moçambique: 1975–1985. Em busca de fundamentos filosófico-antropológicos* (Porto: Edições Afrontamento e Fundo Bibliográfico de Língua Portuguesa, 1995), 193.

76 Of the 33 lecturers working at the FACOTRAV in 1983, 20 were of foreign origin. Abteilung Lehrkörper der UEM, *Abschlußbericht,* Concerning the transfer of the

For example, weekly practice periods in enterprises were part of the studies and the pedagogic concept stressed the formation of a qualified Mozambican leadership personality.[77] The explicit emphasis on the education for combatants, by contrast, drew on the FRELIMO's experiences in the liberated zones and formed a specifically Mozambican aspect of the FACOTRAV's design.[78]

The FACOTRAV most likely existed until 1992,[79] when it was closed "since it was considered that its goals had been achieved."[80] Functioning as a link between adult and higher education, the FACOTRAV was to play a specific role in the post-colonial construction of the Mozambican state, administration, and economy. This role of the FACOTRAV can be assessed more in qualitative than in quantitative terms because of the very low numbers of its students. Only 98 students were enrolled in the first academic year starting in 1983. This number grew only slightly as in 1986 only 124 were enrolled. The mean graduation rate was about 25 %.[81] Although 88 % of the students were indeed children of workers or peasants,[82] only 15 % of them were actually employed as workers prior to entering the FACOTRAV. The vast majority had worked in the administration of enterprises or state institutions.[83]

Through the upgrading to faculty status, the FACOTRAV had become structurally closer to the models of the Soviet Rabfak and the German ABF. However,

---

teaching staff, see Interview with F. J. Cardoso, 24.02.2014 in Lisbon, and Interviews with former FACOTRAV lecturers, April 2014 in Maputo.

77 *Perfil do Finalista - Sintese das Propostas,* Maputo, FACOTRAV, 13.09.1985, AHM, documentation Ganhão, box 16, not paginated; *Curriculum do Curso Pré-Universitário;* Interviews with former FACOTRAV lecturers, February to November 2014 in Lisbon, Maputo, and Rostock.

78 Fernando Ganhão, "The Struggle Continues: Mozambique's Revolutionary Experience in Education," *Development Dialogue*, no.2 (1978): 25–36; Zawangoni, *A FRELIMO e a Formação.*

79 No documents citing the date of closure of the FACOTRAV were found in the AHM holdings. The current rector of UEM, Prof. Orlando António Quilambo, stated to Ingrid Miethe that the FACOTRAV was closed in 1992. Personal conversation, 13.03.2015, Maputo.

80 Universidade Eduardo Mondlane, *Annual Report 1992–1993* (Maputo: The University, 1992), 12.

81 Johnston, *Study, Produce*, 207.

82 *Informationsbericht über die Fakultät für Kämpfer und Arbeiter der Avantgarde,* 1984/85. BArch, DR3, II. Schicht, 1539, not paginated.

83 *Zur Bedeutung der Facultät für Kämpfer und Werttätige der Vorhut im Spiegel statistischer Zahlen,* 30.03.1985, BArch, DR3, II. Schicht, 1539, not paginated.

as the low number of its students indicates, the FACOTRAV did not aim at the entrance of masses of students from the proletariat into higher education, as was the case in the USSR. The influence of the FACOTRAV students and graduates in the politics of UEM was also not as pronounced as in the case of the ABF's impact on politics in the Eastern German universities.[84] In Mozambique, priority was on quickly providing secondary and higher education to select and deserving former combatants and administrative personnel so as to employ them according to the goals of FRELIMO and the construction of an independent, socialist state. In this light, simply improving the education of FACOTRAV students was regarded as expedient, even when the students did not move on to university studies.[85]

Constructive restraint shown by the foreign cooperators was also a critical factor for the successful "internalisation"[86] of the FACOTRAV. The case of cooperation with the GDR serves to illustrate this point. The GDR only sent advisors and lecturers on request by its Mozambican counterparts and to carry out specific tasks that were defined by the Mozambican partners, such as the creation of an "ABF-like institution".[87] Although cooperators from the GDR brought with them their own ideas about the new institution and the transfer process, they were not always able to assert these in the framework of multinational cooperation. Additionally, final decision making power on the design of the FACOTRAV always resided with Mozambican actors, respectively the FRELIMO.[88] Furthermore, GDR cooperators were instructed to contribute to

84 Miethe, *Bildung*; Tandler, "The Workers' Faculty."

85 Interviews with former FACOTRAV lecturers in Lisbon, Maputo and Rostock, February to November 2014.

86 Ochs and Phillips, "Processes," 11.

87 Strobel, *Bericht zur Einrichtung einer ABF-ähnlichen Einrichtung;* See also Helmut Dora, *Bericht über die Arbeit der Ökonomischen Fakultät (II. Halbjahr/1980) der AG-Universität Maputo. Anlage zum Halbjahresbericht II/1980 der AG der DDR-Lehrkräfte an der UEM*, an das MFH, Maputo, 14.11.1980, BArch, DR3, II. Schicht, 1540, not paginated.

88 *Zur Einschätzung der Arbeit im Rektorat.* Report by Hr. Urbanski to MFH, Maputo, 19.06.1981. BArch, DR3, II. Schicht, 1540, not paginated.

For more examples on GDR-PRM cooperation see interviews with former FACOTRAV lecturers in Lisbon, Maputo and Rostock, February to November 2014.

See also: Helmut Dora, *Kokos und bitterer Tee. Tage und Nächte in Mosambik* (Rostock: BS-Verlag, 2009), 85–87; Tullner, *Die Zusammenarbeit*, 396–403.

the long-term “Mozambicanization of the academic staff” at UEM.[89] This goal was achieved at the FACOTRAV already in the 1984/85 academic year in which the number of “national” or “Mozambican” lecturers (17) was already more than double that of the foreign lecturers and cooperators (8).[90] In 1986, there were only one lecturer form the USSR and one from the GDR left at the FACOTRAV.[91]

Like the Vietnamese W-P Schools, the FACOTRAV’s history shows that a “borrowed” educational institution can contribute to the consolidation of a country’s decolonization process. The FACOTRAV successfully promoted the education of former independence fighters, thereby qualifying Mozambicans to contribute to post-colonial state building. While different Mozambican and foreign actors and experiences were influential in its creation, it was nevertheless considered an essentially Mozambican institution because its design and mission differed from the foreign models and took into account the priorities of the FRELIMO government. The internalization of the FACOTRAV was highlighted by the FRELIMO Central Committee’s Secretary for Political Economy when he stressed that the FACOTRAV was “truly our faculty”.[92]

Conclusion: Educational transfers as means of decolonization

Transfers of policies, governmental structures and institutions from the USSR to other socialist countries have often been depicted rather one-sidedly as originating in and following the interests of that country.[93] The term “Sovietization”, sometimes used to refer to the transfer of Soviet institutional models to other countries, invokes pictures of institutional imposition of generic models originating in the USSR.[94] Respective educational transfers would thus be referred to as “imposed” transfers according to the model of Phillips and Ochs. Such a

89 *Einschätzung zum Stand und zu einigen Entwicklungen an der UEM*, Bericht der MHF-Expertengruppe aus Maputo an das MHF, Abt. Auslandskader/Experten, Maputo, June 1986: 17. BArch, DR3, II. Schicht, 1538, not paginated.

90 *Informationsbericht über die Fakultät für Kämpfer und Arbeiter der Avantgarde,”* 1984/85, BArch, DR3, II. Schicht, 1539, not paginated.

91 *Einschätzung zum Stand.*

92 *Mensagem lido pelo sr. Ermelindo Mwya em nome dos ex-alunos da Faculdade,* UEM, FACOTRAV, Maputo, “Semana de Educacao” 13.-20. Abril 1985. AHM, documentation Ganhão, box 55.

93 Oscar Sanchez-Sibony, *Red Globalization: The Political Economy of the Soviet Cold War from Stalin to Khrushchev* (Cambridge: Cambridge University Press, 2014).

94 Connelly, *Captive University*; Theodore R. Weeks, *Russification, sovietization* (Mainz: Institut für Europäische Geschichte, 2010), accessed August 24, 2016,

view paints a picture of Third World actors as people without agency that fall victim to expansionist ambitions, a view that has been questioned by recent research on the role of Third World actors during the Cold War.[95] Our research presented here has shown that educational transfers connected to the Worker-Peasant Complementary Education Schools in the DRV and the FACOTRAV in Mozambique cannot be regarded as "imposed" transfers. Rather, they were motivated by local problems and interests in the newly independent states, based on a shared ideological world-view with the lending countries from the Second World. Although the centralized orientation of socialist countries and the special role of the USSR in the socialist camp might lead one to suspect otherwise, the transfers did not result from pressure exerted on these countries. In contrast, the educational transfers described here were initiated by the ruling FRELIMO and VWP. In the case of the Vietnamese W-P Schools, no foreign actors were involved in either the design, the creation or the running of the schools. While in the Mozambican case foreign advisors involved in creating and running the FACOTRAV tried to advance their own agendas, it was the rector of UEM who ultimately made decisions. Furthermore, despite the importance of international transfers for the creation and design of the respective institutions, through internalization the W-P Schools and the FACOTRAV became quite unique institutions that differed markedly from the foreign models they drew on. After the described transfer processes had led to the creation of these institutions, their further development and eventual closure took place in response to local circumstances and conditions in the DRV and the PRM. We thus conclude that the specific educational transfers associated with the Worker-Peasant Complementary Education Schools and the FACOTRAV furthered the creation of national educational institutions and systems, as well as contributed to the building of post-colonial states by providing relatively well-trained graduates. The described educational transfers and the respective institutions thereby served as means of decolonization, rather than reflecting or resulting in new dependencies.

Archives

Vietnam National Archives Centre 3 (VNAC3), Hanoi

- Fonds of the Ministry of Education

---

http://ieg-ego.eu/en/threads/models-and-stereotypes/russification-sovietization/theodore-r-weeks-russification-sovietization#Conclusions.

95 Westad, *The Global Cold War*; Sanchez-Sibony, *Red Globalization*, 10–11.

- Fonds of the Office of the Premier, 1945–1954

Mozambique Historical Archives (AHM), Maputo

- *Fonds of the Department for the Central Archive of the UEM (2.7), collection on the rectorate of the UEM under Fernando* Ganhão

German Federal Archives (BArch), Berlin Lichterfelde

- Fonds of the Ministry of Higher and Technical Education of the GDR (DR3), 1967–1989/90 (II. Schicht)

Political Archive of the Federal Foreign Office (PAAA), Berlin

- Fonds of the Ministry for Foreign Affairs of the German Democratic Republic (MfAA), ZR

Literature

Aust, Martin. "Russland und die Sowjetunion in der Globalgeschichte." In *Globalisierung imperial und sozialistisch: Russland und die Sowjetunion in der Globalgeschichte 1851–1991*, edited by Martin Aust, 13–38. Frankfurt am Main: Campus, 2013.

Balzer, Harley D. "Workers' Faculties and the Development of Science Cadres in the First Decade of Soviet Power." In *The Social Direction of the Public Sciences: Causes and Consequences of Co-operation between Scientists and Non-Scientific Groups*, edited by Stuart Blume, Joske Bunders, and Loet Leydesdorff, 193–211. Dordrecht: Springer Netherlands, 1987.

Ban Bí thư khóa II. "Thông tri số 82-TT/TW về việc chọn học sinh thành phần công nông để học bổ túc cấp tốc về văn hoá. 21.12.1955." Accessed August 31, 2016. http://dangcongsan.vn/cpv/Modules/News/NewsDetail.aspx?co_id=28340670&cn_id=490786.

Ban Liên lạc Trường Bổ túc văn hóa công – nông trung ương và Trường Phổ thông lao động trung ương. Thông tin về một số giáo viên, cán bộ nhân viên và học viên: Phụ bản cuốn: Một ngội trường cách mạng. Hanoi: Nhà xuất bản giáo dục, 2005.

Barnes, Barbara. "Education for Socialism in Mozambique." *Comparative Education* 26, no. 3 (1982): 406–419.

Beech, Jason. "The Theme of Educational Transfer in Comparative Education: A View Over Time." *Research in Comparative and International Education* 1, no. 1 (2006): 2–13.

Boden, Ragna. "Jakarta, 1965: Zur Rolle kommunistischer Parteien in der Dritten Welt." In *Die Sowjetunion und die Dritte Welt*, edited by Andreas Hilger, 121–141. Schriftenreihe der Vierteljahreshefte für Zeitgeschichte. München: Oldenbourg Wissenschaftsverlag, 2009.

Boden, Ragna. “Globalisierung sowjetisch: Der Kulturtransfer in die Dritte Welt.” In *Globalisierung imperial und sozialistisch: Russland und die Sowjetunion in der Globalgeschichte 1851–1991*, edited by Martin Aust, 425–442. Frankfurt am Main: Campus, 2013.

Bộ Giáo dục. “Nghị định 43-NĐ thành lập trường bổ túc văn hóa cộng đồng [sic! công nông]. 23.01.1956.” Accessed August 31, 2016. http://thuvienphapluat.vn/archive/Nghi-dinh/Nghi-dinh-43-ND-thanh-lap-truong-bo-tuc-van-hoa-cong-dong-vb22858t11.aspx.

Castiano, José P. *Das Bildungssystem in Mosambik (1974–1996): Entwicklung, Probleme und Konsequenzen*. Hamburg: Institut für Afrika-Kunde, 1997.

Christy, Erik E. “Influence of the Soviet Union on Chinese Higher Educational and Scientific Development: 1920–1950.” PhD diss., University of Oregon, 1986.

Connelly, John. *Captive University: The Sovietization of East German, Czech and Polish Higher Education, 1945–1956*. Chapel Hill: University of North Carolina Press, 2000.

Cross, Michael. *An Unfulfilled Promise: Transforming Schools in Mozambique*. Addis Adaba: Organisation for Social Science Research in Eastern and Southern Africa, 2011.

Crossley, Michael, and Leon Tikly. “Postcolonial Perspectives and Comparative and International Research in Education:A Critical Introduction.” *Comparative Education* 40, no. 2 (2004): 147–156.

Dale, Roger, and Susan L. Robertson. “Beyond Methodological ‘isms’ in Comparative Education in an Era of Globalisation.” In *International Handbook of Comparative Education*, edited by Robert Cowen and Andreas M. Kazamias, 1113–1128. Springer International Handbooks of Education 22. Dordrecht [u.a.]: Springer Netherlands, 2009.

Dora, Helmut. *Kokos und bitterer Tee. Tage und Nächte in Mosambik*. Rostock: BS-Verlag, 2009.

FRELIMO. Comité Central. *Documentos da 8 sessão do Comité Central da Frelimo*. Maputo: Departamento de Informação e Propaganda, 1976.

FRELIMO. Comité Central. “Ökonomische und soziale Direktiven.” In *Dokumente des 3. Kongresses der FRELIMO*, edited by Informationsstelle Südliches Afrika, 139–190. Bonn: issa, 1978.

Funada-Classen, Sayaka. *The Origins of War in Mozambique: A History of Unity and Division*. Oxford: African Minds. 2013.

Ganhão, Fernando. “The Struggle Continues: Mozambique’s Revolutionary Experience in Education.” *Development Dialogue* 2 (1978): 25–36.

Gaspar, António da Costa. "Frente Diplomática." In *História da Luta de Libertação Nacional. Volume 1*, edited by Joel das Neves Tembe, 87–188. Maputo: Ministério dos Combatentes, Direcção Nacional de História, 2014.

Gómez, Buendía M. *Educação Moçambicana. História de um processo: 1962–1984*. Maputo: Livraria Universitária, 1999.

Grajek, Rainer. *Berichte aus dem Morgengrauen: Als Entwicklungshelfer der DDR in Mosambik*. Grossbothen: Bücherwerkstatt & Verlag Ute Vallentin, 2005.

Griffiths, Tom G., and Euridice Charon Cardona. "Education for Social Transformation: Soviet University Education Aid in the Cold War Capitalist World-System." *European Education* 47, no. 3 (2015): 226–241.

Griffiths, Tom G., and Zsuzsa Millei, eds. *Logics of Socialist Education: Engaging with Crisis, Insecurity and Uncertainty. Explorations of Educational Purpose v. 24*. Dordrecht, New York: Springer, 2013.

Hegewald, Holger. "Berlin, Maputo und zurück - Dozent an der Eduardo-Mondlane-Universität 1989–1990." In *Wir haben Spuren hinterlassen!: Die DDR in Mosambik: Erlebnisse, Erfahrungen und Erkenntnisse aus drei Jahrzehnten*, edited by Matthias Voss, 463–480. Münster: Lit, 2005.

Hilger, Andreas. "Sowjetunion, Staatssozialismus und Dritte Welt 1945–1991." In *Die Sowjetunion und die Dritte Welt*, edited by Andreas Hilger, 7–17. München: Oldenbourg Wissenschaftsverlag, 2009.

Informationsstelle Südliches Afrika – issa. *Dokumente des 3. Kongresses der FRELIMO*. Bonn: issa, 1978.

James, Leslie, and Elisabeth Leake. "Introduction." In *Decolonization and the Cold War: Negotiating Independence*, edited by Leslie James and Elisabeth Leake, 1–17. London: Bloomsbury Academic, 2015.

Johnston, Anton. *Study, Produce, and Combat! Education and the Mozambican State 1962–1984*. Stockholm: Institute of International Education, University of Stockholm, 1989.

Johnston, Anton. "The Mozambican State and Education." In *Education and Social Transition in the Third World*, edited by Martin Carnoy and Joel Samoff, 275–314. Oxford: Princeton University Press, 1990.

Kaiser, Tim, Tobias Kriele, Ingrid Miethe, and Alexandra Piepiorka. "Educational Transfers in Postcolonial Contexts: Preliminary Results From Comparative Research on Workers' Faculties in Vietnam, Cuba, and Mozambique." *European Education* 47, no. 3 (2015): 242–259.

Katsakioris, Constantin. "Soviet Lessons for Arab Modernization: Soviet Educational Aid to Arab Countries after 1956." *Journal of Modern European History* 8, no. 1 (2010): 85–106.

Katunceva, N. M. *Rol' rabočich fakul'tetov v formirovanii kadrov narodnoj intelligencii v SSSR [The Role of the Workers' Faculty in the Creation of the People's Cadres Intellegentsia]*. Moscow: n.d, 1966.

Langa, Domingos J. "Understanding the Role of Public Universities in Mozambique: The Case of the Eduardo Mondlane University (UEM)." Master Educationis (MEd), University of the Western Cape, 2013.

Mateus, Dalila C. *A Luta pela Independência. A Formação das Elites Fundadoras da FRELIMO, MPLA e PAIGC*. Mem Martins: Editorial Inquérito, 2006.

Mazula, Brazão. *Educação, Cultura e Ideologia em Moçambique: 1975–1985. Em busca de fundamentos filosófico-antropológicos*. Porto: Edições Afrontamento e Fundo Bibliográfico de Língua Portuguesa, 1995.

Miethe, Ingrid. *Bildung und soziale Ungleichheit in der DDR: Möglichkeiten und Grenzen einer gegenprivilegierenden Bildungspolitik*. Opladen, Farmington Hills: Verlag Barbara Budrich, 2007.

Miethe, Ingrid, Tim Kaiser, Tobias Kriele, and Alexandra Piepiorka. *Globalization of an Educational Idea: Workers' Faculties in Eastern Germany, Vietnam, Cuba and Mozambique*. Berlin, Boston: De Gruyter Oldenbourg, 2019.

Mittelman, James H. *Underdevelopment and the Transition to Socialism: Mozambique and Tanzania*. New York: Academic Press, 1981.

Mondlane, Eduardo. *Kampf um Mosambik*. Frankfurt am Main: März Verlag, 1970.

Nguyễn Khánh Toàn. *Giáo dục dân chủ mới*. Chiên khu: Bộ quốc gia giáo-dục, 1947.

Nguyễn Khánh Toàn. "Успехи культурного строительства в Демократической Республике Вьетнам." In *Демократическая Республика Вьетнам 1945–1960*, edited by A. A. Guber, and Nguyen Khanh Toan. 177–199. Moscow: Izdatel'stvo Vostočnoj literatury, 1960.

Nguyễn Thanh Tú. "GS. Nguyễn Khánh Toàn: Nhà kiến trúc sư trong giai đoạn đầu của nền giáo dục cách mạng." Accessed March 8, 2016. http://100years.vnu.edu.vn/BTDHQGHN/Vietnamese/C1778/c1779/2006/05/n7775/.

Ninh, Kim Ngoc Bao. *A World Transformed: The Politics of Culture in Revolutionary Vietnam, 1945–1965*. Ann Arbor: University of Michigan Press, 2002.

Oanh, K. "Gặp mặt gần 1000 cựu học sinh bổ túc công nông". In *ViệtBáo.vn*. Accessed November 14, 2013. http://vietbao.vn/Giao-duc/Gap-mat-gan-1000-cuu-hoc-sinh-bo-tuc-cong-nong/20503189/202/.

Ochs, Kimberly, and David Phillips. "Processes of Educational Borrowing in Historical Context." In *Educational Policy Borrowing: Historical*

Perspectives, edited by David Phillips and Kimberly Ochs, 7–24. Didcot: Symposium, 2004.

Pepper, Suzanne. *Radicalism and Education Reform in 20th-Century China: The Search for an Ideal Development Model.* Cambridge [England], New York: Cambridge University Press, 2000.

Quinn-Judge, Sophie. *Ho Chi Minh: The Missing Years 1919–1941*. London: Hurst & Co., 2003.

República Popular de Moçambique, Assembleia Popular. "Lei no. 4/83 de 23 de Março." *Boletim da República* 1, no. 12: 13–21. http://www.iese.ac.mz/lib/PPI/IESE-PPI/documentos_educacao.html.

Rothermund, Dietmar. *The Routledge Companion to Decolonization*. London, New York: Routledge, 2006.

Sanchez-Sibony, Oscar. *Red Globalization: The Political Economy of the Soviet Cold War from Stalin to Khrushchev*. Cambridge: Cambridge University Press, 2014.

Schuch, Jane. *Mosambik im pädagogischen Raum der DDR: Eine bildanalytische Studie zur "Schule der Freundschaft" in Stassfurt*. Wiesbaden: Springer, 2013.

Seyboldt, Peter J. "Yenan Education and the Chinese Revolution, 1937–1945." PhD diss., Cambridge/Mass.: Harvard University, 1969.

Shipway, Martin. *Decolonization and Its Impact: A Comparative Approach to the End of the Colonial Empires*. Massachusetts: Blackwell Pub, 2008.

Springhall, John. *Decolonization Since 1945: The Collapse of European Overseas Empires*. Houndmills, Basingstoke, Hampshire, New York: Palgrave, 2001.

Steiner-Khamsi, Gita, and Ines Stolpe. *Educational Import: Local Encounters with Global Forces in Mongolia*. New York: Palgrave Macmillan, 2006.

Studer, Brigitte. *The Transnational World of the Cominternians*. Houndmills, Basingstoke, Hampshire: Palgrave Macmillan, 2015.

Tandler, Fredrika M. "The Workers' Faculty (Rabfak) System in the USSR." PhD diss., New York: Columbia University, 1955.

Taylor, Robert. *China's Intellectual Dilemma: Politics and University Enrolment, 1949–1978*. Vancouver: University of British Columbia Press, 1981.

Trần Lực. *Mấy kinh nghiệm Trung-Quốc mà chúng ta nên học*. Hà Nội: Nhà Xuất bản Sư thật, 1958.

Trần Lực. "Cần công, kiệm học." *Giáo dục Nhân dân* 6 (March 1958): 31–32.

Tullner, Mathias. "Die Zusammenarbeit der DDR und Mosambiks auf dem Gebiet der Bildung und die Tätigkeit der Bildungsexperten in Mosambik." In *Wir haben Spuren hinterlassen!: Die DDR in Mosambik: Erlebnisse,*

Erfahrungen und Erkenntnisse aus drei Jahrzehnten, edited by Matthias Voss, 388–406. Münster: Lit, 2005.

Universidade Eduardo Mondlane (UEM). *Annual Report 1992–1993, Volume 5.* Maputo: The University, 1992.

Vasavakul, Thaveeporn. "Schools and politics in South and North Viêt Nam: A comparative study of state apparatus, state policy, and state power (1945–1965)." PhD diss, Ithaca: Cornell University, 1994.

Verber, Jason. "True to the Politics of Frelimo? Teaching Socialism at the Schule der Freundschaft, 1981–1990." *In Comrades of Color: East Germany in the Cold War World*, edited by Quinn Slobodian, 188–210. Oxford, New York: Berghahn Books, 2015.

Voss, Matthias, ed. *Wir haben Spuren hinterlassen!: Die DDR in Mosambik: Erlebnisse, Erfahrungen und Erkenntnisse aus drei Jahrzehnten.* Münster: Lit, 2005.

Weeks, Theodore R. "Russification, sovietization." Accessed August 24, 2016. http://ieg-ego.eu/en/threads/models-and-stereotypes/russification-sovietization/theodore-r-weeks-russification-sovietization#Conclusions.

Westad, Odd A. *The Global Cold War: Third World Interventions and the Making of our Times.* Cambridge, New York: Cambridge University Press, 2005.

Woodside, Alexander. "The Triumphs and Failures of Mass Education in Vietnam." *Pacific Affairs* 56, no. 3 (1983): 401–427.

Zawangoni, Salvador A. A *FRELIMO e a Formação do Homem Novo (1964–1974 e 1975–1982).* Maputo: CIEDIMA - Central Impressora e Editora de Maputo, 2007.

Jane Weiß[1]

Decolonization and Difference in the Context of the German Democratic Republic's Educational Co-operation Programs

Abstract The socialist experience during decolonization was multi-layered and the colonial, understood as a set of representations constructing the other, also played a role during the process of socialist involvement in decolonization. This contribution focuses on unequal relations between metropolitan and peripheral polities within the socialist cosmos. It addresses the educational cooperation between the German Democratic Republic (GDR) and Africa. The author presents the perspectives of a different set of actors, among whom GDR officials feature most prominently. These actors were delegated to provide aid in building new educational systems in Africa under the banner of 'socialist solidarity'. The analysis shows, that there is no easy answer to the question of the influence of these new 'civilizers'. The recipients' colonialist perceptions of educational aid and a genuine interest in the common goal of decolonization of education coexisted.

Keywords: German Democratic Republic, socialist cooperation, difference

Transnational and/or post-colonial studies on decolonization processes often completely dismiss the role of the Eastern bloc or deal with it in a secondary way, which most of the time means they treat it only in their relationship to the efforts of the "West". In the context of global decolonization history and in the post-colonial perspective, the German Democratic Republic's (GDR) Africa policy, for instance, was particularly discussed in its international political dimension as "scene of the East-West German rivalry of systems".[2] Yet this certainly significant dimension reduces the variety of exchange processes and neglects global entanglements in history. This dimension establishes the "East as the defining

---

1 Research for this contribution has been completed in the project "Education for All. Self-perceptions and outside-images in the production and circulation of a central myth in transnational perspective" within the research program "Educational Myths about the German Democratic Republic – a dictatorship and its afterlife", funded by the Federal Ministry of Education and Research (BMBF).

2 Andreas Eckert, "Spätkoloniale Herrschaft, Dekolonisation und internationale Ordnung," *Archiv für Sozialgeschichte 48*, (2007): 7.

other of freedom and progress in the West".[3] In addition, the countries of the global South appear in this perspective as merely reactive forces and their own initiative and agency fades out.

Following the premises of entangled history that postulates a de-focusing of the Eurocentric views,[4] I will propose a complementary widening of perspectives when dealing with the Eastern bloc. Eurocentrism is a Western-dominated concept, and this not only since the crackdown of the Cold-War political blocs.[5] This dominant perspective has to be taken down. On the one hand, through the historiography of marginalized stories and narratives. They dispute the place and monopolistic status of majority narratives. On the other hand, through a historiography that challenges the paradigma of a bipolar confrontation of two blocks as the main perspective.[6] In so doing, the Eastern bloc appears less monolithic and more diverse than usual.[7]

Decolonization processes in the 20th century have been largely neglected when looking at the history of the GDR. This contrasts with the fact that this small country short after its inception in 1949 became involved in processes of global decolonization. The GDR ideally and materially supported liberation movements, provided them with infrastructure and promoted cooperation in the fields of science, technology and education.[8] It is even possible that the small GDR was the most important "education exporter" of the entire Eastern bloc. These hypothetic formulations indicate that I first of all have to rely on my own

---

3 Martin Aust, "Russland und die Sowjetunion in der Globalgeschichte," in *Globalisierung imperial und sozialistisch - Russland und die Sowjetunion in der Globalgeschichte 1851–1991*, ed. Martin Aust. (Frankfurt/New York: campus, 2013) 18.

4 Sebastian Conrad and Shalini Randeria, "*Einleitung. Geteilte Geschichten – Europa in einer postkolonialen Welt.*" in *Jenseits des Eurozentrismus. Postkoloniale Perspektiven in den Geschichts- und Kulturwissenschaften*, ed. Sebastian Conrad and Shalini Randeria (Frankfurt, New York: Campus, 2002).

5 Aust, "*Russland und die Sowjetunion in der Globalgeschichte*," 13.

6 Ibid., 24.

7 Historiography may leave behind the polarizing perspective from Cold War studies and pose a stronger emphasis on the triangle of capitalistic, socialist and bloc-free countries. See Ibid.

8 Hans Mathias Müller, *Die Bildungshilfe der Deutschen Demokratischen Republik* (Frankfurt am Main: Peter Lang, 1995); Hans-Joachim Döring, *"Es geht um unsere Existenz": Die Politik der DDR gegenüber der Dritten Welt am Beispiel von Mosambik und Äthiopien* (Berlin: Chr. Links Verlag, 2001).

source analyses, since there are hardly any historic-systematic works on this topic.[9]

In a general perspective, the question of education in the context of decolonization has remained rather in the shadows of scholarship, although liberation struggles in the countries of the global South education became one of the most powerful forces of emancipation. Moreover, the post-colonial polities declared that the establishment of a non-racist, democratic system of education was one of the most significant problems they had to face.[10]

As a consequence of these and other developments, a big majority of the countries in Africa, South and Southeast Asia, the Middle East and Latin America looked for cooperation and support from socialist countries like the Soviet Union, Cuba and the GDR. From the viewpoint of old and new polities of the global South, socialist countries represented a more promising possibility of development than the model offered by Western capitalist countries.[11] Between the 1950s and the 1980s, 35 out of 53 African countries declared themselves as socialist and people's republics, although some of them did it only for a short time.[12] The result of this situation was a variety of bilateral cooperation agreements and initiatives between socialist countries and the countries of the global South. Education undoubtedly was one of the most critical fields of cooperation. The GDR played

9 The work published by Müller (1995) has done a first attempt in this direction. Nonetheless, he could not include all possible sources, because many documents were not available in the archives at that time. Particularly, he could not consult the repository of the Ministry of Education (*Ministerium für Volksbildung*). The work by Büschel (2014) has considered a wider range of sources; yet he did not analyze the field of education. He focused rather on the comparison of the two German states. Correspondingly, he did not consult the archives of Ministry of Education as well. See Müller, *Die Bildungshilfe der Deutschen Demokratischen Republik;* Hubertus Büschel, *Hilfe zur Selbsthilfe, Deutsche Entwicklungsarbeit in Afrika 1960–1975* (Frankfurt, New York: campus, 2014).

10 Liberation movements such as the PAIGC and the FRELIMO established numerous schools in the liberated areas. cf. Sonia Vaz Borges, *Militant Education. Liberation Struggle, Consciousness. The PAIGC education in Guinea Bissau 1963–1978* (Frankfurt/M.: Peter Lang, 2019); José Paulino Castiano, *Das Bildungssystem in Mosambik (1974–1996): Entwicklung, Probleme und Konsequenzen* (Hamburg: Institut für Afrika-Kunde im Verbund der Stiftung Deutsches Übersee-Institut, 1997).

11 Döring, *"Es geht um unsere Existenz": Die Politik der DDR gegenüber der Dritten Welt am Beispiel von Mosambik und Äthiopien*, 26.

12 Cf. M. Anne Picher and Kelly M. Askew, "African Socialism and Postsocialism," *Africa* 76, no. 1 (2006): 1–14.

a significant role in this context, although it was a young and relatively small state. Of course, the GDR followed the Hallstein-Doctrine about the necessity of broad international recognition of this German state as a path for securing the existence of the new republic. Yet this more strategic point of view was not the only determinant for the GDR's strong involvement in international cooperation. A solidary stance over decolonization, grounded in anti-racist and anti-colonial positions, was determinant as well. For instance, the consequent condemnation against the racist Apartheid regime positioned the GDR as a trustful partner in the view of many countries of the global South.[13] Within the context of the general GDR support for liberation movements, a set of personal relations enabled a close cooperation between the GDR and some countries, being Mozambique a case in point.

This article presents a contextualized view of the structuring of educational cooperation of the GDR with countries of the global South. Following analytical insights from the historiography of entangled histories, it will focus in the constructions of cultural difference within this process of cooperation. I will particularly focus on the constructions of the self and the other as well as on their mutual bonds. I will address this problem by closely looking at the preparation courses for GDR experts designated as specialists in education in the foreign cooperation. I work on the premise that within the instruction of experts going abroad difference as a category played key role and that to build up, to convey, and to construct this difference gives some indication of the awareness and the handling of self-construction and the construction by others as well as its materialization in texts, structures and actions. Particularly interesting in this respect are the lines drawn to construct difference, along with images of the others – the countries of the global South – were enacted.

For this purpose, I will briefly introduce the GDR's development co-operation, particularly in the educational field. I will further explain the criteria that came into play in the selection of the experts for foreign assignments and their preparation for their task. Finally I will on the basis of archival evidence, discuss and analyze the dimension of difference concerning the Own and the Other within the framework of developmental cooperation in the field of education. I mainly refer to those documents of the federal archive concerning the educational preparation of the foreign cadres that I could research for the 1980s

13 Döring, *"Es geht um unsere Existenz": Die Politik der DDR gegenüber der Dritten Welt am Beispiel von Mosambik und Äthiopien*, 23.

so far.[14] These documents include training concepts for the preparation of foreign cadres, consultation records and their realization, presentations specially made for these trainings, correspondence between different ministry levels and the other involved institutions, reports, as for example the mentioned final reports of the foreign cadres, and official documents, as for example the rules of traveling for these cadres. This bulk of documents will be complemented by selected records held at the International Research Library for the History of Education in Berlin (*Bibliothek für Bildungsgeschichtliche Forschung*, BBF/DIPF), particularly published reports and interviews and contemporary documents. In addition, I have conducted some interviews with educational experts, who acted as co-operators in that time. The way in which differences between the self and the others were constructed related to culture, society or the educational system point at the knowledge critically underlying the GDR cooperation with countries of the global South.

The development co-operation of the GDR

In the field of the so-called development co-operation[15], the GDR was, on the side of the Soviet Union, an important actor within the Eastern bloc countries. A study from 1995 asserted that in 1979, putting the Soviet Union aside, the GDR accounted for half of the development aid of all Eastern European countries that belonged to the Council of Mutual Economic Assistance.[16] Already in the early 1950s, when the GDR in some aspects still had to be regarded as a "developing country" itself, the country supported North Korea and Vietnam.[17] Moreover, eleven students came 1951 from Nigeria in order to study at the Worker's and

---

14 I reference to the following dossiers of the ministry for national education in the Federal Archives Koblenz (Bundesarchiv, BArch): DR2 50423, DR2 50556-1, DR2 50556-2, DR2 50614-2, DR2 50514-3, DR2 50665.

15 The concept of development cooperation is only partially applicable to the socialist countries because these countries did not consider, mostly out of an ideological motivation, commercial relations as being commercial in their nature. They rather considered them as being conducive to the development of the respective countries and as an element of the emerging system of socialist trade. In this perspective, some areas of foreign trade as well as direct assistance through the GDR state and population were defined as cooperation for development. Müller, *Die Bildungshilfe der Deutschen Demokratischen Republik*; Döring, *"Es geht um unsere Existenz"*.

16 Müller, *Die Bildungshilfe der Deutschen Demokratischen Republik*, 44.

17 Ibid., 15.

Peasant's Faculty of the Karl-Marx-University in the city of Leipzig[18] and in 1952 around 100 North Korean students went to Leipzig as well.[19] In the course of the 1950s, the GDR constantly expanded its young foreign policy relationships and in 1958 it already had closed 15 trade and payment agreements with African and Asian states.[20] These agreements contained concrete arrangements stipulated that assistance within the "scientific-technical co-operation" would be cost-free for these countries.[21]

The GDR's educational co-operation included countries and liberation movements in Africa (Guinea, Benin, Tanzania, Sudan, Mali, Ethiopia, Angola, Mozambique, Guinea-Bissau/Cape Verde Islands), South Asia and Southeast Asia (Vietnam, Laos, Kampuchea, Mongolia, North Korea, Afghanistan, India, China), the Near and Middle East (South Yemen, Syria, Libya, Iraq, Algeria, Egypt) and Latin America (Cuba, Chile, Nicaragua, Mexico) and it had various forms. However, both the focus areas and the bilateral relations varied subject to global and international political changes and always depended on the political orientation and situation of the respective countries.[22] Out of this extensive list of cooperation partners, GDR developed stronger ties to Ethiopia, Angola, Mozambique, South-Yemen, Vietnam and Cuba.[23] From 1981 onwards, this list incorporated Nicaragua as well.[24]

The educational co-operation professionalized fairly quickly. Already in the 1950s, first institutions for the vocational training of foreigners had been opened, for instance the Herder Institute in Leipzig. While in the 1960s teachers were at first sent out mostly into secondary schools of recently liberated African states and liberation movements still struggling for independence, in the 1970s

---

18 Ibid., 70.

19 Liana Kang-Schmitz, *Nordkoreas Umgang mit Abhängigkeit und Sicherheitsrisiko: am Beispiel der bilateralen Beziehungen zur DDR* (Berlin: epubli GmbH, 2011), 178. The section for "foreign students" at the University of Leipzg emerged out from these preparatory courses and became the "Institute for Foreign Students" in 1956. It was integrated into the Herder Institute in 1961, the organization in charge of German courses in foreign countries and the preparation of foreign students in the GDR. See, Müller, *Die Bildungshilfe der Deutschen Demokratischen Republik*, 79.

20 Müller, *Die Bildungshilfe der Deutschen Demokratischen Republik*, 16–19.

21 Ibid., 51.

22 Cf. Ibid., 32.

23 Cf. Müller, *Die Bildungshilfe der Deutschen Demokratischen Republik*; Döring, *"Es geht um unsere Existenz"*.

24 Cf. Erika Harzer and Willi Volks, ed. *Aufbruch nach Nicaragua. Deutsch-deutsche Solidarität im Systemwettstreit* (Berlin: Ch. Links Verlag, 2008).

the mere personal support expanded already in the direction of education and training, development and production of teaching materials, curriculum work, and finally the conception and implementation of decolonized educational systems, as for example in Mozambique, where GDR experts were heavily involved in establishing the new educational system on the level of the Mozambican ministry for education.[25]

For the educational cooperation programs between the GDR and the countries of the global South, we find the following areas of bilateral cooperation:

- The dispatch of experts, who acted as consultants in all levels of the educational systems such as steering and organization of educational ministries, institutions of teacher training, universities, etc.
- The dispatch of teachers and trainers for the general system of education as well as for higher schools, universities and schools established by the liberation movements; particularly they trained teachers and developed curricula and didactic materials.
- The education and training of persons coming from the global South at the universities, higher schools and professional schools in the GDR. This included vocational training simultaneously to their employment as contracted workers

25 For instance, educational experts were already active in the schools established by the FRELIMO in the liberated areas. There, they worked together with the future leaders of the independend state. cf. Matthias Voß, "Gespräch mit Achim Kindler, der als Lehrer im Auftrag des Solidaritätskomitees der DDR als erster DDR-Bürger bei der FRELIMO arbeitete," in *Wir haben Spuren hinterlassen! Die DDR in Mosambik. Erlebnisse, Erfahrungen und Erkenntnisse aus drei Jahrzehnten,* ed. Matthias Voß (Münster: LIT Verlag, 2005); Mathias Tullner, "Die Zusammenarbeit der DDR und Mosambiks auf dem Gebiet der Bildung und die Tätigkeit der Bildungsexperten der DDR in Mosambik," in *Wir haben Spuren hinterlassen!, Die DDR in Mosambik. Erlebnisse, Erfahrungen und Erkenntnisse aus drei Jahrzehnten,* ed. Matthias Voß (Münster: LIT Verlag, 2005). The relations between the GDR and Mozambique were quite close and intensive. This included a wide range of bilateral agreements between the two states – more than 80 were ratified – as well as personal encounters and relationships. Ca. 1200 GDR citizens worked at the same time in Mozambique. On the whole, around 7000 GDR citizens worked between 1977 and 1990 in the country. Around 21.000 Mozambique citizens worked and studied in the GDR. Many of them were known as contract workers after the signing of a corresponding agreement between the two countries in 1979. cf Döring, *"Es geht um unsere Existenz,"* 142; Castiano, *Das Bildungssystem in Mosambik*; Ewald Weiser, "Vorbemerkung," in *DDR-Bildungshilfe in Äthiopien. Interaktive Erkenntnisse, Erfahrungen und Eindrücke*, ed. Ewald Weiser (Berlin: LIT Verlag, 2013).

as well further education and special qualification measures for high rank officials at the Institute for Administration and Organisation in Potsdam.[26]

The ideological context of this co-operation rested on the interpretation of global socio-political developments in the light of Marxist-Leninist positions.[27] The wave of decolonization of the 1960s accompanied by a growing number of liberation movements was very much approved of as an anti-imperialist fight. The political leadership publicly showed their solidarity with these movements. In addition, the GDR political leaders called the population and the other socialist countries on international solidarity and international actions, being the first term the main slogan.

Countries and liberation movements, assumed that they agreed with Marxist and Leninist ideologies, were called countries with "non-capitalist developmental orientation" or "socialist orientation". Their parties, which for the most part originated from former liberation movements, were considered "vanguard parties" as soon as they adopted concepts of Marxism and Leninism when analyzing society, choose these concepts for their future society and if their developmental strategies including their actual implementation were based on them. The Socialist Unity Party of Germany (SED) declared itself "brotherly" connected to these parties. The young decolonized states were officially coined "nationally freed countries" ("national befreite Länder").

The financing was realized in a variety of ways. It is almost impossible to differentiate between resources mobilized through solidarity networks, resources available from trade agreements and resources coming from service agreements. Payed activities, trade facilitation schemes, resources from public budgets and contributions from the GDR population converged in many ways. For instance, the work done by GDR educational experts in the aided countries was often paid

26 Special educational institutions were established, for instance, the "School of Friendship" (Schule der Freundschaft), in Staßfurt, where 900 young Mozambicans were schooled as specialized workers in a socialist spirit. See Lutz R. Reuter and Annette Scheunpflug, *Die "Schule der Freundschaft". Eine Fallstudie zur Bildungszusammenarbeit zwischen der DDR und Mosambik* (Münster: Waxmann, 2006), Jane Schuch, *Mosambik im pädagogischen Raum der DDR. Eine bildanalytische Studie zur "Schule der Freundschaft" in Staßfurt* (Wiesbaden: Spriner VS, 2013); "Lehrerbildung für junge Nationalstaaten" an der PH Halle/Köthen. See Müller, *Die Bildungshilfe der Deutschen Demokratischen Republik*, 70–125.

27 I refer to scientific publications from several research fields such as education studies, social studies, Asian studies, African studies and Latin American studies – all of them are GDR publications from the 1970s and 1980s.

by these. Yet the GDR sent invited students from Mozambique to study in the country and donated school materials.

In the ideology of the GDR, mirroring a generally accepted view in the socialist countries, political and economic interests were hardly discernible. For instance, trade between their countries was not only an economic question pursued the aim of independence from capitalist world trade. Socialist industrialization of the countries in the global South and the setting of shared, often oversized, projects followed this idea. Nonetheless, there were signs of a stronger commercialization of bilateral relations in the 1980s; securing the interests of the GDR state came to the forefront at cost of the claim of international solidarity.[28] Tellingly, Hans-Joachim Döring titled his book about bilateral relations between the GDR and Ethiopia as "It is about our existence" ("Es geht um unsere Existenz"). He referred to Alexander Schalck-Golodowski,[29] who argued in 1982 with these words against additional resources for Mozambique in its armed struggle again the RENAMO rebels.[30] Although the idea of solidarity remained central, economic interests increasingly gained precedence. In Döring's analysis, new dependencies were being created and the GDR availed itself of the power gap between the nations.[31]

Experts abroad – the foreign cadres of the GDR

The GDR's personnel policy was heavily centralized, bureaucratized, and driven by the maxim to help safeguard the power of the SED. The so-called cadres, especially the leading ones, were supposed to be die-hard defenders of the GDR and its politics. Leading cadres and persons deemed to be qualified were recruited on all levels of the state and the society, in enterprises, universities etc. and centrally processed through a unified data system. The essence of this constant search for the "nomenclature" was the determination of persons qualified for (leading) positions along with a definition of their particular field of expertise and tasks. Even substitutes were determined in case the provided person could not acquire the position. These processes were subject to utmost secrecy, especially as the secret services of the GDR, the *Staatssicherheit* or *Stasi*, was involved in these

28 Cf. Müller, *Die Bildungshilfe der Deutschen Demokratischen Republik*; Döring, *"Es geht um unsere Existenz"*; Büschel, *Hilfe zur Selbsthilfe*.

29 Schalck-Golodkowski was the director of the bureau of trade coordination within the Ministry of Foreign Trade.

30 Döring, *"Es geht um unsere Existenz"*, 13.

31 Cf. Döring, *"Es geht um unsere Existenz"*.

processes on all levels. After the building of the Berlin Wall in 1961, the system of the traveling cadres was gradually subsumed under this personal system. Its implementation served the purpose to control the official trips into foreign countries, particularly into non-socialist foreign countries. It was necessary to reduce the high number of people fleeing from the GDR and to ensure the officially traveling persons to represent the GDR with their political opinion abroad and not to reveal official secrets. Ideally these persons should combine the highest professional quality with an equally high commitment to the socialist cause and absolute allegiance to the GDR, and in such act as a paragon of GDR socialism.[32]

This policy of cadres was clearly reflected in the structures and contents of the educational co-operation. Experts dispatched to foreign countries for the purpose of educational co-operation were traveling and foreign cadres, respectively and were supposed to equally correspond to the ideals of a GDR's representative abroad. Correspondingly, the ministry for national education differentiated between traveling cadres who stayed up to six months abroad and foreign cadres who worked more than six months abroad. Traveling cadres were, for instance, athletes, writers and scientists, who normally spent only a few days in Western foreign countries.[33] Foreign cadres, in contrast, worked many years in non-Western countries, above all in countries of the global South.[34] Following analysis focus on foreign cadres, because educational experts working up to three years in foreign countries received a specific education and preparation in the GDR before departure.

Not much is known about this influent group of experts.[35] If we take the universe of travelling and foreign cadres, an overwhelming majority held a university or a vocational degree. Almost 80 % of the foreign cadres, particularly, were university graduates. Travelling and foreign cadres were normally 26 to 50 years old, women were a minority, and about half of the group was a member of the governing party SED.[36] Niederhuts' central hypothesis about the political selection of these cadres in view of the politicization of their function and to the detriment of their expertise is not even proved by his own evidence. In the field of educational expertise, this interpretation, drawing on my data from the 1980s,

32 Jens Niederhut, *Die Reisekader: Auswahl und Disziplinierung einer privilegierten Minderheit in der DDR*, (Leipzig: Evangelische Verlagsanstalt GmbH, 2005).

33 Niederhut, *Die Reisekader*, 35.

34 Niederhut, *Die Reisekader*, 36.

35 Cf. Döring, *"Es geht um unsere Existenz"*, 220.

36 Niederhut, *Die Reisekader*, 43.

cannot definitely be confirmed. Particularly in this field, a significant number of experts with complete doctoral education were active.

Selection and preparation of the foreign cadres

The GDR's development co-operation was precisely not focused at one place (as for example the Development Service of West Germany, DED), but selectively located in widely different administrations of the GDR. Thus, for the educational field, three definite, separate and partially competing "government bodies" were involved: the ministry for higher education and professional schools (*Ministerium für Hoch- und Fachschulwesen*), the state secretary for vocational training (*Staatssekretariat für Berufsbildung*), and the ministry for national education (*Ministerium für Volksbildung*).

There was a multi-level process that each of the candidates underwent: 1. nomination, 2. selection, 3. confirmation, 4. preparation, and 5. delegation. This proceeding was very complex and carried out most thoroughly. The term most often used for the persons in question was hereby consultant (*Berater*) or expert (*Experte*).

Candidates were usually nominated by their institution – university, the state enterprise, the Academy of Pedagogical Sciences (APW) – at the same time they themselves could signal an interest to be sent out and seek for a recommendation by their superiors, teachers or professors. Then the ministry for national education checked their suitability according to the following criteria:

- professional qualification: Experience in leadership as well as in the education of teachers. A PhD was required.
- political orientation: preferably membership of the SED, political opinion ("firmness") in according to the standards of the SED and the GDR.
- no contacts whatsoever with non-socialist countries/West Berlin, including family members.
- suitability with regard to physical and mental health and language proficiency
- "moral firmness" (preferably married, no criminal record, etc.).

Further aspects were a solid financial situation, the membership in national organizations and the trade union, etc. The children and the wives were checked according to the same criteria. For instance, the children's behavior at school as well as their performance level was inquired.

If the ministry for national education had decided in favor of a candidate, the file went to the Ministry of State Security, which then made the final decision. The respective information was sought in written form from the corresponding authorities. Simultaneously members of the ministry for national education performed so-called delegation talks with the candidates and their families. Families of the children were visited in order to gain a more comprehensive image of the social and economic circumstances. From 1983 on, espouses and children until the age of ten could travel with the candidates and live with them. Before that time, this was possibly only in exceptional cases. This new regulation reacted to the specific situation of the foreign cadres, who lived some years in another country and were definitely not prone to leave behind their families.[37] There were also foreign cadres married to each other, although evidence shows that this was rather exceptional. Female foreign cadres travelling without their families were exceptional as well. Normally, expert missions lasted three years, but sometimes they may be extended.

Some consultants worked in different countries and stayed in the GDR for short periods between their different missions. Consultants in foreign countries worked together in hierarchical groups and were called "expert collective for education". There was a leadership that secured the coordination of activities and represented the group. The expert collective communicated with other GDR citizens in the respective countries, particularly with embassy officials.

Once selected, traveling and foreign cadres had to visit a ten-day preparation training. They attended presentations of experts, workshops and group discussions. The substantial key aspects of these preparation trainings were the following:

1. Instructions and recommendations about correct behavior abroad are well documented. For instance, who was allowed to talk with whom about what, mobility in the country (concerning the risk of flight) safety issues both in non-material and in material terms, as well as medical instructions;[38]
2. country-specific knowledge: "information about country-specific manners and living conditions in the operation country" – through other mostly leading cadres (presumably the group leaders), political situation of the country (including friend/enemy schemes), and particularly prominent: focus on "status and problems of the educational development in the operation countries".
3. political topics: global political developments concerning the question of decolonization (focus on liberation movements, also military components),

37 Niederhut, *Die Reisekader*, 36–37.

38 Some of those partly bring to mind current day safety measures against terrorist threats, Participants were for example encouraged to watch whether one was being followed or whether unknown persons approach apartments or vehicles.

the GDR's attitude towards the struggle, in particular towards its role in the support on the education sector of the liberated countries, the dealing with the influence of western ideas of education in these countries (original term: "bourgeois pedagogy", *bürgerliche Pädagogik*)

4. contents: specific further trainings about teacher training, development of curricula, polytechnic, educational management and inspection related to their particular missions.
5. Transitions form old to new consultants in the form of presentations, working groups, and more informal exchange about the activities in the country.
6. Working groups of the espouses travelling abroad with information, instructions and presentations between experienced and future travelling espouses.

Additionally, there was (at least in the 1980s) a personalized and highly differentiated preparation plan for *every* foreign cadre, which had to be worked through by following exact steps and defined periods of time. This program was individually tailor-made for the qualification of the experts and previous knowledge as well as for the prospective activity. The preparation training was only *one* item on the agenda. Moreover, the self-instruction of selected material, consultations in several ministries and the Academy of Pedagogical Sciences, talks with scientists of relevant fields and skilled foreign cadres, as well as visiting partially certified language trainings were contents of the agenda.[39]

There are some unclear aspects about the materials used for the preparation and training of the foreign cadres. Yet evidence shows that detailed reports and analyses about the political and educational situation of those countries and liberation movements to be assisted was a crucial element of them. Some of these reports and expertise were PhD thesis included in the archival papers.[40]

39 See for example: BArch, DR2 50665, Maßnahmen zur Vorbereitung des Genossen Dr. sc. Rudolf Pfeifer, Dozent in der Arbeitsstelle für Auslandspädagogik der APW, auf eine Tätigkeit als Berater und als Staatlicher Leiter der Expertengruppe Volksbildung der VDR Äthiopien, 1989, 1–5.

40 For instance, International Library for the History of Education, Akademie der pädagogischen Wissenschaften Papers, BBF/APW 15115, Zimare, Jürgen: Zur Entwicklung der Berufsbildung in ehemaligen portugiesischen Kolonien: Informat ionsvergleich. 31 Bl.; BBF/APW 13972, "Renate Martini: Entwicklung, Gestaltung und Wirkung von Frelimo-Schulen in unterschiedlichen Entwicklungsetappen der mozambiquischen Befreiungsrevolution: Thesen zur Dissertation, 12 Bl."; Baselm, Salem: Schulpolitische und theoretische Grundfragen der Lehrplanentwicklung in sozialistischen Ländern – insbesondere in der DDR – und ihre Bedeutung für die Realisierung der Lehrplanreform in der VDR Jemen, Berlin, Akademie der

Similarly, candidates had to read literature and materials written in the Section for Asia, Africa and Middle East Studies at the Karl-Marx-University in Leipzig or they have to make consultations with researchers of this institute. This was a mandatory part of their training. Research works from this Institute had been highly respected in the scholar community from 1950s onwards due to their international and innovative character. They intended a critique of Eurocentric positions, they were strongly historical in outlook and many times crossed diverse discipline boundaries.[41] Particularly a critique of colonial history, research on decolonization and liberation processes, including educational ideas and institutions, as well as African literature were fields of scholarship where the Institute had set new standards.[42]

After successfully undertaking the multi-level process of nomination, selection, confirmation, and preparation, the foreign cadres waited for their delegation. After their work abroad, they had to draw up a detailed report according to predefined structure items about their activity. A critical evaluation of their preparation for the mission in the GDR, positive and negative factors shaping their time in the assisted countries as well as a critical assessment of their own work as consultants and experts, including recommendations for a better preparation training, were essential parts of these reports.

"We" and "Them" – the GDR and the recipients of East German educational aid

As described in the beginning, I am interested in the constructions of difference in the context of these productions of knowledge. My theoretical approach focused on 'difference' is located between the poles of the Own and the Other, whereby this difference becomes an epistemic category of attributions.

First it is apparent that the Own is a very strong focus. The Own covers the global political conditions and the positioning of the GDR in the light of Marxist-Leninist theory. Key words were "revolutionary global processes" and "international class struggle". Aside from this, also topics rather specific for the GDR appear autonomously, as the "antifascist-democratic revolution", which means the transformation of the national socialist society into a socialist society, as well

Pädagogischen Wissenschaften der DDR, Diss. 1978; Weiser, *DDR-Bildungshilfe in Äthiopien*, 411.

41 Felix Brahm and Adam Jones, "Afrikanistik," in *Geschichte der Universität Leipzig, 1409–2009*, ed. Ulrich von Hehl et al. (Leipzig: Leipziger Universitätsverlag, 2009).

42 Brahm and Jones, "Afrikanistik."

as the GDR's educational system and educational policy in their formation and actuality. One example for this is the opening speech for a mandatory preparatory course in Ludwigsfelde in 1982. There, W. Engst, deputy of the GDR's Secretary of Education, which neither addressed "foreign countries" explicitly, nor the relationship of the GDR with the "operation countries", and didn't even contain the well-worn phrases about the international, anti-imperialist, anti-colonialist struggle. The 12 pages, thus about 30 minutes, are merely about internal topics and marginally address the role and the duties of the foreign cadres.[43]

This emphasis on the Own while almost completely dismissing the Other continues also in such a way that it is referred back again and again to the Own GDR experiences, successes, and mistakes of building up a completely redesigned educational system after 1945. Thus, the presentation just mentioned includes the following passage: "The main purpose of this training complex entails making the crucial experiences and lessons learned, which have been collected in realizing universal principles of a socialist education, especially in the period until the end of the 1950s, still more effective for your specific work."[44]

After 1945, the Soviet occupation zone (SBZ) and later GDR took an entirely novel path with regard to the German educational tradition. It abolished most of the older school system's hierarchical structure and introduced instead the ten-year general educational polytechnic secondary school (POS). The administration and management of the educational system was centralized; curricula, teaching material, and teacher training were standardized. "Education for all" was one of the basic principles. In the 1980s, the GDR possessed a broad and high level of general education. The student performances in the scientific subjects and in mathematics, for instance, were notably higher than in West Germany.[45]

The reference to this – from the GDR's view – success story in establishing an entirely new educational system, and the juxtaposition with the situation after the end of the Second World War was a common thread throughout. It reflected an act of reassurance and a sense of pride in the achievements made combined with the conviction, that this very fact had qualified the GDR for leadership in the build-up of educational systems in the liberated countries. Here, a connecting line could be drawn in terms of a transition, between the fight against

43 BArch, DR2 50556, Eröffnungsrede des Gen. W. Engst, STM, ZIW-Lehrgang 1982, 17.08.1982, 1–12.

44 BArch, DR2 50556, Eröffnungsrede des Gen. W. Engst, STM, ZIW-Lehrgang 1982, 17.08.1982, 5.

45 Gert Geißler, *Geschichte des Schulwesens in der Sowjetischen Besatzungszone und in der Deutschen Demokratischen Republik 1945 bis 1962* (Frankfurt et al: Peter Lang, 2000).

the heritage of fascism on the one hand side, and colonialism on the other, which helped to construct an imagined similarity between the GDR and the "socialist-minded" liberated countries The GDR's own experiences of societal transformation, in this case of a European transformation, turned into the means of the transformation processes of the liberated African countries.

Do the sources tell something about the Other, too? Several groups of people fell under this category: Other persons from the GDR like members of the GDR embassies and GDR representations, staff of the United Nations (UNESCO), experts from other socialist or non-socialist countries, and, not to the least, the foreign counterparts. "Partners" was the official name for the latter persons responsible in the respective national states. The latter distinction line I like to specify now.

Those countries having a bilateral arrangement in the educational field along with the people living there stayed relatively stable. Utmost caution or a distance kept can be felt in the documents. A form of respect but also self-defense against persons being perceived as alien or different might have factored in. Being mindful of potential racism, it can be noted that on the surface no racist language is used at all. Not even racist terms occur, neither in the official documents nor in the final reports of the foreign cadres. In these documents I received, the Other in order to distinguish it from the Own is particularly visible in the interaction. In a written report with recommendations on the behavior of foreign cadres towards the "partner", it can be looked closely at this relation. At first, it becomes clear that a strong focus shall be the joint work: "The single tasks and problems are always to be worked out in close comradely co-operation and consultation with the respective partner. A so-called one-man work in private is absolutely wrong."[46] Behind these words seems to stand the acknowledgment, as result of a learning process, that new concepts and their implementations can only be successful if they are completely supported by the persons they are directed at: "All existing experiences confirm that the single recommendations of the expert only can be concretely and practically realized and applied if they are consistently worked out together with the respective partner."[47] However, in the following, this intended and by itself understandable approach is put into a clearly manipulative context: "The consultant should collaborate closely and comradely with his direct working partner in particular and in doing so, he should constantly try to make sure that his ideas, thoughts, and suggestions are always turned into those

46 BArch, DR2 50614, Vortrag Eröffnung ZIW-Lehrgang, 1–50, 45.

47 Ibid.

of the partner. The partner must get the feeling of being the author of any reports and rule suggestions."[48]

Moreover, in this document, there is talk of specific thought patterns and behavior patterns of the respective partners that should be noted in a special way. Here, the superiority of the Own is clearly postulated:

> "In practice, the general mentality of the partner, a partially still distinct pragmatism, and certain still not fully hurdled problems in recognizing and digesting particular abstract coherences often involve explaining certain problems with selected forms and methods of visualization and pictures, respectively the expert should be prepared for."[49]

This supposed "general mentality" is always ascribed to the so-called colonial past or the "colonial heritage" not overcome yet. I have often found this interpretative pattern. A position as the knowing partner is occupied here. The motive of *White Supremacy* appears, for instance, when the lack of abstraction in the people of the global South, even as a temporal occurrence, is being referred to.

Knowledge and the lack of knowledge – difference between the Own and the Other

In the context of educational cooperation of the GDR with countries from the global South, one of the main differences between the Own and the Other affected the constructions of knowledge and non knowledge. The GDR-Own was above all the experiential knowledge of having built up a socialist educational system after 1945. Alone this the own educational system along with the usual teaching methods, material, and curricula qua postulated successes was defined as the superior model. This affirmed superiority in comparison to the countries of the global South was highly precarious. On the GDR side, there was a strong avidity to see the self-defined successful results of the educational system confirmed by the Other. Partners in the countries of the global South provided this confirmation. Again, and again, it is particularly emphasized in the documents that the partners very much appreciate the work of the GDR consultants/experts and that the contacts with the partners were conducted very successfully and in a constructive spirit. The almost obsessive reference to the Own was remarkable and stood always in focus. How the activities of the foreign cadres was perceived during their work and which image of the GDR existed in the respective country remained a central concern:

48 Ibid.

49 BArch, DR2 50614, Vortrag Eröffnung ZIW-Lehrgang, 1–50, 47.

> "I would like here make a general remark. As GDR citizens in Guinea, we do have an excellent reputation. Sympathy feelings, respect and recognition for our country were present in our encounters with people in the most disparate circumstances, during work as well as during our leisure time."[50]

For instance, very much appreciated and supported were the foundations of the "Society of the GDR's friends" in many liberated states, as for example in Benin in 1986. Even the perspectives of other foreign experts and staff members of the UNESCO about the work of the GDR-experts appeared to be of utmost interest, and these motives are an often long part of the concluding reports: "During this cooperation it was clear that the GDR and specially our system of education enjoyed a high reputation among the UNESCO cadres; yet it was also clear that they did not know enough about our experiences and positions."[51]

The positively connoted recognition of the Own through the Other was important. The GDR's self-image was permanently questioned and sharpened in the interactions with foreign counties, which strongly recalls other processes of state building.[52]

The foreign cadres acted very cautiously. It seems that the top-down scheme in their work largely functioned as expected. For instance, a construction manager was dismissed from a building project on the island of Zanzibar in 1968 because he had scolded the working apprentices accusing them of behaving like "Western Germans".[53] Additionally, it is generally recorded that foreign cadres who crossed the political borders, and also the anti-colonialist and anti-racist ideological framework related to them, were immediately expelled and had no chance for a further operation as GDR foreign cadres. The sparsely depicted conflicts tend to be reflected by the GDR consultants in a self-critical way (wrongly applied consultant, wrong estimate of the situation, etc.):

> "Our consultations and active involvement in the elaboration of curricula is still presupposing the special circumstances of our countries. We do lack a detailed knowledge and experiences about other developing countries, for instance, the work in

50 BArch, DR 2 50423, Reinhard Thiele, Abschlußbericht zur Tätigkeit in der Republik Guinea von Oktober 1983 bis Juli 1987, 10 Seiten, 4.

51 Thiele, *Abschlußbericht zur Tätigkeit in der Republik Guinea von Oktober 1983 bis Juli 1987*, 7.

52 See also Brahm and Jones, "*Afrikanistik*", 313.

53 Büschel, *Hilfe zur Selbsthilfe*, 473.

> school classes comprising more than 60 children, the role of religion, the cultivation of traditions in family education, etc."[54]

It was a main concern for the leading persons of the Ministry of Education and for the acting experts not to be perceived as agents of new version of a white neo-colonial perspective. They rather preferred to be perceived as precursors of a new solidary and equitable policy of the global Nord regarding the countries of the global South.

The overall picture reveals a mélange of perpetuated colonialist knowledge and concrete lived solidarity. According to its self-conception, the GDR clearly had an anti-colonialist and anti-racist position and represented such a policy inwardly and outwardly. Nevertheless, on the implementation level of such a policy I described, the dislocations come sharply into view. Documents show that perceptions of superiority and paternalistic views were available on both the leading and the operative level. Many of the development projects failed due to very different reasons.[55] Whether we may speak or not of a general failure on the field of educational cooperation, is not possible to assert considering the state of the art.

In the GDR, racism and colonialism counted as overcome realities after the establishment of the socialist republic. In this view, patterns of meaning and action related to the bourgeois and capitalistic society were no longer effective. In this view, an astounding "identification of programs and realities"[56] masked cultural and political factors. It is on this basis by no means unexpected that the GDR actors neglected the continuity of racist and colonial structures, even their scientific and political knowledge in this respect was considerable.

Archives

Bundesarchiv (Federal Archives, Koblenz/Germany)

Bibliothek für Bildungsgeschichtliche Forschung (International Library for the History of Education), Berlin

54 BArch, DR 2 50423, Hannelore Christoph, Abschlußbericht zur Tätigkeit in der Republik Guinea von 1983–1987, 7 Seiten, 1987, 6–7.

55 Cf. Döring, "*Es geht um unsere Existenz*"; Büschel, *Hilfe zur Selbsthilfe*.

56 Marianne Krüger-Potratz, Annette Kaminsky and Werner Winter, "Völkerfreundschaft und internationale Solidarität," in *Freundschaft! Die Volksbildung der DDR in ausgewählten Kapiteln*, ed. Ministerium für Bildung, Jugend und Sport des Landes Brandenburg (Berlin: 1996), 174.

Literature

Aust, Martin. "Russland und die Sowjetunion in der Globalgeschichte." In *Globalisierung imperial und sozialistisch - Russland und die Sowjetunion in der Globalgeschichte 1851–1991*, edited by Martin Aust, 13–38. Frankfurt/New York: Campus, 2013.

Borges, Sonia V. *Militant Education. Liberation Struggle, Consciousness. The PAIGC education in Guinea Bissau 1963–1978*. Frankfurt: Peter Lang, 2019.

Brahm, Felix and Jones, Adam. "Afrikanistik." In *Geschichte der Universität Leipzig, 1409–2009*, edited by Ulrich von Hehl, Uwe John and Manfred Rudersdorf, 295–32. Leipzig: Leipziger Universitätsverlag, 2009.

Büschel, Hubertus. *Hilfe zur Selbsthilfe, Deutsche Entwicklungsarbeit in Afrika 1960–1975*. Frankfurt/New York: Campus, 2014.

Castiano, Jose P. *Das Bildungssystem in Mosambik (1974–1996): Entwicklung, Probleme und Konsequenzen*. Hamburg: Institut für Afrika-Kunde im Verbund der Stiftung Deutsches Übersee-Institut, 1997.

Conrad, Sebastian and Randeria, Shalini. "Einleitung. Geteilte Geschichten – Europa in einer postkolonialen Welt." In *Jenseits des Eurozentrismus. Postkoloniale Perspektiven in den Geschichts- und Kulturwissenschaften*, edited by Sebastian Conrad and Shalini Randeria, 67–83. Frankfurt/New York: Campus, 2002.

Döring, Hans-Joachim. *"Es geht um unsere Existenz": Die Politik der DDR gegenüber der Dritten Welt am Beispiel von Mosambik und Äthiopien*. Berlin: Chr. Links Verlag, 2001.

Eckert, Andreas. "Spätkoloniale Herrschaft, Dekolonisation und internationale Ordnung." *Archiv für Sozialgeschichte* 48, (2007): 3–20.

Geißler, Gert. *Geschichte des Schulwesens in der Sowjetischen Besatzungszone und in der Deutschen Demokratischen Republik 1945 bis 1962*. Frankfurt: Peter Lang, 2000.

Harzer, Erika, and Volks, Willi ed. *Aufbruch nach Nicaragua. Deutsch-deutsche Solidarität im Systemwettstreit*. Berlin: Ch. Links Verlag, 2008.

Kang-Schmitz, Liana. *Nordkoreas Umgang mit Abhängigkeit und Sicherheitsrisiko: am Beispiel der bilateralen Beziehungen zur DDR*. Berlin: epubli GmbH, 2011.

Krüger-Potratz, Marianne, Kaminsky, Annette and Winter, Werner. "Völkerfreundschaft und internationale Solidarität." In *Freundschaft! Die Volksbildung der DDR in ausgewählten Kapiteln*, edited by Ministerium für Bildung, Jugend und Sport des Landes Brandenburg. 173–241. Berlin: BasisDruck, 1996.

Müller, Hans M. *Die Bildungshilfe der Deutschen Demokratischen Republik.* Frankfurt: Peter Lang, 1995.

Niederhut, Jens. *Die Reisekader: Auswahl und Disziplinierung einer privilegierten Minderheit in der DDR.* Leipzig: Evangelische Verlagsanstalt GmbH, 2005.

Picher, M. Anne and Askew, Kelly M. "African Socialism and Postsocialism." *Africa* 76, no. 1 (2006): 1–14.

Reuter, Lutz R. and Scheunpflug, Annette. *Die "Schule der Freundschaft". Eine Fallstudie zur Bildungszusammenarbeit zwischen der DDR und Mosambik.* Münster: Waxmann, 2006.

Schuch, Jane. *Mosambik im pädagogischen Raum der DDR. Eine bildanalytische Studie zur "Schule der Freundschaft" in Staßfurt.* Wiesbaden: Spriner VS, 2013.

Tullner, Matthias. "Die Zusammenarbeit der DDR und Mosambiks auf dem Gebiet der Bildung und die Tätigkeit der Bildungsexperten der DDR in Mosambik." In *Wir haben Spuren hinterlassen!, Die DDR in Mosambik. Erlebnisse, Erfahrungen und Erkenntnisse aus drei Jahrzehnten*, edited by Matthias Voß, 388–406. Münster: LIT Verlag, 2005.

Voß, Matthias. "Gespräch mit Achim Kindler, der als Lehrer im Auftrag des Solidaritätskomitees der DDR als erster DDR-Bürger bei der FRELIMO arbeitete." In *Wir haben Spuren hinterlassen! Die DDR in Mosambik. Erlebnisse, Erfahrungen und Erkenntnisse aus drei Jahrzehnten*, edited by Matthias Voß, 34–46. Münster: LIT Verlag, 2005.

Weiser, Ewald. "Vorbemerkung." In *DDR-Bildungshilfe in Äthiopien. Interaktive Erkenntnisse, Erfahrungen und Eindrücke*, edited by Ewald Weiser, 5–16. Berlin: LIT Verlag, 2013.

List of Figures

Authors

Sonia Vaz *Borges* is a researcher of the history of education at the Institute of Education at Humboldt-Universität zu Berlin, Germany

Marcelo *Caruso* is Full Professor of the History of Education at the Institute of Education at Humboldt-Universität zu Berlin, Germany

Catriona *Ellis* is Teaching Associate in History at the University of Strathclyde, Scotland

Tim *Kaiser* is Lecturer and Researcher in the Department of Social Sciences and Cultural Studies at Giessen University, Germany

Daniel *Maul* is Associate Professor of History in the Department of Archaeology, Conservation and History at Oslo University, Norway

Ingrid *Miethe* is Full Professor of General Education in the Department of Social Sciences and Cultural Studies at Giessen University, Germany

Alexandra *Piepiorka* is Lecturer and Researcher in General Education in the Department of Social Sciences and Cultural Studies at Giessen University, Germany

Parimala *Rao* is Assistant Professor of the History of Education at the Zakir Husain Centre for Educational Studies at Jawaharlal Nehru University, India

Michael J. *Seth* is Professor at the History Department at the James Madison University, United States

Hakeem Ibikunle *Tijani* is Full Professor for International History, Africa and African Diaspora at the National Open University of Nigeria (NOUN), Nigeria

Jane *Weiß* is Lecturer and Researcher of the History of Education at the Institute of Education at Humboldt-Universität zu Berlin, Germany

Ting-Hong *Wong* is Associate Research Fellow at the Institute of Sociology at Academia Sinica, Taiwan

Studia Educationis Historica

Bildungsgeschichtliche Studien / Studies in the History of Education /
Estudios de Historia de la Educación

Herausgegeben von/ edited by
Marcelo Caruso, Eckhardt Fuchs, Gert Geißler, Sabine Reh, Eugenia Roldán Vera, Noah W. Sobe

Vol. 1 Anna Larsson / Björn Norlin (eds.): Beyond the Classroom. Studies on Pupils and Informal Schooling Processes in Modern Europe. 2014.

Vol. 2 Marcelo Caruso (ed.): Classroom Struggle. Organizing Elementary School Teaching in the 19th Century. 2015.

Vol. 3 Cristina Alarcón / Martin Lawn (eds.): Assessment Cultures. Historical Perspectives. 2017.

Vol. 4 Sonia Borges: Militant Education, Liberation Struggle, Consciousness. 2019.

Vol. 5 Marcelo Caruso / Daniel Maul (eds.): Decolonization(s) and Education. 2020.

www.peterlang.com

Lightning Source UK Ltd.
Milton Keynes UK
UKHW041407310822
408121UK00003B/31

9 783631 674154